650 PRIZE-WINNING BLENDER RECIPES
For Nutrition-Minded People

BLENDING MAGIC

by
BERNARD JENSEN
NUTRITIONIST

DEDICATION

This book is dedicated to those housewives who are seeking, finding, and using the finest equipment and the finest foods in their kitchen to keep their family in the best of health. Into her hands I pray and hope that the finest knowledge and information be given her that those who are depending on her for their health may know what it is to really

"feel wonderful."

H E A L T H   F R O M   Y O U R   B L E N D E R

In one of the most delightful valleys in the entire world, hidden
between mountain peaks, lakes, flowers and trees, is a place
called Hidden Valley Health Ranch.

This ranch is a dream come true, envisioned and built by Bernard
Jensen, author, teacher, lecturer and world-renowned nutritionist,
a dedicated man who has devoted his life to the philosophy of
improved health through correct diet.

Hidden Valley Health Ranch is the embodiment of this philosophy,
and every one of its 130 acres is devoted to health, happiness
and peace of mind.

Every grape vine, every fruit tree, every vegetable is
organically grown without commercial fertilizers or poisonous sprays.

Every meal, every recipe, every menu is the result of careful
planning, experienced preparation and appeals to the eye and
the appetite alike.

Between meals, tempting fruit and vegetable drinks are served.
So popular has this gracious custom become that Bernard Jensen
has gathered all his liquefying recipes together and here presents
them for your health and enjoyment.

It is his hope that you will enjoy a great many of them. While
their number is legion, you will probably discover--as have
others--that a certain few of them will become favorites with you,
and that the discovery of these favorites will more than compensate
you for your efforts in ascertaining just which ones were created
especially for you!

Drink to your own health--and may your days be long and happy.

+   +   +   +

INTRODUCTION

IN PRAISE OF:

A small mechanical device which is the product of man's ingenuity and his creative use of electricity......"The Blender".

This wonderful little machine can create miracles of color, flavor and consistency that can help you build better health, vigor and vitality. At whatever point you are on the ladder of health, it can lift you up one rung higher.

It always stands ready to serve you and to bring forth delicious health-giving concoctions, proof of Nature's bounty, for both young and old, for weak or strong, for big or small; for all.

It helps you to dream up many tempting creations to make of every meal a festive occasion. You may even begin to feel like an Alchemist, turning carrots into molten gold, or like an Artist, setting a pallette of colors on your dining table. Meal time can become a happy creative time resulting in more vitality, strength, endurance and abundance of energy for all.

MAY EVERYONE BENEFIT FROM ITS USE.

TABLE OF CONTENTS

SECTION I

PHILOSOPHY AND NUTRITION

TABLE OF CONTENTS (cont.)

SECTION III

BLENDING RECIPES

TABLE OF CONTENTS (cont.)

TABLE OF CONTENTS (cont.)

KNOW YOUR BLENDER

There have been many changes in the blenders today. We find they are making them better, and they are making them stronger. They are also putting extra gadgets on the machine so that they can serve every idea that may come out of the kitchen needs. For instance, now we can buy liquefiers and blenders with ten different speeds on them, but throughout the book we will refer to only three, Low, Medium, and High. We use the low speed in making butter, cheese, and so forth. Use the medium speed on fine vegetables, cooked vegetables, and those that cannot stand a lot of buffing and churning. And in the high speed, we use the tougher vegetables where we want to give a fine puree to the finished product.

There are a few things that we could consider about this liquefier, and it will last you a long time. Any instrument that is misused will have a short life. When you drive your automobile into the gas station, you do not ask for sawdust to be put in. You ask for the good oil and the good gas. Now, if you will give your liquefier careful handling - do not overwork it or run it until it gets so hot that it actually can heat your food while you are blending, then you can keep this blender a long time. Never expect the blender to do more than it is capable of doing. If necessary, it is better to use two different blendings rather than try to do it all at one time.

Cleansing it carefully is very important. Always wash it out immediately after its use - don't let it stand around.

This Magic Blending Book is strictly for those who want to delve into and deal with the highest nutritional values. We consider that getting into the highest nutritional values comes when we keep our food natural, use natural food to begin with, and keep it as whole as possible. Get only the purest food and keep it this way. The blender should never be used to blend any material into natural food so that it will be a second best food when finished, or will be detrimental to the human body. All flavoring, all coloring, all materials used in this blending operation can be natural and can be good for the human body from a nutritional standpoint.

It is possible this book will become the most valuable book in your life. It may even save your life. I know it will. It can give you better health providing you will realize that a few changes will have to be made in your preparation of food. For instance, natural sweeteners such as honey are much better from a health standpoint. In place of chocolate, try using carob. You will find that we have considered everything for the good of your health in this book.

Originally, the liquefier was used in bars for crushing the ice for mixed drinks. But this liquefing book is strictly for nutritional purposes. It will add to your health, not take away. It is for adding strength, power, energy, and everything you need to supply the body with whatever it needs for rejuvination and regeneration. In many cases, I believe that the liquefier is not necessary in the average kitchen, but is a valuable adjunct. I believe you can prepare foods which are easier to digest for the different age groups, such as in feeding the baby, the aged or elderly, for those who are sick or may have ulcers of the stomach. People who cannot handle heavy, raw salads can have them liquefied.

There are many other uses for the liquefier. Many drinks we are accustomed to having, like milk shakes, can be made natural in the blender and will be much better for you than any you can buy in our commercial outlets today.

Other uses are when the digestive juices may be low or energy may be low. You may want to go the advanced way in making raw vegetable soups. You might have an inclination to make a raw asparagus soup, which would be much better from a nutritional standpoint than a cooked asparagus soup. By using natural ingredients, the herbs, coloring, seasonings, and flavorings, you can be the best cook on your block by way of the blender to keep yourself well.

THE CARE OF YOUR BLENDER

Some suggestions that will help you to get the maximum perform-
and and service from your blender. These suggestions will help
make your blender-preparation of food much more of a pleasure
and more rewarding.

Read Manufacturer's Instructions before using.

Set blender on a clean, firm, and dry surface before starting the
motor. A clean surface is important, otherwise foreign particles
may be drawn into the motor.

Place the food container firmly on the motor base, and rest hand
lightly on the lid before turning the motor on.

Use top opening when adding pieces of food. If your blender is
not equipped with this, just move lid to one side.

Always put the liquids and semi-liquids into the container first,
except where otherwise stated, such as when using seeds and nuts
which have not been previously soaked. These are best ground dry
with the liquids added later. It is generally best to soak seeds
and nuts for several hours in water or other liquid.

A spatula is a necessity when using a blender, to push foods into
the blade section from time to time. It might be necessary to turn
the motor off when using the spatula, but in time you will find
that in most cases you can leave the motor running. Be careful not
to let the spatula go too far down, otherwise it might come in contact with the cutting blades.

Your blender chops very fast, so stop the motor and examine now
and again so as not to "chop" finer than you desire. When whipping
cream, run at Low (L) speed and watch very closely, otherwise you
might end up with butter instead of whipped cream. Experience will
be your best teacher in using your blender.

It may be necessary to increase speed to High (H) when blending if
motor seems to be pulling "heavy". This usually helps release
food which may have become lodged in the blade section. Occasionally it may be necessary to empty the container and take pieces of
food from the blade section. Heavy foods should be blended at Low
speed, then turned on High for a few seconds.

Some foods such as seeds and nuts are best processed in small quantities. Your motor will keep cooler and really makes very little difference as to the time taken to prepare your food.

Always clean blender immediately after using. If your blender is equipped with removable cutting-blade section, take apart, and wash and dry each part thoroughly.

Remove cord from outlet when not in use, and wipe if necessary with camp cloth and push cord into storage area base if provided. If not, carefully wrap cord around base of your blender. Proper care of your blender will reward you with better and longer service.

A FEW TIME SAVERS AND SUGGESTIONS

Handy Bread Crumbs

To use bread crumbs for toppings on casserole dishes, tear a
slice of bread into several pieces and place in container. Turn
speed to (H) and switch motor on and off about twice. If finer
crumbs are desired run a few seconds longer. Store or use as
required. One slice of bread makes about ½ cup of crumbs.

Grating Cheeses

Cut Cheddar or other hard cheeses into cubes of ½ inch size
and grate at (M) speed using ½ cup of cubes at a time. Run
blender for longer period of time if finer cheese is desired.

Grating Nuts and Seeds

When grating nuts and seeds process 1 cup or less at a time. Cover
container and run on (L) speed until chopped as desired. Nuts
and seeds are best ground without liquid and are easier to digest
if soaked overnight before grating.

Grating Fresh Coconut

Put about ½ cubed coconut meat in the blender container, cover
and run on (L) speed until grated. Stop and start blender if
necessary to toss coconut into blade section. Empty into
a bowl and repeat until you have the amount you need.

Dry Chopped Fruits and Vegetables

Raw or cooked fruits or vegetables can be chopped fine enough
for any need. Just use the following method:
Slice or dice fruit, either raw or cooked into 3/4 to 1 inch
pieces and place in container. Do not process more than ½ to
1 cup at one time. Set speed at (L), but tougher vegetables
such as carrots, can be processed on (M) speed. The more
tender the food, the lower the speed. Switch motor on and off
until desired fineness is obtained. To dry-chop onions just
quarter one medium onion and put in container and set speed at
(L). For dry-chopped celery, cut in 3/4 inch lengths, and set
speed at (L) and move to (M) if necessary. Celery is best cut
in smaller pieces as otherwise stringiness may occur in finished.
product. To dry-chop carrots, add carrots cut in 1 inch pieces
into the container. Do not add more than one cup of carrots at
a time. Set speed at (M) and proceed until desired consistency
is obtained.

For Water-Chopping Large Amounts of Vegetables

Cut cabbage, celery, onions, peppers, carrots etc , into 1 inch
pieces. Place loosely in blender container to about 2/3 full.
Add water to 4 cup level, or about 3/4 full. Turn speed to (M)
and run motor just long enough so that vegetables at top have
travelled to blades. Turn motor off, empty contents into sieve,
drain and repeat as needed.

How to Re-constitute Milk Solids

Measure water as desired into blender container. Add dry milk
solids. Start on (L) speed, then turn to (H) speed until well
blended. Use in any recipe where milk is called for.

To Make Soups more Nutritious

You can add Wheat Germ, Soybean Lecithin, liquid or granules, Sunflower seeds, Rice Polishings, Yeast, Dulse etc., to add more
nutrition and smoothness to your soups. Any of these items may be
purchased from your Health Food Store.

For Colder Drinks

Chipped Ice can be added when colder drink is desired. Ice cubes
can also be used. Add one at a time.

To Sour Milk or Cream

When a recipe calls for sour milk or cream and you have none on
hand, just add lemon juice to sweet milk or cream.

To Liquefy Honey

Honey can be liquefied by placing container in warm water until
honey is of consistency desired. To measure solid honey, simply
use knife to level spoon.

To Get the Most Chlorophyll from Your Greens

Put the greens in Blender with water. Turn to (H) speed until
well belnded. Put blended mixture in a muslin bag and squeeze
juice out as much as possible. A potato ricer can also be used
for this purpose. Simply put the pulp in the ricer and press as
you would for ricing potatoes.

BE ORIGINAL

Do not be afraid to venture when using your blender. If one
kind of food called for in a recipe is not on hand, try using
some other food. For instance, if a recipe calls for peaches
and you have no peaches on hand, try using pears, apples etc.
If a recipe calls for Sunflower seeds and none on hand, you can
generally use Sesame seeds. Try to keep in mind the health of
your family, then try to make your foods as nutritious as possible by using one or more of the food supplements such as Wheat
Germ, Lecithin granules, Rice Polishings etc. Use your blender
when guests arrive unexpectedly. Make a drink of chilled Pineapple Juice and ripe Bananas. Put the juice in the blender and
add the bananas cut in quarters. Blend until smooth and see how
your guests will enjoy this pleasant drink. A little Health Ice
Cream can be added if desired. A little ingenuity on your part
will bring you many unexpected compliments from your family and
guests.

A healthy family is a happy family, and it is up to the housewife to see that her family is served the most healthful and
nutritious as well as tastefully served foods. Try making a
delicous fruit cocktail for Dad when he arrives home from work.
Hand him the paper, and let him relax while you continue with
the preparation of your evening meal. Fruit served as a drink
a short time before the main part of the meal is served will be
better from a health standpoint. Fruit digests within half an
hour whereas other foods take a much longer period of time, so
for this reason, it is best to have fruit served beforehand, than
to use it as a dessert at the end of the meal. A blender-made
drink for the children when they come from school will be both interesting and healthful and much better than cookies and cakes.
Let the children participate in making their drinks, under supervision of course until they become familiar with the blender. Be
sure to teach them to wash the blender and put things away in good
order. When your teen-agers have their friends in, let them make
a pleasant and nutritious drink. In so doing, you may introduce
them to a more nutritious and healthful way of serving foods.

If some of the items in the recipes included in this book are unfamiliar to you, such as Sunflower Seeds, Lecithin Granules, Rice
Polishings, etc., they may be purchased at a Health Food Store.

BLENDING FOR HEALTH

Years ago, man could live a simple life close to Nature, eating
well and plentifully from food grown in a live and fertile soil. By
putting back all that was taken out of the soil, he maintained the
endless cyclic relationship between man and Nature. But many
things have changed in the course of civilization and man has been
drawn away from his natural habitat and has lost contact with the
earth.

There is a story in Greek mythology of the final victory of Hercules
over his opponent who was born of Mother Earth and whose strength
was renewed and revived every time he was thrown and touched the
Earth. Becoming so invigorated by this contact with Mother Earth,
he was nearing victory when the mighty Hercules lifted him high
above the ground and kept him there, breaking connection with the
Earth and drawing him away from the source of his strength and
power, finally causing him to weaken and collapse.

Isn't this what has happened to modern man? The pull of civilization has caused man to be separated from Mother Earth and
this has resulted in his becoming weak and under-nourished, with
loss of energy and vibrant health.

POTENTIAL FARMERS DRAWN TO CITIES

In the early days of our country, food was grown in rich soil that
had all the materials necessary for the harvesting of nutritionally

adequate crops. But with the rapid expansion of commercial centers, some of the potentially good farmers were drawn to the cities with the result that not enough men who loved and understood the land were left to protect and till it properly. The evils of tenant farming, where men cannot work the land as their own, have also taken their toll. And finally, the forcing of crops to abnormal growth and size for the commercial market has added to the tremendous problem of a devitalized national market-basket.

Several reasons can be given for the inferior food now grown on small and large farms alike. One of the most important is the lack of understanding by a great majority of the growers of the necessity for a balanced soil to produce nutritionally-balanced food. Also, there are too few agricultural schools turning out farmers with the know-how to cultivate crops from properly cared-for soil. If men knew how to till the land, there would be fewer dust bowls and a much hardier nation today. Good soil is generally followed by good health, and poor soil by poor health. Our health deteriorated in proportion to the degree to which our soils are depleted.

BALANCED SOIL, BALANCED FOOD, HEALTHY PEOPLE

One of the glaring proofs of the need for better food was found

in the draft rejections during World War II. Ninety per cent of
the men from the South were rejected from wartime service because they were not considered physically fit to serve their country. However, only ten per cent of the men from Colorado were
refused admission to the military ranks. Surely this eighty per
cent difference between the men of the Heartland and the men
from the South has something to do with the food they ate during
their growing years, and the foods they lived on at the time of
their service applications.

What, then, can we do to recapture and maintain some of the hardi-
ness and natural vigor of our grandfathers? How can we get
through a normal work day, whether it is in the factory, home or
office, and not fall into the habit of using the "crutch" of harmful
stimulants that actually rob us of the very energy we need? Must
we feed our bodies the devitalized foods that are in the markets
today?

We know that we should live a sane, balanced life, based on reason. The emotional appeal to our senses from unethical adver-
tising must be turned aside, and we must make our choice according to what our reason tells us is right, rather than what our over-
stimulated emotions clamor for.

LIQUEFIED FOODS--IMPOVERISHED SOIL

Now, no one claims that liquefied foods are the entire answer to
a healthier nation; they are only a part of the answer, but never-
theless, an important part. Because Americans generally buy
foods grown in impoverished soil, they must somehow make up
in bulk for the below-standard foods they consume. For example,
a carrot grown in Sweden will probably be many times more nutritious than a carrot grown on one of the big forced-production
farms on the California Imperial Valley. The Swedish carrot
may be smaller, but it will have less water and more vitamins,
consequently being of more value from a nutritional standpoint.
The American carrot produced for the big market centers is
often larger than normal but of inferior quality because, in many
cases, it is grown with chemical fertilizers and is forced to
mature quickly. The real crux of the problem is that our food
can be no better than the soil from which it springs. Inferior
soil must produce inferior food. Soil that does not have the proper minerals and the other factors needed for healthy plant life is
not going to produce healthy fruits and vegetables. If we were
getting the quality of food that enabled our "iron ancestors" to
work 16 hours a day, six days a week, American radio and tele-
vision commercials would not be filled with hawkers crying the
merits of vitamin tablets.

HEALTH ALSO DEPENDS ON MENTAL ATTITUDE

In planning a nutritional program, remember that the body molds
to the kind of fruits and vegetable we put into it. But we also have
to use our minds in this molding process. The body itself has no
method for refusing harmful foods; the mind must do that. Unless
our mind regulates the ingestion of starches, you will get fat. If
you live on too many proteins, you will definitely get a putrefactive bowel--a bowel that will cause excessive fermentation. The
basis of all art is selection, and so it is with the art of eating in-
telligently and healthfully. You must learn how to select your foods,
how to choose the right combinations in order to have a balance that
will not only build health but maintain it.

Emotions have a great deal to do with the way food is handled in the
digestive process. If you are the type who does not know when to
stop--when to say "No!"--when to put on the brakes, you may find
that you are inviting digestive troubles.

Here is something interesting to think about. The psychologists today tell us that penny-pinchers invariably develop constipation. A person who is squeezing his mind and squeezing everything out of everybody else has a tight bowel. The reflex condition from the mind is always manifested in the rest of the body. Freedom of mind creates freedom of body. Ease of mind begets ease of body.

Nine out of ten people who go to hospitals with ulcers of the stomach go there as a result of fretting, worrying and stewing over love or money troubles. If an operation is being considered for the patient who is suffering from stomach disorders, or colitis, it should start in the head, not in the stomach. What we think affects our entire physical makeup. Learning to control our emotions helps us to receive more benefit from the foods we eat.

IMPORTANCE OF FRUITS AND VEGETABLES

As you learn to build your diet healthwise, you should have more fresh fruits and vegetables and try to cut down the meat intake to only three times a week. It is interesting to know that I have never had a person come to me who was ill or in difficulty from eating too many fruits and vegetables; the trouble lies mainly with eating too many starches or proteins. We should learn to balance all the good things meant as food for man, and the rewarding dividends will be great. Eating less of the concentrated foods and adding more of the fruits and vegetables is one way of achieving the balance that will give us these dividends.

Fresh raw vegetables are rich in certain vitamins and minerals essential to good health. Salads give you these precious elements. You cannot get well without raw food. However, there are some people who cannot eat raw salads because they are too irritating and rough on the intestinal tract. They should use the blender to liquefy these foods.

VARIETY

To understand the role that liquefied food plays in the diet, we must realize that good health is built on a foundation on which the whole body is fed. We must have a protein every day and a starch every day; we must feed the brain, nerve and muscle structures every day. We must have all the different kinds of vegetables, the green, the yellow, and the red--as each one of these colors represents certain minerals in the earth kingdom. There will be an imbalance if we concentrate on trying to eat only special foods high in sodium, or high in silicon, or high in one or another mineral. If we follow the color patterns in nature, we will soon learn how to balance our vegetable diets. Remember, if our plates are filled with a variety of color, we will not

have to be too concerned with the KIND of diet that is best for us. However, if our condition requires certain foods, we will, of course, have to consider these, but under normal conditions we do not have to worry as long as we maintain a variety of color when eating.

USE BLENDER TO BUILD LOST RESERVES

It is also beneficial to have variety in combinations. Experience has shown us that at least half of our daily food should be raw. This does not mean that we must take only raw salads. Here is where liquefied fruits and vegetables can be of great advantage, especially if the digestive system is not able to take the raw salads. Almost everyone is able to take raw fruits and vegetables in liquid form, and these liquefied salads are also easy to make. However, try to avoid taking both fruits and vegetables at one time. They serve the needs of the body best when they are taken separately.

Some of you may protest against the little trouble it takes to liquefy your foods, but just remember that the reserves in

certain areas of the body have been overdrawn. For example, if there are cavities in the teeth, it means that the reserve of calcium has been depleted. If the joints are aching, the sodium reserve must be replenished. And although these can be built up in a number of ways, one of the most natural and least expensive is by drinking raw vegetable juices.

If the problem is one of weight, we can use juices either to add or subtract. By proper selection, we can help solve the problem either way. Of course, it is important to check with your doctor before adding or subtracting from your weight. Do not try to solve your problem without professional assistance, as abnormal weight can mean more than an excess of starch or a lack of certain nutritive elements. There are times when abnormal weight can be a sign of a serious internal condition that is much more important to your life than the overweight or underweight problem. We must all constantly keep before us the importance of seeking out causes, rather than trying to correct symptoms.

GET COMBINATIONS CORRECT

In planning a liquefied food program, divide the drinks into the
proper classifications; such as, vegetable, fruit, protein, etc.
In liquefying foods follow the same combinations that are followed
in a solid diet regime. For example, do not combine peaches with

barley, or other fruits with other starches. And certainly avoid
such combinations as soy bean milk with potatoes. If you will
remember the rules for maintaining balance in your solid combinations,
you will have little trouble with the liquefied combinations. If you
cannot take raw salads at present because you find them too difficult
to digest, then liquefy your salads and receive the benefits in this'
way. If you cannot take some cooked foods because of the fibers
in them cause disturbance, then liquefy these cooked foods. People
with ulcers of the stomach should remember that they have a liver
to keep up, teeth to feed, hair to grow, etc. and they must have a
balanced diet for this. Just living on milk is not enough, for they
are only soothing the stomach with a food that is insufficient.

for proper body balance. To maintain a balanced diet the whole body must be built up. An ulcer patient must still have a starch, a protein, vegetables and fruits in the daily diet.

GREATER FOOD VALUE, LESS BULK

Liquefied food enables us to get more vitamins and minerals from our market baskets than we would ordinarily be able to consume. The market baskets will have to be bigger and filled more often, but as a result, we will be more vital, more energetic, and more able to work without fatigue or the need of harmful stimulants. Numerous examples can be cited of how fresh vegetables can be liquefied to provide the necessary quantity of food elements for a good diet. It is important to remember that the blender enables us to consume more vitamins and minerals from fresh produce than would be possible for the average busy person who cannot, or will not, take the time to chew large quantities of food thoroughly.

LIQUEFIED FOOD MUST BE WELL CHEWED

The Blender has become so useful because of the fact that we have lost the proper use of our teeth. The average person today

does not know how to chew. Some time ago there was a man by the name of Fletcher, who advocated chewing each mouthful of food 32 times in order to derive the best benefits from our meals. This chewing process was called "Fletcherizing" the food. As the average person will not do this, liquefied or or juiced food seems to be the next best solution. This does not mean that we should chew our solid foods less; it merely means that liquefied food, being broken into fine particles, is more easily salivated. So, consider the tremendous importance of the liquefier in the number one spot in every kitchen in America today.

However, vegetable and fruit juice drinks can be of great benefit only if they are consumed properly. They must be drunk slowly--almost eaten--to aid the saliva in mixing with the juice. The Blender grinds up the fruit or vegetable in the way the human teeth would grind them, but it does not furnish the saliva to mix with the juice! In fact, the thorough salivation of the liquefied food against the roof of the mouth to get rid of all the air unavoidably whipped into it, is essential or it will cause much discomfort from gas in the stomach and intestines. Juices must never be consumed like drinking water, even though the broken-down particles are largely water. There are still some solid food particles contained in the juice, and these must be mixed with the natural saliva before they are swallowed.

There is another important factor to consider in liquefication of food. Once the vegetable or fruit is juiced, the process of oxidation occurs very rapidly. This is the reason why we should begin drinking the juice as soon as it is made. Liquefied food spoils quickly unless consumed within a reasonably short period of time. If liquefied food is to be stored, it must be filled to the top of the container so that no air remains to unite with the juice.

Too much liquefication can cause gas, because air is forced into the juice by the machine blades when making the liquid. Also, many times we find that foods do not get broken down sufficiently when they are raw. In such cases they should first be steamed to tenderize them and then liquefied. The combination of cooked food with liquefied food works out very well, since at least half of the daily food intake should be raw.

USE OF THE BLENDER

Now, let us take up the different ways the Blender can be put to use. In my cookbook, "VITAL FOODS FOR TOTAL HEALTH", there is a section devoted to liquefied drinks and liquefied salads, some of which may be repeated here. It is suggested that you refer to this part of the cookbook for additional ideas and information.

In combining the foods for a liquefied drink, remember that it is sometimes necessary to liquefy one ingredient more than another. For instance, a bell pepper, summer squash and parsley may be chosen to make a drink. The bell pepper and parsley will take a little longer to break down than the squash, so allow less time to liquefy the squash, by breaking down the other ingredients first, and adding the squash at the last minute.

Celery usually has heavy strings, and it is best to break down the celery first because of its heavy fiber content; it should be liquefied from three to five minutes. Tomatoes, on the other hand, are more easily broken down, and liquefy much more quickly. However, they putrify very rapidly, so be sure to clean the liquefier thoroughly soon after making fresh tomato drinks. Unless the liquefier is kept free from spoiled food particles, illness may result from drinking the liquids containing these spoiled food particles.

LIQUEFIED FOODS AS AN AID TO BETTER HEALTH

Liquefied foods act as an aid in the correction of different disease conditions of the body. Practically any food or supplement to food can be taken in this form and even those who are very ill can digest and assimilate food that is broken down in this way. For example, if the trouble is a liver or gall bladder condition, then the fruits or vegetables can be liquefied in a base of dandelion tea, which, in itself, is a marvelous natural remedy for diseases in these organs of the body.

Whenever there is difficulty in taking raw, rough salads, as in colitis cases, liquefy the raw foods for easier digestion. To further eliminate all bulk, sieve the liquefied vegetables, making an excellent drink. We often find that a person with a fine sensitive mind also has a body that is fine and sensitive, and raw foods cannot be assimilated easily. To such a person the Blender is a boon.

CORRECT LIQUID BASE FOR LIQUEFIED DRINKS

All liquefied drinks require a liquid base, and to make fruit or vegetable drinks properly, you must select the correct base. To be really correct, a vegetable concoction should have a vegetable base, and a fruit drink a fruit base. Water may be used, but if the drink is being prepared for a specific purpose, such as re-mineralizing the body to replace the minerals that are lacking, or if we are trying to gain or lose weight, then the drink should be more concentrated, to speed up the process we are aiming for. Incidentally, avoid using table salt to season. Learn to rely on the salts in the vegetables themselves, or use natural flavoring such as a vegetable broth, made from either dehydrated vegetables or fresh vegetables. This makes a wonderful base as it is both tasty and nutritious, blending with any of the vegetable health drinks. Tomato juice is another fine base. Use it with the above combination of bell pepper, parsley and squash. Add endive or watercress, if desired. Vegetables may be cooked, just to tenderize, if you wish, but it is best to take them uncooked if you can, for greater food value. Endive, watercress, parsley and celery tops are all excellent vegetables to use as 'toppers' for drinks. Not only does each have its own particular vitamin and mineral value, but their distinctive flavoring adds interest to any vegetable drink. Dry vegetable powder makes an excellent seasoning for any liquefied vegetables, whatever the base.

HERBAL TEAS AS A BASE

Teas used as a base can also enrich the mineral content of a drink. However, the bitter flavor of some teas make them difficult to take. Combining them with the liquefied ingredients utilizes these herbal teas in the best way. Strawberry tea is one of the more delicious-tasting teas and is a fine tea for all intestinal difficulties. Natural foods liquefied in this tea can be used with great benefit for people with colitis.

Another mild-flavored tea, which may be used is oatstraw tea. Oatstraw tea is high in silicon, and using it as a base is a good way of getting silicon into the diet. Huckleberry tea may be used in the starch drinks. This tea has been found to be especially valuable in any difficulty with the digestion of starches by the pancreas. Elderberry and parsley teas have their own specific purposes in a body-building routine and can also be used as a base in the Blender. To make a drink more specific in its action, use the medicinal herbal teas as a base. This is the best way to get these teas down, especially those which are bitter.

We should learn to take some drinks whether we like their taste or not, for their value in body-building. If we learn to use the right combinations, we can make the less palatable drinks more tasty. Take time to experiment with your Blender and you will find it lots of fun.

All herbal teas may be used in either fruit or vegetable concoctions. Use from 1 to 1-1/2 teaspoonsful for each cup. Add boiling water and allow to steep for 3 to 5 minutes. Do not boil. Strain and sweeten with honey, if desired. Refer to "VITAL FOODS FOR TOTAL HEALTH" for further suggestions and measurements.

We might add that papaya tea as a base for fruit drinks is wonderful to help digest a protein meal, and is particularly good for an acid stomach, or a stomach with too little hydrochloric acid. Use this tea as a base in your liquefied protein drinks.

PROTEIN DRINKS

Some of these protein foods may also be used as a base:
yogurt, eggs, buttermilk, skim milk, soy bean milk, or soy
bean milk powder mixed with water, cottage cheese or nut
butters. These may need an additional base, depending on the
other ingredients. Soy bean milk, although considered a protein, may be combined with either fruits or vegetables. This
milk is a fine body-builder, containing all of the essential amino
acids, which feed your brain and nervous system. It is a good
protein for the stomach. If used in the powdered form, first
liquefy it with water, before adding the other ingredients.
Keep your protein nutrition high by taking it in this manner.

CARBOHYDRATE DRINKS

Cooked cereal may be made into a drink, using soy bean milk
as a base, except that this does not combine well with wheat
cereal. Liquefy your cereals to eliminate subjecting the
grains to heat. Use sprouted, soaked or freshly ground
grains--grind them in your own kitchen. If your liquefier will
not handle them, then one of the tiny electric mills that are
available will do it speedily, and all of the essential nutrients
will be retained. Add some soaked raisins, dates, dried figs
or some carob powder for a delicious and sustaining carbohydrate meal. The addition of flaxseed, which should also be
ground, makes for a smoother, thicker consistency. These
are only a few suggestions. Try out your own ideas to suit
your own particular taste and needs.

In making the many fruit drinks, vary them with added sweetness

using date sugar, apple concentrate, maple syrup and even blackstrap molasses. These not only sweeten but flavor and supplement as well. Carob powder, available at the Health Food stores, may also be used for added nutrition. Carob powder is a sweet flavoring, also called "St. John's Bread". It is the pod of a tropical tree and is mentioned in the Bible. It has been known to man since ancient times. It is highly nutritious and can be used instead of cocoa or chocolate.

REVIVED FRUIT

When using dried fruits--and they may be used as the basic ingredient of the drink or as flavoring--soak them first. Even raisins and dates should be soaked first. The reason we do not recommend using the unsoaked, dried fruit is because the fruits cannot be soaked through sufficiently in the Blender, no matter how long they are liquefied.

However, unsoaked, dried fruits, which have been liquefied, are better than unsoaked dried fruits eaten as they are. The maximum benefit is received from dried fruits if they are soaked first, as unsoaked dried fruits almost always cause gas before the digestive juices can get to them. The normal digestive process for dried fruits lasts about ten hours, and before the unsoaked dried fruits are adequately soaked up by the digestive juices, the body is ready to expel them. Thus, we do not get the good out of them unless they have been pre-soaked.

There is an art to soaking the dried fruits properly. Wash, add cold water to cover, and bring slowly to a boil. Remove from fire and allow them to stand all night. The boiled water kills all insects and parasites that might otherwise cause trouble. Remember to start with cold water, so that the increasing heat will penetrate into the inside of the fruit. We have called these "revived" fruits in the recipe section.

LET THE CHILDREN HELP

Everybody seems to like the fruit concoctions because most of us have a sweet tooth. Children, particularly, love sweet drinks and the natural sweetenings will definitely not harm them. Use them for the children's breakfast fruit, for in-between-meal snacks, as desserts, and before going to bed. Natural foods can be relied on to build their bodies healthfully, and to waylay sickness.

Allow the children to mix some of their own drinks, and let them find their own way of doing things, with supervision, of course. Their combinations may surprise you and turn out to be real good. Delectable combinations of foods which are compatible may be easily made, and these will help them and you to both feel better and look better. Where there are several

children and you cannot please them all, you may solve the
personal preference problem by assigning a separate day for
each on which they can treat the family to their own favorite
mix. You may be sure they will rarely be vegetable drinks,
for most everyone seems to prefer the sweet drinks. The
fruit concoctions usually win approval everywhere, even with
the sick. However, there are many ways of disguising the
less tasty, or more medicinal type of drink. Black walnut
flavoring is one way to dress these up, and mixed with soy
bean milk it is especially good.

FRUIT CONCOCTIONS

Ripe fruit should be served as soon as it is prepared in the
blender, because ripe fruit when it has been broken up and
the air allowed to get to it will oxidize very quickly. But be
sure to use the ripe fruits whenever they are in season. On
a hot day, when you don't wish to serve a heavy meal, let
the liquefied drink take its place. They are a meal in themselves as a drink or as a liquefied salad, and when protein
is added they make a completely balanced menu.

To make a fruit salad, you may combine fresh peaches and pears, adding to this combination a raw egg-yolk or soy bean milk. Oat-straw tea also makes a good base, as does strawberry or peach leaf tea. Or in place of the egg-yolk or soy bean milk, consider using cottage cheese, or fresh, raw milk, preferably goat's milk.

WITH NUTS

As a good protein in fruit salads, nuts or prepared nut butters may be used, but the nuts should be soaked overnight. Raw, hard nuts are difficult to chew, and unsoaked nuts react in the digestive tract the same way as the unsoaked dried fruits. Soak them in a little apple or pineapple juice, overnight, or in a little honey water. When ready to make the liquefied drink, the nuts will be soft, and the drink will be zesty and contain the full protein value for the digestive system. Sesame seeds or sunflower seeds soaked overnight also make fine seed milks.

MELON DRINKS

Cantaloupe or watermelon liquefied (using the entire melon, the seeds, flesh and rind for greater food value, as the different colors represent mineral elements) make delectable drinks, as do the other melons. Strain after blending to remove hulls.

Liquefy all the cantaloupe seeds, add a little soy milk or water and strain. This makes a highly nourishing seed milk drink.

25

FOR GAINING WEIGHT

As an in-between-meal snack, or as a food to gain weight, combinations of dried fruit, banana and pineapple juice are very good. For that extra weight-building, add flaxseed tea, as this tea will help put on pounds very quickly. Flaxseed tea is not too appetizing by itself, but when added to a liquefied fruit drink of bananas, dried peaches, prunes or raisins, with either a little soy bean milk or a tablespoon of nut butter, the taste of the flaxseed tea is camouflaged. When making liquefied drinks for gaining weight, use the sweet bases, such as apple juice concentrate, rather than the citrus juices.

FOR LOSING WEIGHT

For reducing use the low-calorie foods, leaving out the sweet flavorings and using grapefruit juice as a base, including the pulp. The pulp neutralizes the citric acid that is contained in the grapefruit, and prevents the stirring up of body acids. People with stomach disturbances should pay particular attention to this. Even when losing weight, fresh fruits can be used in the diet--peaches, pears and apples--particularly apples. Fresh apples are delicious liquefied. A tasty weight-losing drink is a sectioned orange with pulp, a cut apple, and a little pineapple juice for the base.

NIGHTCAPS

Although pure maple syrup may be the preferred sweetening in liquefied drinks, due to its high mineral and vitamin content, honey may also be used, particularly in its raw form. However, heated honey is not good for us. If a warm drink is preferred, use carob powder instead as a sweetener. Carob powder in a cup of warm water twenty minutes before retiring at night is a good relaxer and will help you to sleep. The

sweetening stimulates the heart activity, and, as relaxation
begins in the arterial and heart system, you will find that you
want to go to sleep. Most people need only a start to get to
sleep, due to body tension. If additional nutrition is needed,
mix the carob powder in warm soy bean milk or in broth.
Apple juice concentrate in a glass of warm water before going to bed will also help you to sleep.

In cases of heart condition, the sweetened drinks are very
good. Merely using a teaspoonful of honey in a glass of
water three times a day is a good remedy. The carbohydrate
drinks are particularly good for heart cases. If there is any
special trouble on the left side of the body, consider having
the starch drinks; while any trouble on the right side of the
body seems to benefit most from the protein drinks.

THERAPEUTIC DRINKS

Taking Vitamin C is one way of getting rid of infections in the
body. Bell peppers are one of the vegetables highest in
Vitamin C. If catarrhal troubles are the problem, a bell
pepper and tomato juice drink is a wonderful help. For arthritis and rheumatism, not only is Vitamin C necessary for
breaking down the calcium deposits in the joints, but sodium
is also needed in abundance. Celery is very high in sodium,
and with tomato juice as a base is beneficial for arthritic
and rheumatic conditions. If a little watercress, or endive,
is added to the foregoing combination, it makes a tasty

liquefied salad, which acts not only as a good cleanser and fortifier for the body in the above conditions, but is a good, balanced salad for the daily diet. This salad is also good for those who suffer with various stomach disorders and who cannot take raw salads.

Liquefied vegetable salads can be used as both fortifiers and eliminators. To make these liquefied vegetable salads more palatable and interesting, do the same as you would to a salad that was not liquefied, to add interest and to create a desire to eat it. Some cooked vegetables may be added, such as squash, peas, green beans, or sweet corn. Soaked raisins, dates, or other dried fruit add much to a vegetable salad, especially liquefied salads made with green leafy vegetables. Children especially love the flavor of dried fruit with these vegetables and will gladly eat these much-needed foods prepared in this way.

VEGETABLE SOUPS

Liquefied vegetables and fruits need not be served only as cocktails or salads. They also make delicious soups--raw, warmed or cooked. For example, a parsley, green pepper and summer squash combination, with some added herbs, warmed a little and seasoned with butter, can be served as a soup.

There is an infinite variety--try a cream soup as a hot dish. Heat your favorite liquefied soup, remove from the stove and add a little sweet raw cream, nut milk or ordinary milk.

If you like a cream sauce as a base, try using arrowroot. First blend the arrowroot with your milk or cream, or soybean powder and water if preferred, making a smooth consistency. Then cook gently in a double boiler, stirring until thickened.

Add the liquefied vegetables, and heat just to serving point. A little butter may be included when ready. Here are some suggestions. Liquefy spinach, kale or other green leaves for two or three seconds, and then add to the hot cream sauce with a little butter or cold-pressed oil. Remove from heat and serve immediately.

SOUPS FROM SPROUTS
Learn to make delicious soups by using sprouted legumes. Every household should have a sprouting program--grains, seeds, legumes, for their high nutritive value. Then these should be processed in the liquefier, with a suitable liquid or water and a little carrot juice. Add some sliced leek, a few green vegetable leaves, vegetable broth powder, oil, and some slippery elm powder to give it a smooth consistency and to benefit the stomach. When a warm soup is desired, heat only the liquid used as the base, and serve immediately with warm toast or croutons.

Try barley and green kale soup, first liquefying the soaked or sprouted whole barley. Or you may experiment with other grains, as well as other green leafy vegetables. This is a good way to utilize the coarser greens without cooking and destroying their nutritive value. These can be seasoned with vegetable broth powder. Flaxseed, freshly ground, is a good addition to the grain soups.

For additional information and suggestions on soups, refer to my cookbook, "VITAL FOODS FOR TOTAL HEALTH".

ILLNESS CAN RESULT FROM CHEMICAL DEPLETION:

Most people are short of some element in the body, and it is a good idea to supplement the liquefied diet with vitamins,

Missing Elements

minerals, and the amino acids in pill form. Take the concentrated foods, such as liquid chlorophyll, in your liquefied drinks to help put back what your body is short of. If you have been sick, or are sick now, remember that no sickness exists without a chemical depletion in the body. Every sickness is the result of some missing element, so use the concentrated foods to get you back on the road to health again. Incidentally, the food supplements in tablet or capsule form, which are to be taken along with meals, may be blended with the liquefied vegetables, fruits or soups.

ADD PROTEINS

Proteins added to the liquid salads not only furnish the dietary needs but serve as flavoring to enhance the less palatable taste of some vegetables. The whole raw egg or any of the unprocessed cheeses--the hard, yellow cheese, Swiss cheese, or cottage cheese are all very good for building the nervous system. Instead of eating a coddled egg on spinach, try eating a raw egg liquefied with comfrey (or other greens) and pineapple juice. If the body is protein-starved, due perhaps to overuse of the mind in studies or on the job, feed the brain and the nervous system with a teaspoon of sunflower seed three times daily. Also, use these sunflower seeds, which are so high in protein, to flavor liquefied drinks. Wheat germ may also be added. The Vitamin E in wheat germ feeds the glands and the nerves. A tablespoon daily is not too much for a run-down, worn-out body to absorb. At least six months of this daily diet regime may be needed for a depleted body.

THE QUESTION OF EGGS

If sodium is one of the elements you are concentrating on, take this mineral by adding whipped-to-a-froth egg white to a liquefied drink. The white of an egg is one of the highest sodium foods there is, and an aerated egg white will not damage the kidneys. As stated before, the whole egg, whipped with other ingredients, is very good as it has large amounts of lecithin, iron and nerve salts. For ulcer cases, top the drink with a well-beaten egg white.

The question has often been asked whether to use the whole egg, including the eggshell. Liquefied eggshells may be taken, but the carbonate form of calcium in eggshells is difficult for the digestive system to handle. The digestive juices do not break down the eggshell too easily, even though it is liquefied. However, if used, first soak the shell in orange juice or citric acid to break it down, or crush it into a broth and cook out all the soluble calcium contained in the shell.

CALCIUM

Calcium is found in green kale, which is one of the highest calcium foods; also in raw bone meal. Bone meal may be mixed into either fruit or vegetable drinks.

HERBS FOR SEASONING

The herbal seasonings are excellent with liquefied vegetables; sweet basil, rosemary, thyme, or mint--in fact, almost any of the herbs that are commonly used as kitchen aids to flavor or season. Experiment with herbs according to your own taste, but do not blend too many in one drink. At the most. two are suggested, for they are very penetrating. And in powdered form they are highly concentrated. A tomato salad made with tomato juice base, fresh tomato, a little olive oil, a touch of garlic, sweet basil and a few mint leaves is very tasty. Drink this salad slowly, immediately upon liquefying, because of the fresh tomato contained in it.

For those who can digest raw vegetable salads without liquefying, the liquefier can be used to make interesting dressings. Olive, sesame seed, soy bean, sunflower seed or peanut oil may be used as a base for the oil dressings. Use lemon juice instead of vinegar. Vary the oil dressings by adding tomato juice or avocado; and add dehydrated vegetable powder instead of salt to season. Celery powder or garlic powder may be used, and almost any of the herbs.

Instead of an oil dressing you can use sour cream or yogurt as a base and add one of the nut butters for flavoring; or use whipped sweet cream. A liquefied nut butter or sesame butter may be used as a dressing by itself.

A BALANCED HEALTH ROAD WITH THE BLENDER

IT'S TIME FOR A CHANGE

It isn't easy to break away from the old habits of living, and
sometimes we can't do it in a hurry. Serious illness may have
to be experienced before a right-about-face in the direction of
the more natural way to live can be made, and then we will
have to be educated to this new way. So let us not be impatient
if it takes time to learn. If we were living in a Garden of Eden
today, we could forget all about vitamin pills, glandular foods
and other supplementary aids to our present-day diets. But,
we are living in the Garden of Man, and we find ourselves in
difficulties because of man's inventions and man's money-
making activities. We are supposed to be our brother's keeper,
but there are very few people in food production who are think-
ing about what is best for the people from a health standpoint.
Certainly the people who distribute the so-called 'foods',
such as coffee, doughnuts, fried foods, cola, etc., are not in
business for the health of the people; they are in business for
themselves.

BALANCE YOUR DIET

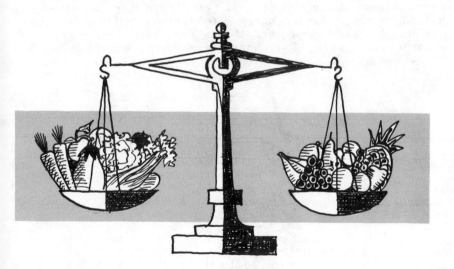

If we are going to keep well, we have to have a strong foundation on which to work; we have to feed the WHOLE body. When we eat, each meal should play its part in the daily program of feeding the whole body--one meal supplying the protein requirements and another the carbohydrate requirements, in combination with compatible fruits or vegetables to provide us with the essential vitamins and minerals. If we have a putrefactive bowel from overburdening the body with too many meat proteins, or with too much starch, we have to clean the body before healing can begin.

COLOR GIVES NATURAL VARIETY AND BALANCE

Healing starts as soon as we begin balancing our daily diet with plenty of vitamins and minerals. The Blender can be of the greatest help in this respect. When making the daily drinks, make them with plenty of color, as variety in the color of fruits and vegetables is your insurance against a depleted diet, or one which is not balanced. Use all the colorful fruits in season; use both underground and aboveground vegetables, and vary these daily. Having only peas and carrots is not variety enough. As explained before, the body molds to the fruits and vegetables we put into it and an overabundance of one kind of food, even though it is a healthful food, is not good. If a horse is fed too much alfalfa, it gets diarrhea and cannot work; if it is given only oats, it gets so hot it cannot work. Even horses must have a balanced diet.

DON'T LET YOUR BLENDER BECOME AN ORNAMENT

For the more healthful way to live, use the blender not only at
every mealtime, but in-between meals also. Liquefied foods
are both basic in the diet and adjuncts to it, to increase the
consumption of foods which may be needed. Concentrate on
drinks which are high in protein, the body-building food element, which is our most important nutritional requirement.
This routine is given only to help you get the best of health
and to use the liquefier for the future preparation of your
food.

IMPORTANCE OF PROTEINS

There are many sources of proteins--animal and vegetable
--some complete in amino acids and others not. All of the
eight essential amino acids, or ten according to some author-
ities, must be taken together to derive full benefits. Then in
the marvelous process of the digestive function, the body can
manufacture all of the others it requires, there being some
32 amino acids which have been discovered.

Use as great a variety of vegetable proteins as possible, such
as the nuts, legumes, grains, seeds, peanuts, wheat germ and
yeast. Yeast has the highest content of all. Learn about the
different types of yeast (popularly known as "brewer's"), for
newly developed biologically-active yeast is now on the market.

Probably the most important nutritional knowledge which should
concern everyone is the study of these proteins, because of their
widespread deficiency. Carefully examine all the facts, and
then each one should determine the regime which he can best
adapt for himself. Always keep in mind the most ideal diet
--simplified to the utmost--from sources and channels through

which the dignity of man and the balance in the economy of nature have been maintained to the highest possible degree. This is really food-for-thought!

ECONOMY AND HEALTH

The Blender will effect a measure of economy for you in the purchasing of fresh fruits and berries; if you will plan to use the fully ripened ones which can be made into delicious lique-fied nectars.

By making regular trips to your local market, you can avail yourself of those varieties which have reached their full stage of maturity, and which if not immediately disposed of would suffer deterioration and be a complete loss. Therefore, you can avail yourself of reduced prices, not only for the sake of your own pocketbook, but for general conservation. We should all practice this in an endeavor to avoid waste and to help control the price level of foods during the harvesting season.

A word of caution should be given regarding the use of these fully ripened products, which have the highest content of natural sugar and are superior in flavor. Use them at once before the chemical change of spoilage begins.

You and your family are on the road to thrilling adventures with foods! And you, the homemaker, will be released from much time and energy consuming food preparations by these new "instant" delectables, which will give you far more of the live food elements--the only materials your body can make use of. Let us no longer "kill" those wonderful life-containing forms of flavor and fragrance which nature gives us in her bounty, but rather encourage the growers to produce more of these "live" foods by natural methods for their maximum nutritional content.

Remember that everything in this book is written with the idea that you be given a basic understanding of how you can use foods and use the Blender. These are suggestions and helps to guide you in your own experiments for your own needs. You can change them, make them different, fit them into your own household requirements.

HEALTH IS EVER WITHIN YOUR REACH

Learn the right combinations of food and have variety in your diet. Use your Blender daily to get fresh food in greater amount,

to build stronger bodies and to help everyone enjoy a more
healthful way of living. Let us always treat ourselves and others
to the best and to the most natural food we can get. Let us use
the Blender to unlock the wonderful live juices in the cellulose
of plants and to bring us the golden nuggets within these tiny
cells and the treasures of minerals that are waiting to be used.
Natural remedies and drugs will do very little good unless we
change our habits of living, correct our diet and start living
the natural life. You will find that natural remedies will be
of little help if you continue to use coffee and alcohol which
can ruin the kidneys.

And let us also treat ourselves to the other priceless gifts of
Nature....fresh air, pure water, sunshine, exercise and proper
rest. Then, too, we can begin to educate ourselves in mind-
ease. As the body responds to our mental attitude, and since
our mind is subject to the power of suggestion, let us substitute good healthy, loving suggestions to help both the body and
the mind to function harmoniously. Body tension or relaxation
is developed through our thought, so we should be careful to
keep our mental attitude in order. Finding peace with ourselves
and with our fellow man is necessary for the good of our
physical well-being.

Remember: Health is ever within your reach.

GENERAL DIET FOR DAILY USE

BALANCED EATING REGIMEN

Make a habit of applying the following GENERAL DIET REGI-
MEN to your everyday living. THIS IS A HEALTHY WAY TO
LIVE BECAUSE when followed, you do not have to think of
vitamins, mineral elements or calories. After you have made
this daily regimen automatic, you can then be given more specific instruction for any troubles you may have.

The best diet, over a period of a day, is TWO different fruits,
at least 4 to 6 vegetables, ONE protein and ONE starch, with
fruit or vegetable juices in between meals. Eat at least TWO
green leafy vegetables a day. One-half the food you eat daily
should be raw. Consider this regimen a dietetic law.

Daily Menu:

	Before Breakfast:	On rising, take any natural, unsweetened fruit juice.
	Breakfast:	Fruit, Protein or Starch, Health Drink
	10:30:	Vegetable Broth, Vegetable Juice or Fruit Juice
	Lunch:	Raw Salad (or as directed) One or two Starches (if following strict regimen, use only one of the first 7 Starches daily.) Vary the Starch from day to day. Health Drink
	3:30:	Juice, Health Cocktail or Fruit
	Dinner:	Two cooked Vegetables, Small Salad, One Protein, Broth or Health Drink, if desired

Do not eat starch and protein together. Eat at separate meals.

Between fruit juice and breakfast, follow this program: Skin
brushing, exercise, hiking, deep breathing or playing. SHOWER:
Start warm and cool off until your breath quickens. Never shower

immediately on rising.

You may exchange your noon meal for the evening meal, but follow the same regimen. It takes exercise to handle raw food, and we generally get more after our noon meal. That is why a raw salad is advised at noon. If one eats sandwiches, it should be at noon. . . and with raw vegetables.

RULES OF EATING

1. If not entirely comfortable in mind and body from the previous meal time, you should miss the next meal.
2. Do not eat unless you have a keen desire for the plainest food.
3. Do not eat beyond your needs.
4. Be sure to thoroughly masticate your food.
5. Miss meals if in pain, emotionally upset, not hungry, chilled, overheated, and during acute illness.
6. Before retiring, use the slanting board.

FRUIT JUICES: Grape, prune, papaya, pineapple, black cherry, fig, or apple. On Doctor's advice you may have orange, grapefruit, lemon or tomato juice.

FRUITS: AT LEAST 2 Fruits Daily

Nectarines, peaches, apples, pears, apricots, sapota, watermelon, honeydew, casaba, grapes, berries, ripe strawberries, papayas, mangoes, persimmons, plums, fresh seedless figs. Use fruit in season.

* Revived dried fruits, such as prunes, raisins, figs, apricots,

Dates, ripe bananas. Sun dried or regular olives.

* All dried fruits must be put into cold water and brought to a boil. Turn off the flame at boiling point and let set overnight, using fruit the next day.

VEGETABLES: AT LEAST 4 to 6 Vegetables Daily

Raw Salad	Cooked Vegetables
asparagus	artichokes and Jerusalem
avocado	artichokes
bean sprouts	asparagus
beets and young tops	bean sprouts
broccoli (s)	beets and beet tops
cabbage (s)	broccoli (s)
carrots	Brussels sprouts (s)
cauliflower	cabbage (s)
celery	carrots
chives	cauliflower (s)
corn	celery
cucumber	corn
Jerusalem artichokes	eggplant
lettuce (green leafy type	lima beans
only;i.e., romaine,	okra
endive)	onions (s)
okra	parsnips
onions (s)	peas
parsley	spinach
peas	squash
peppers - red and green	string beans
radishes and tops	Swiss chard
spinach	tomatoes
sprouts	turnips and tops (s)
Swiss chard	zucchini
tomatoes (citrus)	or any vegetable other than
turnips and young tops (s)	potatoes.
young string beans	
watercress	
zucchini	
(s) - sulphur vegetable	

STARCHES: HAVE ONE starch daily.

1. Yellow corn meal
2. Baked potato
3. Baked banana (or at least dead ripe)
4. Barley
5. Steamed brown rice or wild rice.
6. Millet
7. Banana squash or Hubbard squash

Steel cut oatmeal, rolled oats

STARCHES   (Cont'd.)

      Rye meal or grits
      Buckwheat
      Whole wheat cereals
      Roman meal
      7 Grain Cereals

      Whole grain breads; e.g., whole wheat,
         whole rye, soy bean, mixed meal.

      Corn bread, bran muffins (see recipe section)
      Rye Krisp

PROTEINS: HAVE ONE protein daily

Once a week: Fish... Use a white fish having fins and
                 scales; such as, sole, halibut,
                 trout or sea trout.

Three times a week: Meat... Use only lean meat. Never
                 use pork, fats or cured meats.

Twice a week: Cottage Cheese... or any cheese that
                 breaks.

Once a week: Egg omelet, etc.

If vegetarian, use soy beans, lima beans, cottage cheese
                 or any cheese that breaks, meat
                 substitutes or vegetarian proteins;
                 sunflower or sesame seeds; nuts
                 and nut butters.

DRINKS:

Vegetable broth, soup, buttermilk, raw milk, goats milk,
whey, dandelion root (coffee substitute), carob powder
(chocolate substitute), oat straw tea, alfamint tea,
huckleberry tea, papaya tea or any other health drink.

Don't forget the daily supplements: Rice bran, sunflower seed,
wheat germ and dulse. Yeast, flaxseed meal, molasses and
whey are some of the other health-aids. These may be liquefied along with drinks or food.

GENERAL DAILY DIET

SAMPLE MENUS

Our daily program must include:

> Two different Fruits
> At least four to six Vegetables
> (Two green leafy vegetables)
> One Protein
> One Starch
> Fruit or Vegetable Juice between meals

About 60% of the food we eat should be raw.

BEFORE BREAKFAST--Upon arising, drink:

> Any natural, unsweetened fruit juice.

BREAKFAST:	Revived Fruit	Prunes with dash of lemon rind.
	Starch	Rye grits, honey, butter.
	Health Drink	Oatstraw Tea
	Fresh Fruit	Fresh peaches with raw apple sauce* and sprinkle of ground nuts*
	1 Protein	Scrambled egg*
	Health Drink	Hot Mock-Choc Drink (Carob). *
10:30 A.M.:	Vegetable Broth	
	Vegetable or fruit juice	Green Drink*
LUNCH:	Vegetable Soup	Split Pea soup*
	Raw Salad	Jellied Beet salad *
		Green Onions, cucumber slices, shredded carrot, Pimento Dressing. *
	1 Starch	Cornmeal Muffins *
	Health Drink	Alfamint Tea
3:30 P.M.:	Vegetable or fruit juice or fruit	Persimmon in whey. *

*Made in Blender - See Recipes

42

DINNER:	Small raw salad	Slaw*
	2 Cooked vegetables	Asparagus
		Garlic Butter*
		Baked carrots
	1 Protein	Nuttose Mushroom
		Loaf*
	Health Drink	Lemon Grass Tea
	Health Dessert	Raspberry Cream*
	(Permitted but not recommended.)	

ANOTHER SAMPLE MENU

FOR GENERAL DAILY DIET

BEFORE BREAKFAST--upon rising, drink:

Any natural, unsweetened fruit juice.

BREAKFAST: Revived Fruit   Revived Black
                                     Mission Figs, Coconut,
                                     Sliced Banana with
                                        Cream.
              Starch   Rolled Oats
              Health Drink   Shavegrass Tea

              Fruit   Baked Apple stuffed
                                        with raisins, Papaya
                                        Sauce*. or half Canta-
                                        loupe with Strawberries.
              1 Protein   Cottage Cheese or Nut
                                        Butter*
              Health Drink   Golden Seal Tea

10:30 A.M.:   Carrot Juice

LUNCH: Vegetable Soup   Cream of Spinach Soup*
              Raw Salad   Lettuce, Tomato, Pep-
                                        per Salad.
                                     Shredded Raw Beet*
                                     Celery Sticks, Olives
                                     Roquefort Dressing*
              1 Starch   Baked Potato
              Health Drink   Peppermint Tea

3:30 P.M.:   Fruit Cocktail

DINNER: Small Raw Salad   Tossed Salad
              2 Cooked Vegetables   String Beans, Steamed
                                        Cauliflower with
                                        Cheese Sauce*
              1 Protein   Herb Omelet*
              Health Drink   Strawberry Tea
              Health Dessert   Sea Foam*
                 (Permitted but not recommended)

                 * Made in Blender-See Recipes.

                              44

HEALTH DIVIDENDS...FROM EXTRAS IN THE DIET

There are a few foods which have long been symbols of
"health foods" in general. These include yogurt, blackstrap
molasses, wheat germ, powdered skim milk and brewer's
yeast. We have added sprouts, whey and vegetable broth
powder and seasoning because of their highly nourishing qual-
ities and versatility and their actual goodness. This important business of nutrition should be fun! Have you ever experienced how really delicious yogurt and blackstrap molasses
can be?

One should let the full flavor of each individual food be
developed by thorough salivation in the mouth in order to be
able to realize the distinctive taste inherent in each one.
To derive the utmost in nutrition, there should be an appeal
to the senses of smell, taste and sight which will stimulate
the flow of digestive juices and cause the "mouth to water".

Make these foods standard in any dietary regimen. And
remember the adage, "Variety is the spice of life". We,
therefore, give you some additional "health-ideas" with
which you may not be familiar and which have been used
in the following recipe section.

Agar Agar: A vegetarian substitute for gelatin, made
                    from seaweed. Use in place of gelatin.

Arrowroot: A good thickening powder--high in cal-
                    cium and alkaline in reaction.

*Bran Water: An extract of minerals from simmering
                    common wheat bran. See recipe.

Carob: Chocolate-flavored powder with none of
                    the disadvantages of cocoa and with
                    higher nutritional value. A chocolate
                    is now made from carob flour.

Dandelion Root Coffee:
Has "coffee taste"--made from roasted root of dandelion.   Good for the liver.

Dessicated Liver: For building the blood stream.

Dulse:
A Nova Scotia powdered seaweed very high in iodine and manganese.   A good supplementary food.   Can be used as a salty seasoning.

Flaxseed Meal and Tea:
Healing for intestinal tract; good natural laxative.

Fruit Juice Concentrates:
Pure concentrates of whole fruits prepared by a special vacuum method without high temperatures.   Cherry, apple and grape in Hidden Valley Brand Products.

Gelatin:
Use a pure 100% gelatin as put out by Hidden Valley Brand Products.   A valuable protein supplement, handy in normal and reducing diets.

*Health Cream Cheese:
Regular Cream Cheese is made by a quick acid process which makes it undesirable healthwise.   Make your own from recipe given.

Herbs: See list.

*Herb Teas:
Healthful drinks made from steeping various herbs in boiling water.   See recipe (also list).

Molasses:
High in iron and sugar carbohydrate (Use the unsulphured Blackstrap).

*Oatstraw Tea: A rich silicon tea--see recipe.

*Oils and Fats: See information following.

* See following pages for recipes.

*Revived Dried Fruits:	To kill bacteria and eggs, and to soften dried fruits, such as figs, prunes, apricots, we have a special method. See recipe.
Rice Polishings:	High in silicon and source of Vitamin B.
Soy Milk:	A milk substitute, non-catarrh forming. Obtainable in powder form from Health Stores.
Soy Sauce:	Flavoring derived from soybeans. Use in broths, in cooking vegetables, in gravies and vegetarian loaves, instead of salt.
*Sprouts:	See recipe.
Wheat Germ:	Source of Vitamin B and Vitamin E.
*Whey (liquid):	See recipe.
Whey (Powdered):	A high sodium food, good for arthritis and reducing diets, in handy powder form, made from fresh raw milk. Obtainable as a Hidden Valley Brand Product.
*Vegetable Broth Powder and Seasoning:	See following.
Vegetable Water or Vegetable Stock or Vegetable Broth:	Juices in which vegetables have been cooked, free from meat stock. Rich in minerals.
Yeast:	Source of Vitamin B--high in Protein. Brewers Yeast may be sprinkled on cereals, fruits, in drinks, etc.
*Yogurt:	See recipe.

Any ingredients in the following recipes with which you are not familiar with may be purchased from a Health Food Store.

*   See following pages for recipes.

BRAN WATER OR WHEAT BRAN TONIC
(For nutritional deficiencies)

Bran is one of our highest foods in silicon. It has the structural elements that give tone and power to the body that most of us are lacking. The 16 chemical elements can be found in very good proportion in bran water, if properly made.

To get the greatest good from this bran tonic, make and use it in the following manner:

Take one cup of sifted bran to about three cups of water and bring to a boil. Do not boil for even a moment. Remove from the fire and allow to cool. Strain off the liquid into a quart mason jar and refrigerate overnight if possible. The starch will settle to the bottom of the jar. Pour off very carefully without disturbing the starch and stop pouring the moment the starch begins to come up. Drink three or four cups of this liquid daily, half an hour before meals, if possible. Do this for two or three months for the best results. Add a little celery salt, garlic salt or vegetable seasoning, and take either warm or cool. By adding a cherry concentrate to the bran tonic, it becomes a wonderful drink for the children and one they will not refuse. Another fine variation is to add liquid chlorophyll, one teaspoon per cup. This is one of the greatest tonics I know for the blood stream. Be convinced by trying it over a period of one month.

This tonic also makes a good stock for soup, being interchangeable with vegetable broth and herb teas for this purpose. We have used it in our soup recipes occasionally to give you the idea.

HEALTH CREAM CHEESE

1/2 cup Cottage Cheese
1/2 cup Yogurt
1/2 cup Sour Cream
1 tsp Gelatin

Blend in liquefier, scraping down frequently until a smooth consistency is arrived at. Leave in refrigerator an hour or two to thicken. Develops sharpness on keeping a couple of days.

HERB TEAS

Take 1 tsp. to 1-½ tsp. Dried Herbs; e.g., Mint, Papaya, Clover, Comfrey and add to 1 cup really boiling water. Then steep 3 to 5 minutes. Strain.

OATSTRAW TEA

Cover ordinary clean Oat Hay, Oat Straw, or Chaff with cold water, bring to boil. Boil gently 10 minutes. Strain carefully.

OIL AND FATS

It is not advisable to use much Oil or Fat in the diet. These are unnatural concentrations and are very hard on the liver. Much, too, has been made of cholesterol in these times. Cholesterol is a waxy, white, fat-soluble substance that is an essential part of the composition of the body cells and the functioning of blood circulation. However, in excess amounts it creates a health hazard. This can result from an over-indulgence in Fats and Oils.

On the whole, vegetable oils--Sesame, Safflower, Soy, Corn and Cottonseed are to be preferred as they are highest in poly-unsaturated fatty acids. Avocado oil will be the oil of the future. Do not use any oil which has been heated or hydrogenated. Never fry or otherwise cook food in oil. Choose some other method of cooking, and add a little oil to flavor when cooking is completed. Heated oils are your worst enemy. They put the greatest amount of cholesterol in the bloodstream.

TO REVIVE DRIED FRUITS

Wash Fruits, cover with cold water and bring to boil. Turn off heat and leave stand overnight.

SPROUTS

Sprouts are the finest thing for helping our health. When you are green inside, you are clean inside. Chlorophyll has been used for various purposes and is one of the finest foods for fast assimilation and for getting into the blood stream quickly. The freshest way you can get chlorophyll is in sprouts. They are the finest food for adding basic vitamins and minerals to the diet.

Recipes for Making Sprouts

Alfalfa seeds and mung beans (which are soybeans) are among
the most easily sprouted. There are many ways of growing
them.

Get a porous, unglazed clay dish--shallow, like a pie pan--and
sprinkle seeds generously over the bottom of it after putting a
small amount of water in the dish. Cover with a cheesecloth to
keep out dust, and put in a dark place. Cover with a black
cloth if that is easier. Dampen two or three times a day, or
just enough to keep the sprouts moist.

Another method is to take a wide-mouthed glass jar and put a
quarter cup of untreated alfalfa seeds or mung bean seeds into
the jar. Fill the jar with water so that the seeds are well
covered, and let stand at room temperature for a half hour, pour
off the water, then every three or four hours put water in the
jar and pour off, leaving the sprouts just damp or wet. The
average kitchen temperature is about right for growing sprouts.
They do not need to be in the sunlight. In about three days you
will have a harvest of delicious sprouts. (Keep jar lying on side
with lid off.)

Liquefying Sprouts:

The liquefying of sprouted grains, seeds and legumes (beans of
all varieties, peas, lentils) provides a variety of ways to enjoy
these wonderful foods. You should set up a sprouting schedule
in your food planning program and always have them on hand
as an accompaniment to your salads, for they have an unusual
flavor and benefit. Expand your sprouting program until you
include in rotation a variety of the whole grains--our "staff of
life". You will want to give these the prominent place which
bread has for so long held in the human diet. Sprouting changes
the chemical structure, converting a concentrated carbohydrate
into a green vegetable state, creating an important factor in
maintaining the proper acid-alkaline balance in the organism.

Liquefy them in juices and soups. Mix in salads and omelets.
Use in sandwiches combined with date paste, or with avocado
dressing.

WHEY

Whey is the fluid in milk which remains after the cream and
casein (protein) have been removed in the process of making

cheese. It is one of the greatest foods--very important in intestinal management and one of the highest foods in sodium content. May be used by itself as a drink or in combination with a wide variety of foods, especially in liquefied drinks.

Recipe For Whey and Homemade Cottage Cheese:

Pour two quarts of raw whole milk (goat's milk if available) into an enamel pan, cover and allow to stand at room temperature until sour, then place at a temperature around 100° until it clabbers (thickens). Do not stir. Put on a very slow burner and heat gradually, but do not allow it to become too hot, so that the fluids will begin to separate. Put the thick curd into a cloth bag and tie. Hang to drip until dry. Overnight is best. Remove and place in a jar or dish then refrigerate. This makes cottage cheese supreme. And every drop of the whey which has drained off should be used in the various liquefied whey drinks.

VEGETABLE BROTH POWDER AND SEASONING

Truly the "salt of the earth", made from raw vegetables and concentrated grain amino acids which impart a natural salty taste. Contains organic minerals needed by the body. This is an excellent seasoning for general purposes instead of ordinary table salt, a Hidden Valley Brand Product.

Use it also for a broth between meals or at bedtime and in all liquefied vegetable preparations. (See Recipe Section following.)

YOGURT

Yogurt is a cultured milk, originally developed in the Balkan countries where longevity is attributed to its extensive use. It is an excellent protein food, containing "friendly bacteria" necessary for proper intestinal hygiene; it is easily digested, especially for those to whom milk and milk products present difficulties. Learn to eat it plain, or with a little vegetable broth powder, honey, molasses or fruit juice concentrate, with berries or fruit in any form.

Liquefy Yogurt with fruit juice or fruit, making an excellent fruit whip. Use as a salad dressing.

Try making your own, using raw goat's milk if possible.

Recipe for Yogurt: With one quart of goat's milk or raw milk.

Put one quart of milk in a 2-quart saucepan. Allow to boil till milk rises to top of pan. Remove immediately from fire.

Pour milk into Pyrex container (which has a cover). Allow to cool till little finger can be inserted to the count of ten without too much discomfort.

Remove skin forming on milk.

Use 1 Tbsp. of starter from previous batch (or 2 Tbsps. if in area of high altitude).

Mix starter in cup with little of the warm milk to fill cup and stir. Then add to bowl of milk and mix thoroughly.

Put all the milk in the bowl and place into the gas oven (with pilot). Allow to stand two hours to jell (possibly more). It should have the consistency of custard.

Finally, cool in refrigerator. Cover before storing in your refrigerator.

RIGHT COMBINATIONS

ALKALINE-FORMING, ACID-FORMING FOOD CHART

Generally speaking, the acid-forming foods, such as bread, grain, eggs, fish, meat, etc. are the builders of the body, while the alkaline-forming foods, such as fruits and vegetables, are the cleansers. We need both. But we need these foods and elements in the right amounts. Only when they are taken in excess are they harmful. However, more of the cleansing or alkaline-forming foods should be consumed to help neutralize the waste acids in our body. If the body is kept clean and balanced by an abundance of alkaline-forming foods, then a surprisingly small amount of acid-forming, or so-called nourishing foods, will be needed. A good proportion to try is 80% alkaline-forming foods and 20% acid-forming foods.

Foods Preceded by the Letters "AL" are <u>ALKALINE-FORMING</u>.

Foods Preceded by the Letters "AC" are <u>ACID-FORMING</u>.

<u>Column No. 1</u>	<u>Column No. 2</u>	<u>Column No. 3</u>
Non-Starch Foods (Vegetables)	Proteins and Fruits	Starch Foods (Carbohydrates)

Foods in Column No. 1 and Column No. 2
may be combined.
Foods in Column No. 1 and Column No. 3
may be combined.
<u>Do</u> <u>not</u> combine foods in Column No. 2 and
Column No. 3.

AL Alfalfa	AC Beef	AL Bananas
AL Artichokes	AC Buttermilk	AC Barley
AL Asparagus	AC Chicken	AC Beans (Lima)
AL Beans (String)	AC Clams	AC Beans (White)
AL Beans (Wax)	AC Cottage Cheese	AC Bread
AL Beets (Whole)	AC Crab	AC Cereals
AL Beet Leaves	AC Duck	AC Chestnuts
AL Broccoli	AC Eggs	AC Corn
AL Cabbage(White)	AC Fish	AC Crackers
AL Cabbage (Red)	AC Gelatin	AC Cornstarch
AL Carrots	AC Lamb	AC Gluten Flour
AL Carrot Tops	AC Lobster	AC Lentils
AL Cauliflower	AC Mutton	AC Macaroni

Column No. 1	Column No. 2	Column No. 3
Non-Starch Foods (Vegetables)	Proteins and Fruits Proteins	Starch Foods (Carbohydrates)

Column No. 1	Column No. 2	Column No. 3
AL Celery Knobs	AC Nuts	AC Maize
AL Chicory	AC Oyster	AC Millet Rye
AL Corn	AC Pork	AC Oatmeal
AL Cucumbers	AC Rabbit	AC Peanuts
AL Dandelions	AC Turkey	AC Peanut Butter
AL Eggplant	AC Turtle	AC Peas (Dried)
AL Endive	AC Veal	AC Potatoes (Sweet)
AL Garlic		AL Potatoes (White)
AL Horseradish	Fruits	AL Pumpkin
AL Kale		AC Rice (Brown)
AL Kohlrabi	AL All Berries	AC Rice (Polished)
AL Leek	AL Apples	AC Roman Meal
AL Lettuce	AL Apricots	AC Rye Flour
AL Mushrooms	AL Avocados	AL Squash (Hub'd.)
AL Okra	AL Cantaloupes	AC Tapioca
AL Olives (Ripe)	AL Cranberries	
AL Onions	AL Currants	- - - - - - - -
AL Oysterplant	AL Dates	
AL Parsley	AL Figs	AL Honey (Pure)
AL Parsnips	AL Grapes	AC Raw Sugar
AL Peas (Fresh)	AL Grapefruit	
AL Peppers (Sweet)	AL Lemons	
AL Radishes	AL Limes	
AL Rutabagas	AL Oranges	
AL Savory	AL Peaches	
AL Sea Lettuce	AL Pears	
AL Sorrel	AL Persimmons	
AL Soybean (Products)	AL Pineapple	
AL Spinach	AL Plums	
AL Sprouts	AL Prunes	
AL Summer Squash	AL Raisins	
AL Swiss Chard	AL Rhubarb	
AL Turnips	AL Tomatoes	
AL Watercress		

The above table of foods is taken from Ragnar Berg of Germany.

FRUIT COMBINATIONS

Fruits should be eaten in a natural harmony. Oranges, grapefruits, tangerines and lemons, as the natural-acid fruits, go nicely with the other acid fruits like pineapple, cranberries, etc. They do not combine well with the sweet or dried fruits, such as prunes, figs, raisins or dates.

The slightly acid, or sub-acid fruits, such as apples, pears, plums, peaches, apricots, persimmons combine fairly well with the acid fruits, but I do not especially recommend the combination.

Melons and berries should always be eaten alone. There is no more disagreeable surprise for your stomach, for example, than watermelon eaten in conjunction with another food.

With fruits, the safest procedure is the simplest one. You can use cream, if you must, but never sugar. White sugar is actually a poison to your system, no matter how much energy you may seem to get from it, and brown sugar is like gilding the lily. The fruit itself has plenty of sugar--you do not need to put sugar on your sugar!

In general, remember that sweet milk goes best with the acid fruits, while sour milk, like clabber, yogurt or even cottage cheese, goes best with the slightly acid or sub-acid fruits. In other words, a glass of milk at orange juice time is a permissable combination. However, remember to keep your diet simple.
- - - - - - - - - - - - -

Foods in Column A and Column B may be combined.
Foods in Column B and Column C may be combined.
Do not combine foods in Column A and Column C.
(Do not combine acid fruits with sweet dried fruits.)
    Berries and melons are best eaten alone.

Column A	Column B	Column C
Acid Fruits	Sub-Acid Fruits	Sweet or Dried Fruits
Oranges	Apples	Dates
Lemons	Pears	Figs
Grapefruit	Plums	Raisins
Limes	Peaches	Prunes
Cranberries	Pineapple	Bananas
Tomatoes	Grapes	
	Apricots	
	Persimmons	

THE VITAMINS

Talk about vitamins is more or less on the tongue of every
dietitian, housewife, doctor and groceryman today. They first
commanded attention probably back in 1747 when oranges and
lemons were found to prevent scurvy. To date, science has
found some seven vitamins and will probably find many more in
years to come. Vitamins seem to offer the "kick" to the
minerals that enter our bodies. They are little invisible help-
ers ready to right every wrong that may come about in the com-
plicated processes of building and maintaining a perfect body.

Natural foods contain all the vitamins that have been discovered
and will be discovered. Scurvy, pellagra, beri-beri, and most
all diseases are the result, partially at least, of vitamin-starv-
ed foods. Cheat the body of vitamin-rich food, and you are on
a disease producing diet. Quality foods count--not quantity.
And remember, vitamins essential to our bodies are best found
in all natural foods.

VITAMIN A

Foods Rich in Vitamin A :

Yellow Vegetables, Green Leafy
Vegetables, such as Spinach
Swiss Chard, Green Lettuce;
Tomatoes, Carrots, Green Peas,
Sweet Potatoes, Endive, Beet
Leaves, Cabbage, Mustard
Greens, Brussels Sprouts,
Green Celery, Yellow Squash.

Bananas, Apricots,
Peaches, Melons, Cherries,
Papaya, Avocados, Mangoes,
Prunes and Pineapple.

Milk, Butterfat, Egg Yolk,
Whole Milk, Cheese.

Injured by high temperature.

Conditions Caused by Lack of Vitamin A:

Loss of weight and vigor.
Loss of vitality and growth.
Loss of strength and glandular balance. Eye infections,
emaciation, acne, poor vision,
poor digestion, diarrhea,
nephritis, rough and dry skin.
(Children require this
vitamin more than
adults.)

Conditions Controlled by Vitamin A:

Tissues become more resis-
tant, especially to colds and
catarrhal infections in respiratory organs, sinuses, ears,
bladder, skin and digestive
tract. Increases blood plate-
lets. Promotes growth and
feeling of well-being.
Anti-ophthalmic.

Vitamin A (Cont'd.)

Stability: (Fat Soluble)

Cooking temperatures do not
affect this vitamin much, but
it is destroyed by heat when
in the presence of oxygen.

Storage:

This vitamin is stored in the
body for future needs. The
surplus is depleted quickly
under strain and stress.

VITAMIN B

Foods Rich in Vitamin B:

Yeast, Egg Yolk, Whole Milk,
Lean Beef, Liver, Kidney,
Asparagus, Spinach, Tomatoes,
Peas, Turnip Greens. Mus-
tard Greens, Chard, Celery,
Potatoes, Carrots, Cabbage,
Beet Leaves, Cauliflower,
Lettuce, Broccoli, Onions,
Peppers, Grapefruit, Lemons,
Oranges, Bananas, Pineapple,
Apples, Melon, Peaches,
Avocados, Grapes, Prunes,
Dates, Cherries, Pears, Whole
Grains, Wheat, Rye, Corn,
Rice, Barley, Oats, Almonds,
Walnuts, Chestnuts, Brazil
Nuts, Pecans, all Legumes.

Injured by high temperature.

Conditions Caused by Lack of Vitamin B:

Nervous exhaustion, loss of
growth, loss of reproductive
function, loss of appetite.
Beri-beri, polyneuritis, intestinal gas, fermentation,
faulty nutrition and assimilation, indigestion, convulsions,
soreness, pain, lack of diges-
ive juices, slow heart beat and
impaired insulin secretions.

Conditions Controlled by Vitamin B:

Better absorption of food and
normalizes the brain and
nervous system by increasing
metabolic processes.

Anti-neuritic.

Vitamin B (Cont'd.)

Stability: (Water Soluble)

Ordinary cooking does not affect
Vitamin B, although heat might
affect it. Soda added to keep
vegetables green destroys Vitamin B.

Storage:

Limited quantities of Vitamin
B are stored in the body.

VITAMIN C

Foods Rich in Vitamin C:

Oranges, Lemons, Grape-
fruit, Limes, Melons,
Berries, Apples, Pineapple,
Cabbage, Tomatoes, Spinach,
Peas, Broccoli, Rutabagas,
Collards, Brussels Sprouts,
Celery, Parsley, Endive,
Watercress, Turnips, Cucum-
bers, Cauliflower, Radishes.

Destroyed by high temperature.

Stability: (Water Soluble)

Destroyed by heat, cooking,
low temperature and oxidation.

Storage:

Vitamin C is not stored in the
body--we must get a fresh supply
every day in our diet.

Conditions Caused by Lack
of Vitamin C:

Tender, painful swelling of
joints, poor health, faulty
nutrition, scurvy, loss of
appetite, loss of weight,
irritable temper, poor complexion, loss of energy, ir-
regular heart action, rapid
respiration, reduced hemo-
globin, reduced secretion of
adrenals, cataract, hemorr-
hage.

Conditions Controlled by
Vitamin C:

A marvelous health promoter,
as it wards off acidosis.

Anti-ascorbutic

VITAMIN D

Foods Rich in Vitamin D

Fish oils, Cod Liver Oil, Halibut, Halibut Liver Oils, Egg Yolk, Butter and Milk, Green Leafy Vegetables grown in the sunshine.

Injured by High
        Temperature.

Stability: (Fat Soluble)

Heat or oxidation does not affect Vitamin D.

Storage:

Nature expects us to get this vitamin from the sun. We tap our greatest source by exposing the skin to sunlight. This sunlight contains ultra-violet rays which change the ergosterol in the skin into limited amounts of Vitamin D.

A limited amount of Vitamin D is stored in the body.

Conditions Caused by Lack of Vitamin D:

Rickets, soft bones, lack of body tone, fatigue, respiratory infections, irritability, restlessness, constipation, ptosis, prolapsus, dental caries, retards growth. Instability of nervous system.

Conditions Controlled by Vitamin D:

Facilitates absorption of calcium and phosphorus from foods, consequently a great bone builder. Guards against tuberculosis. Regulates mineral metabolism.

Anti-rachitic

VITAMIN E

Foods Rich in Vitamin E:

Milk, Cottage Cheese and Wheat Germ. Vegetable Oils, such as Olive Oil and Soybean Oil. Green and Leafy Vegetables, Yellow Corn and Raw Fruits.

Quite Stable.

Conditions Caused by Lack of Vitamin E:

Sterility, loss of adult vitality.

Conditions Controlled by Vitamin E:

Essential in reproduction,

Vitamin E (Cont'd.)

Stability: (Fat Soluble)

Heat or oxidation do not affect
Vitamin E.

Storage:

Limited supply is stored in
body.

Conditions Controlled by
Vitamin E: (Cont'd.)

poor lactation, menstrual
disorders, miscarriage, dull
mentality, pessimism, des-
pondency and loss of courage.

Anti-sterility.

VITAMIN F

Foods Rich in Vitamin F:

Yeast, Whole Grain and Eggs,
Root Vegetables and Fresh
Spinach, Fruits--particular-
ly Orange Juice, Nuts.

Stability: (Water Soluble)

Long cooking destroys Vitamin
F.

Storage:

More Vitamin F is necessary
as the metabolic rate in-
creases in the body.

Conditions Caused by Lack
of Vitamin F:

Stunted growth, sexual im-
maturity, falling hair, bald-
ness, loss of appetite, skin
disorders, nervousness and
eczema.

Conditions Controlled by
Vitamin F:

Vitamin F is necessary for
an all-round development.

Growth Promoting.

VITAMIN G (B2)

Food Rich in Vitamin G:

Whole Milk, Buttermilk,
Cheese, Cream, Eggs,
Meats, Wheat Germ, Yeast,
Green Leafy Vegetables.

Injured by High Temperatures.

Conditions Caused by Lack of
Vitamin G:

Nerve disorders, irritability,
pellagra, skin eruptions, loss
of hair, stomach disorders,
cataracts, old age, lack of
growth, poor appetite, digestive disturbances.

Vitamin G (B2) (Cont'd.)

Stability: (Water Soluble)

Heat does not affect Vitamin
G.

Storage

A limited amount is stored
in the body. It must be added
daily.

Conditions Controlled by
Vitamin G:

Prolongs life span, increases
adult vitality.

Anti-pellagric

- - - - - - - - - - -

THE MINERALS

T. . . . .Injured or destroyed by
              high temperatures
W. . . . .Dissolves in water.
O. . . . .Oxidizes rapidly.

CHEMICAL ELEMENT ANALYSIS CHART

Essential Mineral Salt	Principal Sources	Mineral Salt Activity in the Body
CALCIUM: Found and needed mostly in structural system. Tooth and bone mineral. (W. T. O.)	Milk, Cheese, Raw Egg Yolk, Apricots, Figs, Prunes, Cranberries, Gooseberries, cabbage, Spinach, Parsnips, Lettuce, Onions, Dates, Bran, Tops of Vegetables.	Tone building in the Body. Builds and maintains bone structure. Gives vitality and endurance. Heals wounds. Counteracts acid.
CHLORINE: Found and needed mostly in digestive system and secretions. (T.)	Goat Milk, Cow Milk, Salt, Fish, Cheese, Coconut, Beets, Radishes, Common Salt.	Cleanser in the Body. Cleans. Expels waste. Freshens, purifies, disinfects.

Chemical Element Analysis Chart (Cont'd.)

Essential Mineral Salt	Principal Sources	Mineral Salt Activity in the Body
FLUORINE: Found and needed mostly in the structural system. Tooth enamel. Preserves bone. (T.)	Cauliflower, Cabbage, Cheese, Raw Goat Milk, Raw Egg Yolk. Cod Liver Oil, Brussels Sprouts, Spinach, Tomatoes, Watercress.	Disease resister and beautifier. Strengthens tendons. Knits bones.
IODINE: Found and needed mostly in nervous system. Gland and brain mineral. (O. T.)	Powdered Nova Scotia Dulce and Sea Lettuce (very high), Sea Foods, Carrots, Pears, Onions, Tomatoes, Pineapple, Potato Skins, Cod Liver Oil, Garlic, Watercress.	Metabolism normalizer in the Body. Prevents goiter, normalizes gland and cell action. Ejects and counteracts poisons.
IRON: Found in blood. Stored in liver. (O. W.)	All Green Leafy Vegetables, Blackberries, Black Cherries, Egg Yolk, Liver, Oysters, Potato Peelings, Whole Wheat.	Essential in blood as oxygen carrier. Promotes vitality and ambition. Prevents anemia.
MAGNESIUM: Found and needed mostly in the digestive system. Nerve mineral. Nature's laxative. (W. T.)	Grapefruit, Oranges, Figs, Whole Barley, Corn, Wheat, Coconut, Goat's Milk, Raw Egg Yolk.	New Cell Promoter in the Body. Relaxes. Refreshens system and prevents and relieves constipation and autointoxication.
MANGANESE: Found and needed mostly in nervous system. Tissue strengthener. Memory mineral. (W.)	Nasturtium Leaves, Raw Egg Yolk, Almonds, Walnuts, Watercress, Mint, Parsley, Wintergreen, Endive and Pignolia Nuts.	Controlling Nerves in the Body. Increases resistance. Co-ordinates thought and action. Improves memory.

Essential Mineral Salt	Principal Sources	Mineral Salt Activity in the Body
PHOSPHORUS: Found and needed mostly in nervous system. Brain and bone mineral. (T.W.)	Sea Foods, Milk, raw Egg Yolk, Parsnips, Whole Wheat, Barley, Yellow Corn, Nuts, Peas, Beans, Lentils.	Body and nerve builder in the Body. Nourishes brain and nerves. Builds power of thought. Stimulates growth of hair and bone.
POTASSIUM: Found and needed mostly in digestive system. Tissue and secretion mineral. (W)	Potato Skin, Dandelion, Dill, Sage, Cress, Dried Olives, Parsley, Blueberries, Peaches, Prunes, Coconut, Gooseberries, Cabbage, Figs, Almonds.	Healer in the Body. Liver activator. Strongly alkaline. Makes tissues elastic, muscles supple, creates grace, beauty, good disposition.
SILICON: Found and needed mostly in structural system. Nails, skin, teeth and hair. (W.)	Oats, Barley, Spinach, Asparagus, Lettuce, Tomatoes, Cabbage, Figs, Strawberries.	Surgeon in the Body. Gives keen hearing, sparkling eyes, hard teeth, glossy hair. Tones system and gives resistance to the Body.
SODIUM: Found and needed mostly in digestive system. Gland, ligament and blood builder. (W.)	Okra, Celery, Carrots, Beets, Cucumbers, String Beans, Asparagus, Turnips, Strawberries, Oat Meal, Cheese, Raw Egg Yolk, Coconut, Black Figs.	Youth maintainer in the Body. Aids digestion. Counteracts acidosis. Halts fermentation. Purifies the blood.

Chemical Element Analysis Chart (Cont'd.)

Essential Mineral Salt	Principal Sources	Mineral Salt Activity in the Body
SULPHUR: Found and needed mostly in the nervous system. Brain and tissue mineral. (O. T.)	Cabbage and Cauliflower, Onions, Asparagus, Carrots, Horseradish, Shrimp, Chestnuts, Mustard Greens.	Purifies and activates the Body. Purifies and tones the system. Intensifies feeling and emotion.

- - - - - - - - - - - - - -

SUPPLEMENTS AND FORTIFIERS

Tablets, powders, protein and amino acid preparations, mineral and vitamin supplements, oils such as wheat germ oil, capsules (discard the "shell"), medicinal herbs and other necessary supplmentary preparations can be added to liquefied drinks so that one wouldn't know they were there. Their taste can be camouflaged with a counteracting flavor.

Here are some of the tablets and powders that can be used with benefit by including them in liquefied drinks:

Alfalfa Tablets	For alkalinizing.
Bone Meal Tablets (or Powder)	For extra calcium needed in the Body.
Green Kale Tablets (or Powder)	For extra calcium needed in the Body.
Parsley Tablets	For the kidneys.
Okra, Celery Tablets	High in Sodium.
Whey Powder	High in Sodium.
Papaya Tablets (or Powder)	For digestion.
Prune, Apricot Powder	Good for its laxative effect.
Peach Powder	Good for its laxative effect.
Watercress Tablets	For reducing (high in Potassium)
Lecithin	Good in all high cholesterol cases.

Then there are the four supplements which should always be served on the dining table to overcome the fact that most of us have shortages from the past to make up. They can, of course, also be added to any liquefied drink, salad, dessert, etc.

Dulse: The highest source of iodine for the thyroid gland.

Sunflower Seed: The vegetarian's best source of protein, and a valuable gland and nerve food.

Rice Polishings: Very high in silicon--for skin and hair health, and a source of Vitamin B for nerves and brain.

Wheat Germ: Vitamin B and Vitamin E--the heart and muscle vitamin.

Then, there is always Blackstrap Molasses for its high iron content; Brewers Yeast for Vitamin B and dessicated liver for building the bloodstream.

- - - - - - - - - - - - - -

NATURAL REMEDIES AND TONICS

It is best not to use a remedy for a specific condition unless your whole diet is nutritionally balanced. Eating atrocious foods and trying to find a remedy for conditions you are producing doesn't make good sense. Use the general Daily Eating Regimen as a guide for a nutritionally balanced diet.

Alkalinizing System

1/2 cup Grapefruit Juice
1/4 cup Pineapple Juice
Few Spinach leaves
Liquefy

Appetite

3/4 cup Pineapple Juice
Dandelion Leaves
Liquefy

Arthritis

Alfalfa Seed Tea : Put one Tbsp. Alfalfa seeds in 1 pt. water. Bring to boil and let set overnight. Strain off and drink.

Blood Builder

(a) 1 cup mixed Celery, Parsley and Spinach
1 Tbsp. Cherry Concentrate
1 cup desired Vegetable Juice base

(b) 1 cup Cherry, Grape or Pineapple Juice
1 Tbsp. Whey Powder
1 Egg Yolk
1 Dulse Tablet or 1/4 tsp. Dulse Powder

Body Builder

1/2 cup Coconut Milk
3 fresh or revived Dried Figs
Liquefy

Brain and Nervous System

Liquefy protein drinks, especially with Raw Whole Egg or Egg Yolk, or a hard, unprocessed Cheese, Cottage Cheese, Sunflower Seeds, Soaked Nuts (see recipe section for nut and seed milk drinks), Wheat Germ; Rice Bran or Polishings-- 2 to 3 tsp. daily. (Papaya Tea as a base aids protein digestion.)

Radish, Prune Juice and Rice Polishings for nervous disorders.

Celery, Carrot and Prune Juice for nervous tension.

Lettuce and Tomato Juice: nerve quieter.

Complexion

(a)
1 Tbsp. Apple Concentrate
1/2 cup water
1/2 Cucumber - Liquefy

(b)
Cucumber Juice
Pineapple Juice
Endive - Liquefy

Coronary (Heart)

Any sweet, sweetened or carbohydrate drinks; e.g., Carrot, Pineapple Juice and Honey.

Coronary (Cont'd.)

1 tsp. Honey in glass of water three times daily (in lieu of other sweets.)

Deficiencies:

(a) Calcium

Add raw Bone Meal to Fruit or Vegetable drinks;
Egg Shell, if first soaked in Orange Juice, or boil Egg Shells in broth. Strain out.

Kale Greens in Vegetable Drinks or liquefied Barley Soup. Liquefy Green Kale tablets or powder, in drinks, also Bone Meal Powder or Tablets.

(b) Sodium

Add whey in any broth, soup, milk or liquefied drink.

Add liquid Chlorophyl to any liquefied drink, or in water to which may be added 1 Egg White, whipped to a stiff froth.

Add Celery or Okra Tablets to liquefied drinks.

(c) Silicon

Use Oat Straw Tea with Rice Polishings
Soybean Milk
(d) Iodine

Use leaf or two of Nova Scotia Dulse soaked overnight then put in liquefier.

Deficiencies:

(d) Iodine (Cont'd.)

1/4 to 1/2 tsp. of Dulse Powder added to any drink.

(e) Vitamins

Vitamin A - - Carrot Juice
Vitamin B - - Brewers Yeast
Vitamin C - - Citrus Fruit
  juices, mango, pineapple,
  rose hips, or any of the
  berries.
Vitamin E - - Wheat Germ
  Flakes or Wheat Germ
  Oil
  Corn Germ Oil
  Oat Germ Oil
  Rice Germ Oil
Vitamin K - - Alfalfa or
  Liquid Chlorophyl: 1
  tsp. (also high in iron
  and potassium).

Diarrhea

Try Carob Powder to control.

Gastro-Intestinal

Use any combination of vegetables. Sieve after liquefying. (Various stomach and
intestinal disorders cannot
tolerate fibrous material.)

1 cup Tomato Juice
1 stalk Celery
Few leaves Watercress or
Endive
Liquefy, then strain.

Whey: Use Whey in any milk
or liquefied drink for intestinal management. It is the
highest food in sodium. It (Cont'd.)

Gastro-Intestinal (Cont'd.)

may be used plain as a drink
or in combination with a wide
variety of foods, especially
in liquefied drinks.

Carrot Juice and Coconut Milk
(for colitis, gastritis and gas).

An aid in ulcer conditions is
Egg White, beaten to a stiff
froth, and used as a topping
on liquefied drinks.

Gland and Nerve

1 Tbsp. Cherry Concentrate
1 tsp. Chlorophyl
1 Egg Yolk
2 Tbsps. Wheat Germ
Blend in liquefier.

Hair (For Sheen)

1 Tbsp. Cherry Concentrate
1 cup Oat Straw Tea

Kidneys

Parsley Tablets - Blend into
drinks.

Laxatives

Prune Powder
Apricot Powder
Peach Powder
These may be added to any
liquefied drink.

Respiratory-Catarrhal

Foods high in Vitamins A and
C: Bell Peppers (especially
ripe ones) have high content of
Vitamin C. Parsley is (Cont'd.)

Respiratory-Catarrhal (Cont'd.)

rich in Vitamin A. Use as a base juice or ingredient in liquefied drinks; e.g., Tomato Juice and Green Peppers liquefied.

Rheumatic

Whey: Use Whey with Cherry Concentrate, with any broth, soup, milk or liquefied drink.

Foods high in Vitamin C and Sodium hold Calcium in solution to maintain suppleness in joints; e.g., Tomato Juice and Celery Juice.

Skin

1/2 cup Pineapple Juice
Sprigs of Parsley
1/3 Cucumber, chopped
Liquefy.

Oat Straw Tea and Rice Polishings

Virus and Other Infections

Liquefied foods high in Vitamin C. Concentrate of liquids.

Vitality

1 Tbsp. Apple Concentrate
1 Tbsp. Almond Nut Butter
1 cup Celery Juice

Liquefy.

Weight Gaining

Dried Fruit, revived
Pineapple Juice
Liquefy.

Flaxseed Tea (liquefied if you wish to use the seed) added to any liquefied Fruit or Protein drink.

Sweet bases, such as Fruit Juice Concentrates, rather than Citrus Juices in fruit drinks.

Weight Reducing

Use low calorie foods.

Liquefied Protein drinks; e.g., for a satisfying noon meal: Cottage Cheese in Soy Milk or Whey, with Apricot or Peach Nectar, Apple Juice or Apple Concentrate for flavor.

Use fresh fruits in preference to dried. Fresh Apples are wonderful liquefied; e.g., diced Apple in Pineapple Juice.

Good bases are Tomato, Papaya or Pineapple Juices. For a citrus base use Grapefruit pulp liquefied (after removing the outer peel and dicing); liquefied sections of orange with pulp.

Nut and Seed Milks (see recipes) Soybean Milk: may be made with   Low Fat Soybean Powder,

(Cont'd.

Natural Remedies and Tonics (Cont'd.)

Weight Reducing (Cont'd.)

                    obtainable at
Health Food Stores.

e.g. Soy Bean Milk
     1 Egg Yolk
     Honey
        Fresh Strawberries
Liquefy. (Other fresh
fruits or juices may be
used.)

Try Watercress Tablets
liquefied in drinks.

Use Gelatin Whey
1/4 cup cold water
2 tsps. Plain Gelatin
Blend the two then add
3/4 cup boiling water
and blend.
3 Tbsps. Whey Powder -
Add and blend.

Variations:
Vanilla - add a few drops of
    pure Vanilla.
Orange - add 1 Tbsp. Orange
    Juice and a little grated
    rind.
Cherry - add 1 tsp. Cherry
    Concentrate
Mint - Use Mint Tea instead
    of water.

Youthfulness

1/2 cup Cucumber juice
a few Radishes
1/2 chopped Green Pepper
Liquefy.

- - - - - - - -

FOR:	USE:
Anemia	Parsley and Grape Juice
Asthma	Celery and Papaya Juice
Bed Wetting	Celery and Parsley Juice
Bladder Ailments	Celery and Pomegranate Juice
Catarrh, Colds, Sore Throat	Watercress and Apple Juice (add 1/4 tsp. pure Cream of Tartar)
Constipation, Stomach Ulcers	Celery with a little Sweet Cream, Spinach and Grapefruit Juice.
Colds, Sinus Troubles	Celery and Grapefruit Juices (add 1/4 tsp. pure Cream of Tartar)
Diarrhea, Infection	Carrot and Blackberry Juice
Fever, Gout, Arthritis	Celery and Parsley Juice

FOR:	USE:
Gall Bladder Disorders	Radish, Prune, Black Cherry and Celery Juice
General House Cleaning	Celery, Parsley, Spinach and Carrot Juice
Glands, Goiter, Impotence	Celery Juice, 1 tsp. Wheat Germ and $\frac{1}{2}$ tsp. Nova Scotia Dulse
High Blood Pressure	Carrot and Parsley Juice and Celery
Indigestion, Underweight	Coconut Milk, Fig Juice, Parsley and Carrot Juice
Insomnia, Sleeplessness	Lettuce and Celery Juice
Kidney Disorders	Celery, Parsley and Asparagus Juice
Liver Disorders	Radish and Pineapple Juices
Neuralgia	Cucumber, Endive and Pineapple Juice
Overweight, Obesity	Beet Greens, Parsley and Celery Juice
Poor Circulation	Beet and Blackberry Juice
Poor Memory	Celery, Carrot and Prune Juice and Rice Polishings
Poor Teeth	Beet Greens, Parsley and Celery Juice and Green Kale
Reducing	Parsley, Grape Juice and Pineapple Juice
Rheumatism, Neuritis, Neuralgia	Cucumber, Endive and Whey
Rickets	Dandelion and Orange Juice
Scurvy, Eczema	Carrot, Celery and Lemon Juice

The above health suggestions have been taken
from "Vital Foods for Total Health".

- - - - - - - - - -

HERBS

Herbs offer a great variety of flavors. If you have a small
plot of ground, you may have them fresh, and there probably
will be a surplus left over for drying. Dry them on a tray in
the sun and turn them every 2 or 3 days until they are completely dried out. Then place them in a closed top jar or container.

Herbs are rich in vitamins, aid digestion and since ancient days have been known for their curative value. They also enhance the taste of your health preparations. (See list of the Herbal Teas.)

Allspice:	Sauces, steamed puddings, pumpkin, raisin and other pies, fruit salads and fruit cups, spiced cakes and cookies.
Anise:	Use whole or crushed in fruit and vegetable salads; cakes, breads and rolls.
Basil:	Salads--tomato, mixed green, cucumber, cheese and fruit; sauces; vegetables; egg and cheese dishes.
Bay Leaves:	Vegetable and tomato soup; tossed green and vegetable salads, French dressing; potatoes and carrots; dessert custards and creams.
Caraway:	Cheese dishes; coleslaw, cucumber, potato and tomato salads; crushed in salad dressings; vegetables.
Cardamom:	Cardamom cakes, cookies and breads; with honey to flavor fruit, whipped cream; with spices in pies, puddings and desserts.
Celery Seed:	Breads; butter and spreads; dips; ground in egg and cheese dishes, vegetable juices, salads and salad dressings; sauces; vegetables.
Chervil:	Egg dishes, sauces, soups, salads.
Cinnamon:	Beverages--hot spiced fruit drinks, hot "chocolate", eggnogs, milk shakes, spiced tea or fruit punches; desserts and puddings; fruits. Use whole in hot drinks; when cooking dried fruits or spiced fruits.
Cloves:	Whole in fruit punches, when cooking fruit; ground in spiced cakes and cookies; egg dishes; sauces; vegetables--beets, sweet potatoes and tomatoes.
Dill:	Seed--cream cheese dips and spreads, butter, vegetables--cooked green beans, cabbage, squash and turnips.

Dill:	Herb--rich sauces, appetizers, vegetables as above; salads--avocado, cucumber, vegetable; coleslaw; soups.
Garlic:	Appetizers; salads--green and vegetable, potato; dressings; sauces; soups; entrees; butters.
	Available as salt, powder and chips now.
Ginger:	Green in tiny quantities to vegetables, salads, savory rice, and most Chinese recipes.
	Whole dried: some cooked fruits.
	Ground: Ginger cookies, cakes and puddings; fruit sauce; winter squash, glazed carrots, onions and sweet potatoes.
Horseradish:	Sauces, dips and spreads; salad dressings; vegetables.
Mace:	Whole in cheese sauce, cooked apples, prunes, apricots, fruit salads; sauces and marinades.
	Ground: Breads and cakes;"chocolate" puddings fruits; vegetables.
Marjoram:	Soups--spinach, onion; cream sauces; egg dishes; vegetables--mushrooms, carrots, peas, spinach, zucchini.
Mint:	Appetizers; fruit and gelatin salads, coleslaw; vegetables--carrots, peas, potatoes, zucchini, cabbage; mint-sauce; fruit, gelatin and ice desserts; beverages--hot and iced teas, "Chocolate", fruit punch.
Mustard:	Whole: Salads--coleslaw, salad greens, vegetable and potato salads; vegetables--cabbage, buttered beets.
	Ground: Salads, dressings, sauces, butters, vegetables.
Nutmeg:	Beverages--milk shakes, eggnog, spiced hot drinks, hot "chocolate"; breads, cakes, pies, desserts. Fruits--grated over applesauce, compotes, mincemeat.

Oregano: Vegetables--zucchini, eggplant, tomatoes;
                 hot sauces.

Paprika: Appetizers--cheese; salad dressings; sauces;
                 butters.

Rosemary: Soups--split pea; cornbread and biscuits;
                 vegetables--potatoes, green beans, peas,
                 spinach, chard, zucchini; fruit compotes,
                 punches, jellies.

Sage: Soups--cream and chowder; salads; vegetar-
                 ian stuffings; vegetables--lima beans, egg-
                 plant, onions, tomatoes.

Savory: Soups--bean and lentil, consomme; salads--
                 mixed green, vegetable, potato; sauces--
                 horseradish; vegetarian stuffings.

Tarragon: Mixed green and fruit salads; sauces; egg
                 dishes.

Thyme: Tomato salad, aspics; tomato juice; sauces;
                 vegetables--onions, carrots, beets.

Turmeric: Salad dressings; cream soups and chowders;
                 for coloring; scrambled eggs.

                 - - - - - - - - - -

HERB TEAS

Alfalfa Leaf: Stimulating--for kidneys, bowels, appetite
                 and digestion. Highly alkaline.

Alfalfa Seed: Silicon. Liver cleansing. Arthritis and
                 similar pains.

Alfamint: Minerals and vitamins. Arthritic conditions.
                 digestion. Alkalinizing.

Buchu: Stimulant and diuretic. Genito-urinary tract.
                 Uric-acid gravel. Lungs.

Blue Violet: Catarrhal conditions. Lymph gland drainage.
                 Healing sores. Severe cough.

Catnip: Carminiative, diaphoretic and tonic. Relaxes nerves. Colds.

Chamomile: Aids digestion. Clears complexion. Discharging catarrh. Potassium. Calcium.

Comfrey: Root: gets toxic material out through lungs, loosens colds.
Leaves: Mineral rich. Tonic. Fevers. Kidneys. Bladder. Internal healing.

Cornsilk: Kidney and bladder. Genito-urinary tract. Magnesium. Mucus linings.

Dandelion: Purifies blood (iron). Colds, dyspepsia, diabetes, tuberculosis, rheumatism, arthritis, kidneys, gall bladder, liver. Calcium.

Elderberry: Catarrhal conditions. Colic, diarrhea, ovarian disturbances. Blood.

Eyebright: Tonic. Astringent. Clears and tones. Gastric trouble. Eye beauty.

Flaxseed: Demulcent. Constipation. Enema for bleeding bowel. Silicon. Vitamin F.

Fenugreek: Soothes Mucus surfaces. Ulcers, poor digestion, fevers. Healing.

Golden Seal: Stimulates gastric juices, speeds up digestion. All mucus membrane problems. Colitis. Catarrhal discharge problems. Increases potency of other herbs. Try first for correcting any condition in body.

Horsetail: Diuretic. High in silicon and calcium.

Huckleberry: Digestion of starches. Diabetes, high blood pressure, diarrhea.

Juniper: Weak stomach, foul breath, flatulence. Kidney, liver, blood cleansing.

Oatstraw:	Silicon. Tonic. Mineralizer. Potent solvent. Soothes, stimulates.
Papaya:	Digestion of protein. Dyspepsia, stomach weakness, pyorrhea.
Parsley:	Best diuretic--kidneys, gallstones, diabetes, jaundice. Iron, Manganese.
Peppermint:	Digestion. Circulation of blood. Eliminating toxins. Manganese.
Raspberry:	Poor circulation. Tones female organs. Easier confinement period.
Red Clover:	Cleansing tea (drug deposits). Iron. Vitamin C. Diarrhea.
Rose Hips:	High in vitamin C. Kidneys and bladder. Bladder stones.
Sage:	Cleansing, clears complexion. Sedative. Heart, liver, kidneys. Strength.
Sassafras:	Purifies blood. Spleen, liver. Digestant. Reducing. Catarrh.
Sarsaparilla:	Blood purifier. Rheumatism. Iodine.
Senna:	Purgative. Cleanses digestive tract. Relieves constipation.
Shave Grass:	Silicon. Kidneys, bladder, gas, varicose veins, mucus membranes.
Slippery Elm:	Inflammation of mucus tissues, colitis, diarrhea. Healing.
Spearmint:	Diuretic. Nausea, vomiting, flatulence. Antidote to febrile conditions. Iron.
Strawberry:	Liver. Blood purifying. Diuretic. Heals mucus membranes. Sodium. Iron.

Uva Ursi:	Diuretic. Useful for kidney complaints.
Valerian:	Natural tranquilizer, relaxes nerves. Despondency, pessimism, coughs.
White Oak:	Diarrhea, dysentery, bowel problems. Enemas. Iodine. Potassium.

DIET SECTION

<u>BLAND FOOD DIET</u>

FOR COLITIS, SPASTIC BOWEL, ULCERS, GAS

A program in which the whole body is fed is the foundation in which good health is built. When we cannot take the foods necessary for health in their normal form and are using the blender as an aid, we must not forget that a "Balanced Daily Eating Regimen" is still required. It is no use living on milk and mush to sooth stomach ulcers, while starving the rest of the body. Good health depends on balanced nutrition, and, although when we are sick we often have to favor a weak organ, we dare not neglect all the other needs of the body.

Here is a program in which we are following the dietetic law of balanced eating and using the Blender almost exclusively. Do not forget that <u>chewing</u> well is necessary for a healthy body. Even though the food is liquefied, it must be chewed to mix with saliva.

Use the following foods raw, in liquefied salad form, wherever possible; or cooked and liquefied; or cooked, liquefied and then strained for severe colitis or ulcer cases.

People on a bland diet usually don't get all the variety that healthy people do. Have four to six vegetables daily, two fruits daily, one starch daily, 1 protein daily, with juices or liquids between meals.

DAILY MENU

BEFORE BREAKFAST:	On rising take any natural, unsweetened fruit juice.
BREAKFAST:	Fruit - Protein or Starch
10:30 A.M.:	Liquid or Fruit
LUNCH:	Two vegetables - One Starch Tea or drink.
3:30 P.M.:	Fruit Juice, Tea or Fruit
DINNER:	Two Vegetables - one Protein Tea or Drink.

Do not eat starch and protein together. Eat at separate meals.

RULES OF EATING

1. If not entirely comfortable in mind and body from the previous meal, miss the next meal.
2. Do not eat unless you have a keen desire for the plainest food.
3. Do not eat beyond your needs.
4. Be sure to thoroughly chew your food.
5. Miss meals if in pain, emotionally upset, chilled, overheated, not hungry, or during acute illness.

FRUIT JUICES:

> Black Cherry, Fig
> Grape, Prune
> Papaya, Pineapple

FRUITS: Use two fruits daily (best taken by themselves between
meals.)

Nectarines, Peaches
Apricots, Sapota
Watermelon
Honeydew, Casaba
Grapes (no peels or
seeds),
Ripe Strawberries
(without seeds -
sieve).

Papayas, Mangoes,
Raisins, Prunes
(may have to be pureed
because of peels)
Dates, Fresh seedless
Figs, Persimmons,
Bananas (remove seed
vein). All stewed fruits
(except Pears), Apple
Sauce, sundried or
regular Olives.

All dried fruits must be put into cold water and brought to a
boil. Turn off the flame when at the boiling point and let stand
overnight, using them the next day.

VEGETABLES: Use four to six vegetables daily.

Raw: Avocado

Carrots) Finely
Beets) grated or
Squashes) ground

Leaf Lettuces)
Tender Greens)
Okra)
Celery) Liquefied
Asparagus)
Parsley)

Sprouts)Liquefied and
Corn) strained to
remove hulls

Cooked: Carrots
All Squash family
Egg Plant
Peas
Asparagus
Celery
Okra
Jerusalem Artichokes
Tender String Beans
Tender Beets and Tops
Swiss Chard, Spinach
(cooked very little)
Less tender vegetables
--cook and liquefy (strain
in severe cases)

Legumes and Corn - al-
ways strain.

VEGETABLE SOUPS :
Asparagus - raw or cooked. Strain if necessary.
Corn Soup - raw or cooked but strained to remove hulls.
Other bland Vegetable Soups and Cream Soups - strain
if necessary. (Cont'd.)

78

Vegetable Soups (Cont'd.)

> Legume Soups - strained
> Vital Broth made of Potato, Celery, Carrot and Parsley
> Potato Peeling Broth

Gas-Producing Vegetables (Sulphurous)

Do not eat

> Cabbage, Cauliflower, Onions, Broccoli, Brussels
> Sprouts.

PROTEINS: Have one Protein daily.

Eggs, scrambled or lightly boiled	Raw Milk
Fish	Fresh Goat's Milk
Meat - lean (no fat) (no pork)	Buttermilk
	Yogurt
	Tofu
Gelatin	Cream of Legume Soups
Cheese, any kind	Nut Butters

If possible, milk should be taken as soon as drawn from the
cow or goat.

STARCHES: Have 1 Starch daily.

Breakfast cereals, such as:
  Rolled Oats, Millet Rice
Rye Meal ; Cornmeal

Agar-Agar can be mixed with
  cereals

Soy Toast

White Potatoes) Cooked
Yams   )   and
Sweet Potatoes) mealy

Brown Rice
Wild Rice
Banana Squash
Hubbard Squash
Bananas - dead ripe and
  seed vein removed

GRUELS

Barley Soup (does not
  cause a lot of gas)

Rice Gruel
Millet Gruel

DRINKS: All herbal teas are bland. Mint tea is the best for eliminating gas. Huckleberry, oatstraw, papaya, mint are the four teas which should be used the most. Bran tea is also good.

Soy milk drinks; whey drinks; Acidophilus milk, buttermilk.

Nut and sesame seed milks with dates or carob flour or rice polishings. (Strain to remove fibers)

JUICES: Vegetable juice with milk or flaxseed tea, half and half. Or use liquid chlorophyl instead of the fresh juice, one teaspoon to glass of water.

SWEETS: Maple syrup, honey, date sugar.

SUPPLEMENTS: As prescribed and checked by Doctor.

Springreen Tablets	Acidophilus culture
Whex (goat whey)	Okra Powder
Liquid Chlorophyl	Apple Concentrate
Slippery Elm Food	(with Yogurt)
Flaxseed Meal	Veico #77
Reliable protein supplements	

Everyone on this diet should be taking a bulk, such as, Sea Klenz, Deturge, Meta-Mucil, or Flaxseed Meal.

ENEMAS: People on these diets usually take enemas. Flaxseed tea enemas are best.

EMERGENCY FOODS:

Diet brand canned foods only in an emergency. Nutra-diet brand, diabetic foods, canned baby foods, Oateena, Ryeena, Loma Linda, Nuteena, vegetable cheese.

Foods either too hot or too cold should be avoided. Pureed and soft foods are easy on the digestion--cause less gas. Hot foods and drinks should not be taken as they weaken the mucus membranes; result in spongy gums and weaken the stomach. Cold foods and drinks absorb the heat of the stomach and contract the glands of the stomach so that the hydrochloric acid will not flow freely. This arrests the digestion and produces oppression and irritation.

These bland foods are given with the idea that they will not produc

as or irritate the stomach and intestinal tract. There are many
and foods that are harsh and irritating to the intestinal tract
ecause of roughage. When foods (whether cooked or not cooked)
ave lots of fibers, strings, peelings, or seeds, they should be
quefied or pureed.

BLAND DIET

SAMPLE MENU

ur daily program must include:

> Two different fruits
> At least four to six vegetables
> One protein
> One starch
> Juice or fruit between meals

EFORE BREAKFAST: Upon rising -
Take any natural, unsweetened fruit juice.

REAKFAST: Pureed prunes *
A little nut butter *
Creamed cornmeal mush with honey *
Oatstraw tea

:30 A.M.: Vegetable broth, vegetable juice, or fruit
juice. If something more substantial is required, have a nut or seed milk *, or even a
fruit whip with yogurt *.

JNCH: Celery Soup *
Liquefied Salad *
Blended Sweet Potato *
Huckleberry Tea

30 P.M. Cantaloupe seeds in whey, strained *
Or, fruit or vegetable cocktail *

NNER: Liquefied Salad *
Creamed Asparagus *
Cottage Cheese Custard *
Carrot Milk * (using sesame milk)

GHTCAP: If desired, carob and soy milk drink. *

your diet forbids any roughage, follow the above plan and then
ve all foods after liquefying.

ndicates made in Blender. See Recipe Section.

Special Pre Natal Care Section

The Mother-to-be needs special foods to take care of the baby
that is to be born. Start the day with a glass of good orange
juice blended with egg yolk. Try to use lots of raw carrots,
sunflower seeds, sesame seeds, and almond nuts.

Raspberry leaves steeped and the tea used as a basis for various
vegetable drinks will help in many ways to assure easier birth.
Raspberry leaves also contain many valuable vitamins which will
help supply the body with what it needs at this time. Try to use
one pint of the Raspberry tea as a basis for your drinks every
day. To make the tea, just use an ordinary teapot or any other
dish, one handful of leaves, cover and steep for one hour or more.
Strain and use the tea as stated above. To your drinks try to
include some of the following: ½ tsp. Alfalfa Powder, 1 tsp.
Rice Polishings, 1 tbsp. Lecithin Liquid or granules (see the
chart on page   for other food supplements that will give you
many of the vital requirements of your body at this time).
Remember: how you care for your body during this important time
will depend a great deal on how healthy your baby will be. In
fact, preparation whould really be started some time ahead of con-
ception.

Mothers-to-be should never smoke during this time as Vitamin C
is readily destroyed through smoking. The seed from an unhealthy
father and nurtured by an unhealthy mother cannot be expected to
produce the healthy child as was meant to be. When the right
preparation is made, and baby fed on proper foods after birth,
everyone will benefit as baby will be healthier and more contented
Remember, a healthy baby is a happy baby. Study how to feed
yourself before the baby arrives and then continue to feed yourself and baby on healthy nutritious foods, and both will benefit
from your efforts.

If possible, do breast feed the baby, as this is the way nature
intended. If there is not enough of mother's milk for baby's
need, the mother should take lots of greens such as tops of
vegetables (beet greens and carrot tops),   spinach and comfrey.
As a result your little one will be better adjusted as it grows
up. Baby needs to feel the closeness of the mother at feeding time
Do not force the baby or any children to eat when not hungry.
Often mothers make the mistake of forcing food down their children
when actually their little body needs a rest from the digesting
process. A day now and again on some good fruit often will bring
good results with baby or older children. It is not what we eat,
but what our body is able to utilize that brings results.

The Blender will prove itself invaluable for making tasty meals
for your baby as time goes along. Just introduce gradually
various fruits and vegetables to your baby. A little food properly digested is better than a lot of food forced down. Do try
to use fruits for one meal and vegetables at the other meal. If
using fruit, then serve about half an hour before the other part
of the meal. Remember, fruits digest within a half hour. Other
foods take longer to digest so are best served separate. Try to
use your own preparation of baby foods instead of using the processed kind. Try to let your baby learn to enjoy food more as
nature made it rather than using a lot of salt or other flavorings.
A little honey is better than white sugar, a product that should
never be used by anyone who is interested in good health. Serve
your foods attractively and in small amounts, keeping in mind
the color of food makes for better appetite. Do not use all one
color at one meal. Try to use a combination of green and yellow.
Many children find that soy milk is easier to digest than cow's
milk.

Prunes revived and blended makes a good breakfast food for baby,
followed later by cereal. Study carefully the list of healthful
items that can be gradually added to your baby's diet, and this
also goes for older children. A little molasses (unsulphured,
from a Health Store) is a wonderful addition to the milk for
children. Often a little orange added to baby's milk makes the
milk easier to digest.

If baby is properly fed as to right amounts and right combinations,
you should be rewarded with a healthy happy child. Your sleep
should be less disturbed at nights. Often a baby is restless at
night because of some food eaten before retiring, such as a
pudding made with sugar and corn starch. This sets up a little
disturbance in the digestive system which will often disturb
baby's sleep.

Do study the right combinations of food as listed elsewhere in
this book as to when to use starches and when to use the proteins.
You will be well rewarded by giving careful study to the pre-
natal care of your own body and also as to how you feed yourself
and your little one ofter the birth takes place.

You and your Blender will become very close friends when preparing baby's foods. The more you experiment with your blender
the more valuable it will become.

Don't forget the daily supplements--rice bran, sunflower seed, wheat germ and dulse. These can be liquefied along with food or drinks. Yeast, flaxseed meal, molasses and whey are some of the other useful health-aids.

WEANING THE BABY

Goat's milk is the ideal food for weaning the baby, it being more like mother's milk in composition. If cow's milk is used, it is sometimes necessary to take off some of the cream, whereas goat's milk is naturally homogenized.

Occasionally babies thrive better when a little whipped avocado is used to take the place of cream. There are many babies who cannot take much fat or cream because it disturbs the liver. Use one heaping tablespoon of avocado to eight ounces of milk. The liquefier will whip it into the milk very nicely. (Don't make it frothy, however, or the baby will get gas.)

For carbohydrate value, the average formula uses a milk sugar, 1/2 teaspoon to 8 ounces of milk. This helps to digest the milk. Revived (soaked) apricots or prunes may also be used for sweetening as a change, or the milk can be liquefied with dates, after these have been soaked and peeled. Use two or three to 8 ounces of milk. We can vary these combinations if the baby cannot handle them or if the blends are too rich.

If the baby is underweight, add half as much again of the carbohydrate called for in the formula; if the baby is overweight, use only half the amount.

Occasionally, a wonderful drink can be made with the addition
of arrowroot, which will also take care of the carbohydrate
value of the milk.

A suggested "Weaning Formula" from Dr. Jensen's book, "The
Joy of Living and How to Attain It":

> 1 oz. Goat or Certified Raw Milk
> 1/2 oz. Pure Cream
> 1 tsp. Milk Sugar
> 3 oz.   Distilled Water

Milk is the most important food for the first few months of a
baby's life. The following suggestions can gradually be intro-
duced in addition to the formula, and as weaning time approaches,
they can take a bigger place in the baby's diet with a resulting
reduction of milk intake. However, it sometimes happens that
unusual circumstances make these vegetable drinks useful much
earlier. If an infant cannot tolerate his formula; if he suffers
from diarrhea, or other digestive upsets, they can be invaluable
as a substitute.

Carrot Bottle Feed

4 tsp. cooked Carrot   )   Blend for 2 minutes,
1/4 cup juice from Cooked Carrots   )   strain. Fill baby's
3/4 cup Soy Milk   )   bottle. Heat in hot
2 Tbsp. Millet   )   water.

Spinach Bottle

3 or 4 Spinach leaves   )   Blend for 2 minutes,
  Dip in hot water to wilt.   )   strain. Fill bottle.
2 slices Cooked Carrot   )   Warm.
1/4 tsp. Raw Sugar   )
1 cup Soy Milk   )

Tomato Bottle

1 small Tomato   )   Blend for 2 minutes,
1 cup Milk   )   strain, bottle, and
2 Tbsps. Cereal-Millet,   )   warm.
  Oatmeal or Arrowroot   )

Orange Milk

1-1/2 cups Milk
Juice of 1 Orange
2 Tbsps. Honey

Liquefy until perfectly blended

Apple Bottle

1/4 Apple, cut up
2 half-inch slices Banana
1/4 tsp. Raw Sugar
3/4 cup Milk
2 Tbsps. Arrowroot

Blend 2 minutes, strain, fill bottle, and warm.

INTRODUCING SOLIDS

Banana Soup

1/2 cup Milk
1/2 cup Grape Juice

1/2 Banana
A little Honey or Raw Sugar

Blend till emulsified

Carrot Soup

1/4 cup Carrots, chopped)   Simmer till tender
1/4 cup Water   )

1 tsp. Arrowroot or)
  Agar Agar   )   Thicken with; remove from heat.

1 tsp. Butter   )
1/2 cup Warm Milk)   Add and blend until emulsified.

Recipe Section

Following are a few recipes to assist you in giving your baby nutritious and interesting foods:

Vegetables for Baby

½ cup Freshly Cooked Vegetables
2 tbsp. Milk

Blend together at (M) speed until very smooth.

Baby's "Meal in One"

½ cup Milk
2 tbsp. Chicken Broth
2 tbsp. Cubed Chicken
2 tbsp. Cubed cooked carrots
1 tsp. Butter
1 tsp. Millet, or other quick-
        cooking cereal

Put all in blender and run on (L) speed until chicken and carrot are finely chopped. Pour into saucepan and cook 5 min., stirring constantly. (Celery or peas could be used in place of carrots.)

Vegetable-Meat Dish for Baby

¼ cup Freshly Cooked Veget-
     ables
¼ cup Diced Chicken or Beef
2 tbsp. Milk

Blend together on (M) speed until very smooth.

Vegetable-Egg Dish for Baby

2 tbsp. Milk
½ cup Freshly Cooked Veget-
     ables
1 Egg Yolk
  Dash of salt (sea) if
  necessary, or dulse

Blend all together on (M) speed until very smooth. To make the above more nutritious for Baby, add ¼ tsp. alfalfa leaf powder.

- - - - - -

Baby Pleaser

Put 2 tbsp. Pineapple Juice in Blender
Add ½ Banana, cut in 1" pieces

Blend together until smooth (L). Watch how Baby will go for this delicious treat. Any other fruit juice may be used. To make this more nutritious, add yolk of one egg.

If too much food is made for baby at one time, store the balance in small jar. Sprinkle over top a few wheat germ flakes or finely ground seeds, such as sesame or sunflower seeds, or a little milk over top. This helps to seal the air out and retains the vitamins. Stir together for using the next time which will add variety to dish.

Toddler and Junior Foods Do Not Need to be Blended as Fine:

Banana Apple Delight

1 small, Ripe Banana 1 small Apple, peeled and cored 1 tbsp. Honey 1 tbsp. Lemon Juice	Blend all together on (L) speed until smooth, using spatula where necessary to push food into blades.

- - - - - - - -

"Honey-of-a-Fruit" for Baby

3/4 cup Fresh Fruit 1/2 tsp. Honey 1 tbsp. Water	Blend all together on (L) speed until smooth. Can also be made in small Mason jars for easy storing. Screw Mason jar on blender onto cutting section. (Check for smoothness by taking a small amount from blender and rubbing between fingers.)

- - - - - - - -

Special Kiddie Treat

1 cup Sesame Seeds
1 cup Cashew or any other nuts

Turn to low speed, then (H) until finely ground, but not
powdered. Take one slice or one scoop ice cream and insert
into each section. Then roll or dip in ground seeds until
well coated. The children will love this.

DRINKS

Your liquefier can make the smoothest, most perfect beverages you can imagine, from frosty milk shakes, fizzes, egg nogs, frothy protein-rich soy and nut milk drinks, to healthful, zestful vegetable cocktails.

BASES

(1) For Fruit Drinks choose your liquid base from the fruit juices, as they add flavor and value:

> Apple, grape, pineapple (unsweetened), blackberry, elderberry, pomegranate, mulberry, wild cherry, blueberry, raspberry.

> Juice concentrates, such as apple, cherry, grape. These are high in energy-giving fruit sugars. They are available in Hidden Valley Brand Products at health food stores.

(2) For Vegetable Drinks try to choose a vegetable base:

> Carrot, celery, mixed greens, etc.

> Tomato juice

> Chlorophyll, which is liquid alfalfa. One teaspoon to

one cup water.

Whey - powdered: 1 Tbsp. to 1 cup water.

Or liquid--left from making homemade cottage cheese. See recipe.

Herb teas with leaves or seeds, such as fenugreek or alfalfa. Select according to preference or for any particular medicinal need, as papaya for beneficial effect on kidneys and digestion of proteins; comfrey for general healing and for bowels; huckleberry for starch digestion, or camomile. Oatstraw tea is mild.

Vegetable Seasoning - 1 teaspoon to about 1 cup water. Makes an excellent protein drink.

For both fruit and vegetable drinks, you can use goat's milk also as a base, as well as raw milk, soy, coconut and nut milks.

Drinking raw vegetable cocktails is one of the best ways of supplying needed minerals to the body. They should not be used in place of raw vegetable salads, but rather to supplement them. Drink them at any time of the day or with any meal. Any water left over after steaming vegetables should be used in cocktail bases, never discarded.

SWEETENERS

Soaked raisins, dates, figs, or sweet prunes are permissible to improve taste; soaked black walnuts are also very good to cover a "nasty" taste. The presence of solid particles makes vegetable juices conducive to chewing. These are concentrated foods and not to be taken as a "drink". They should be chewed to mix with the saliva.

Unsulphured molasses (try granules as well as liquid) has healthful properties for use as sweetener in beverages. Also use date sugar, apple concentrate, maple syrup or carob powder.

PROTEIN DRINKS

Make protein drinks by adding cottage cheese, egg yolk, nut butters, and milks, seed and soy milks, protein or amino-acid powders (prepared supplements).

CARBOHYDRATE DRINKS

Add barley or other whole grain, cooked or soaked. Baked potato with the skin is a good way to use up leftovers--with one or two root vegetables, leeks, green leafy vegetables, parsley, herbs, and seasoning.

Raw potato is especially good for you, but when used serve <u>immediately</u>, as this will spoil if allowed to stand.

<u>AND</u>

For an especially nutritious drink, have one of the nut or seed milks; the carrot milk, or the banana milk.

VEGETABLE DRINK SUGGESTIONS

Vegetable Cocktail

2 cups Tomato Juice	1 slice Green Pepper
1 small stalk Celery	1 slice Onion
with leaves, cut up	1/4 tsp. Vegetable Seasoning
2 or 3 sprigs Parsley	1/2 tsp. Honey
2 slices Lemon	1 cup cracked ice

Blend till liquefied. (H)   - - -   3-4 servings

Beet Borsch Drink

1/3 cup Carrot Juice	1/4 cup Cucumber Juice
1/3 cup Beet Juice	1 Tbsp. Lemon Juice

Blend on (H) speed
Serve with a spoonful of Sour Cream or Yogurt on top.

- - -

Carrot Juice Cocktail

1 cup Carrot Juice	2 sprigs Parsley
1/4 cup any Green Juice and/or	1/2 tsp. Vegetable Seasoning
1 or 2 green leaves (outer leaves	or any desired Herb for
of endive or romaine are good)	flavoring.

Liquefy. (H)

- - -

Garden-Fresh Tomato Juice

Bring really ripe tomatoes in off your vines, rinse, slice and blend
(Cont'd.)

91

Garden-Fresh Tomato Juice (Cont'd.)

without adding liquid. A little Vegetable Seasoning may be added, and a pinch of your favorite herb.

Once well blended, strain through a fine sieve; chill.
- - -

Watercress Cocktail

2 cups Pineapple Juice, unsweetened   1 thick slice Lemon or
1 bunch Watercress   2 Tbsps. Lemon Juice
3 Tbsps. Honey or Raw Sugar   1 cup cracked ice

Blend until Watercress is liquefied. (H)
- - -

Borsch-Yogurt Drink

1 cup Yogurt   1/2 cup diced Carrot
1/2 small Lemon, Peeled and   1/4 diced Cucumber
   seeded   1 tsp. Vegetable Seasoning
1/2 cup diced Beets

(H) speed
Blend velvety smooth in liquefier. If desired, pulp may be strained out through sieve. Top with spoonful of sour cream.
- - -

Carrot-Parsley Cocktail

2/3 cup Carrot Juice
6 sprigs Parsley

Liquefy.   (H) speed.   1 serving
- - -

Carrot-Pineapple Drink

1/2 cup Carrots, cubed   1-1/2 cups Pineapple Juice
1/2 cup Celery, cubed

Blend smooth. (H)   - - -   2-3 servings

Dr. Kirschner's Therapeutic Green Drink

Soak overnight in water:

   15 Almonds
    4 Pitted Dates
    5 tsps. Sunflower Seeds
Liquefy with 8 oz. unsweetened Pineapple Juice   (Cont'd.)

Dr. Kirschner's Therapeutic Green Drink (Cont'd.)

Now Liquefy: (H)

8 oz. Pineapple Juice
4 large handfuls Green Leaves
(such as, alfalfa, parsley, mint, spinach, beet greens, watercress; and, if obtainable, comfrey and such nutritious herbs as fillaree, malva, or lamb's quarters--do not use stems.)

Combine the two mixtures and stir.   3-4 servings

Caution: Do not have the mixture too thick. Some like to put it it through a coarse sieve or strainer to eliminate the pulp.

Variation: Use any combination of green vegetable juices instead of all or a portion of pineapple juice for higher chlorophyl value.

- - -

"Coffee Taste" Drink

4 tsps. Dandelion Root Coffee
4 cups Water
Pinch Vegetable Seasoning

Brew as ordinary coffee. Strain into cup and serve with cream and raw sugar. (A touch of molasses brings out the coffee taste.) This is a good base for the Mocha Drink.

- - -

Hot Mocha Drink

1 Tbsp. Honey	2 Tbsps. Whey Powder
1 Tbsp. Butter	1 Tbsp. Carob Powder
1/2 tsp. Pure Vanilla	1 Tbsp. Rice Polishings
Dash of Sea Salt	1 Tbsp. Sunflower Seed Meal

Place these in blender and gradually add 4 cups boiling dandelion root coffee (made as above) and pour into hot cups. (H) speed

Serve with cream and honey to taste. 4-5 servings

FRUIT DRINK SUGGESTIONS

Melon Cocktail

Liquefy the whole melon, seeds, rind, and pulp, for a delicious
(Cont'd.)

highly nutritious cocktail. Melon is better used alone, but occasionally include fresh apricots, prunes, apple, peaches, or pineapple for variety.

- - -

Whole Watermelon Drink

Take desired quantity of watermelon and cut into cubes, using fruit, including seeds and rind. Just a little water in the blender will start it off, and the cubes of the whole melon can be piled loosely in to three-quarters fill the container. Blend smooth. Repeat until all cubes have been blended. Strain the drink through coarse wire strainer to catch seed hulls.

Blend till smooth. Use fruit juices or diluted concentrates for base and treat other fruits similarly.

Note: By using 2 Tbsps. juice to 1/2 cup of fruit, beautiful fruit purees can be made.

- - -

Orange Flip

1 cup fresh Orange Juice
2-1/4 cups water or Oatstraw Tea
2 or 3 Eggs
2 Tbsps. Raw Sugar or Honey

Blend for 20 seconds. (H)   3-4 servings

- - -

Rose Elixir

1 cup Apples, cut up   )   Blend together
1 cup Beets, cut up   )   thoroughly. (H) speed.
1 cup Pineapple Juice   )

Serve in tall sherbet glasses and eat with a spoon.   2-3 servings

- - -

Blended Fruit Drinks

1 Tbsp. Fruit Concentrate: Cherry, Apple or Grape
1 cup Pineapple Juice, Milk, Nut Milks, or Coconut Milk.
  Combine as desired.

Other fruits which can be added are:
Bananas	Blueberries
Strawberries	Plums
Peaches	Apricots
Blackberries	Raspberries

Tahina Pineapple Drink

½ cup Sesame Seeds or
   Sesame Butter
2 cups Chilled Pineapple Juice
A Few drops Lemon Juice

Put Sesame Seeds in blender
and blend on (H) speed until
very fine. Add Pineapple Juice
and Lemon Juice and blend again.
Good as a bedtime sleep Coaxer.
Makes about 3 servings.

Cool Summer Evening Cocktail

2-½ cups Tomato Juice
1 slice Lemon, rind included
1 quarter of Orange, peeled.
1 sprig Parsley
1 sprig Watercress
1 tsp. Vegetable Seasoning
¼ Green Pepper
1 stalk Celery, cut in 1" pieces
2 slices Cucumber, ¼ "slice,
   quartered
1 dash Cayenne Pepper
½ tsp. Paprika

Put Tomato Juice, Lemon, Orange,
Parsley and Watercress into
blender and run on (L) speed.
With motor on add rest of ingredients. Then turn to (H) speed
and blend thoroughly. Chill and
serve. Makes about 3-4 servings.

Golden Pink Punch

3 cups Cold Milk
1 tsp. Honey
2 cups Fresh Strawberries, or
   1-10 oz. Frozen Strawberries
2 cups Fresh Peaches. or Frozen

Golden Pink Punch (Con't)

Blend rest of ingredients
with 2 cups of Milk on (H)
speed until smooth. Pour
into punch bowl and add
remaining 1 cup of Milk.
Makes 6-7 servings.

Tuti Fruit Whirl

1 Orange, peeled and quartered
2 cups Pineapple Juice, chilled
   and unsweetened
1 small Apple, cored and
   sliced (peel if desired)
½ Pear, cored, sliced and
   peeled
½ Peach, peeled
1 tbsp. Lecithin Granules
1 tsp. Yeast Powder

Blend all together on (M)
speed until very smooth. If
not all fruits available, use
more of what you have. Makes
3-4 servings.

Pineapple or Orange Yogurt
Supreme

1-½ cups Yogurt
2 tbsp. Honey
½ cup Orange or Pineapple Juice

Blend all together until
smooth. This is a very
wholesome drink, and if
desired you can add 1 tbsp.
Lecithin Liquid, 1 tsp. Rice
Polishings or any other food
supplement as listed on
page 64   3-4 servings

Lemon Sunrise Drink

1 Egg
4 tbsp. Lemon Juice
1 Cup Water, hot or cold
1 tsp. Honey

Blend all together on (H)
speed until well blended.
Makes about 2 servings.

Blackberry Cocktail

2 cups Blackberries
1 cup Water
2 tbsp. Honey
1 cup peeled Orange sections
½ Lemon, peeled.

Put all ingredients into
blender. Use (H) speed until
smooth. For finer textured
drink, strain before chilling.
For more nutrition, add 1 tbsp.
Lecithin Granules before blending.
Makes 3-4 servings.

Fruit Cocktail Drink

8 oz. Pineapple Juice
4 oz. Black Cherry Juice
2 tbsp. Soyalac
1 tbsp. Cocoanut
1 tbsp. Honey
¼ cup Black Walnuts
1 Egg
1 Banana

Blend all together at (H)
speed until well liquefied.
Serve at once. Makes about
3 or 4 servings.

Carrott Pineapple Supreme

½ cup Cubed Celery
½ Cubed Carrots
1-½ glasses Chilled Pineapple Juice
1 tbsp. Lecithin Granules

Blend on (H) speed until smooth.
Makes about 2 servings.

Lime Strawberry Whirl

1- 10 oz. package Frozen Straw-
    berries or 3/4 qt. Fresh
    Strawberries
2 cups Chilled Water
1 tbsp. Honey
1 tbsp. Lecithin Granules

Blend all together until well
blended on (H) speed. Then add
4 ice cubes, one at a time.
Makes about 5-6 servings.

Pecan Apple Fruit Drink

6 Pecans
1 Apple, diced with skin
3 tsp. Raisins
1 Banana, peeled and quartered
1 glass Pineapple Juice

Put all in blender and turn on (H)
speed until well blended.
Makes about 2 servings.

Plain Lemonade Drink

½ cup Lemon Jucie
1 tbsp. Honey
2 cups Crushed Ice

Blend on (H) speed until ice is
crushed. Makes about 2 servings.

Carrot Sunflower Milk Whirl

3 cups Carrot Juice
3/4 cup Sunflower Seeds

Blend Sunflower Seeds on (H)
speed until finely ground.
Add previously made carrot
juice, blend for a few seconds.
For extra nourishment add 1
tbsp. Lecithin Liquid when
blending. Makes about 4 servings.

Orange-Apricot Flip

1 cup Orange Juice
2 cups Apricots (revived as on
  page 49)
½ cup Lemon Juice
2 cups Water, or milk
1 tbsp. Lecithin Liquid
2 cups Health Ice Cream (see
      recipe on page 228)

Blend all together until very
smooth. If thinner consistency
is desired, add more water or
milk. Garnish with an apricot
half. Makes about 7-8 servings.

Health-For-All Cocktail

2 cups Cold Milk
2 Eggs
1 cup diced Cheddar Cheese
1 tbsp. Lecithin Granules
1 tsp. Rice Polishings
1 tbsp. Wheat Germ
2 tbsp. Sesame Seeds

Blend Sesame Seeds until fine,
then add the other ingredients.
Blend on (H) speed until smooth.
Makes about 3-4 servings.

Orange- Strawberry Delight

1 cup Fresh or Frozen Strawberries, partially thawed
1 cup Orange Juice
2 tbsp. Honey
1 cup Ice Cream, or 1 cup
  cracked ice.
1 tbsp. Lecithin Granules

Put Orange Juice in container,
add the rest of the ingredients,
and blend on (L) speed until
smooth. Garnish with a strawberry or a piece of orange.
Makes 3-4 servings.

Pineapple Sunflower Whirl

½ cup Sunflower Seeds
2 cups Pineapple Juice
1 Banana, peeled and quartered
1 tbsp. Lecithin Granules
A Few drops Lemon Juice

Blend Sunflower Seeds on (H)
speed until finely ground. Add
remaining ingredients and
blend on (H) until smooth. Any
fruit juice can be used in
place of Pineapple Juice. Makes
3-4 servings.

Pineapple-Grape Chiller

3 cups Chilled Grape Juice,
  unsweetened
1 cup Orange Juice
2 thin slices Lemon, rind included
2 cups Chilled Pineapple Juice,
  unsweetened
2 tbsp. Lecithin Liquid

Blend all together at (H) speed
until smooth. Makes about 7-8
servings.

Alfa-Mint Iced Tea

1 cup Water
1 Lemon, peeled and quartered
1 inch piece Lemon Peel
1 tbsp. Honey

Put all above ingredients in
blender and blend well. Add
to this:

1-½ Qts. hot Alfamint Tea (made
  as directed on package)
4-5 sprigs fresh Mint (optional)

Let stand 25 minutes. Strain
and chill until ready to
serve. Honey may be used
when serving if desired.
Makes 8-10 servings.

Fresh Mint Freeze

½ cup Honey
1 cup Water
1 cup Whipped Cream (page 205)
1 cup fresh Mint Leaves
¼ cup Lemon Juice
A little Chloryphyl for coloring

Heat Honey and Water until Honey
is well dissolved, add Mint
Leaves to this and blend in
blender on (L) speed until
leaves are finely ground.
Cover and let stand until cool.
Stir in Lemon Juice and add
green coloring. Strain into
ice tray, discarding mint pulp.
and freeze until mushy. Turn
into chilled bowl and beat with
electric or hand beater until
smooth. Fold in Whipped Cream
and freeze until firm. Makes
about 3 servings.

Quicky Breakfast in a Glass

1 cup Skim or Whole Milk
1 tsp. Honey
1 Egg
½ cup any fresh Fruit
1 tbsp. Lecithin Granules
1 tbsp. Wheat Germ Flakes
1 tbsp. Flaxseed Meal
1 tbsp. Sesame Seed, finely
  ground
2-3 drops Lemon Juice (optional)

Blend on (H) speed Flaxseeds,
Sesame Seeds and Lecithin Granules
until finely ground. Then add
balance of ingredients and blend
on (M) speed until smooth. (This
should be eaten as a food, so as
to mix with the saliva.
Unfamiliar items may be purchased
from a Health Food Store.

"Ahead-of-Time" Lunch Drink

2 tbsp. Sunflower, Sesame Seeds
  or Almond Nuts

Blend until finely ground and then
add:

1 cup Apple Juice
¼ cup Orange Juice
¼ cup chilled unsweetened
  Pineapple Juice
½ Carrott, cut in small pieces
1 Egg Yolk
1 tsp. Raisins
1 Celery Stalk, cut in 1" pieces
2 tbsp. Wheat Germ
1 tsp. Rice Polishings
2 Leaves of Spinach
1 sprig Parsley or Watercress
1 tbsp. Lecithin Granules
1 cup Ice Water

Blend all together on (H) speed
until smooth. Makes 3-4 servings.

Minted Lime Drink

1 cup Boiling Water
2 tbsp. Honey
1 cup Fresh Mint Leaves

Blend all together at (H) speed
until finely ground. Chill.
Strain into large container,
then add the following:

1 Qt. Chilled Water
1 cup Lime Juice
$\frac{1}{4}$ cup Lemon Juice.

Stir until well mixed. If desired
colder for serving, just add an ice
cube to each glass. Makes 6-7
servings.

Delectable Strawberry, Mint Punch

3 cups Fresh Strawberries or
    1-10 oz. package Frozen Straw-
    berries (thawed)
2 cups Lime Juice, chilled
$\frac{1}{2}$ cup Lemon Juice
2 tbsp. Mint flavored Tea
1 tbsp. Honey
6 cups Water, chilled

Blend all together at (H) speed
until smooth with the exception
of the water. Put in punch bowl
and add chilled water. Makes 10-
12 servings.

Orange Lemon Nectar

1 pt. Distilled water
1 dash of Mint
Juice of 3 Oranges and 3 Lemons
Sweetened to tast with Maple
Sugar or Honey

Blend on (H) speed until well
blended. Makes 3 servings

Pomengranate Juice and Whey

2 cups Whey
2 large or 3 small
    Pomengranates

Extract juice by splitting
and placing all but skin in
loosely woven muslin bag.
Squeeze tightly. Add to
Whey and serve immediately.
Makes about 3 servings.

Pineapple Fig Nectar

2 cups Pineapple Juice
1 cup Fig Juice
1 tbsp. Lecithin Liquid

Blend on (H) speed until very
smooth. Top with whipped
cream. Makes about 3-4
servings.

Fruit Punches

Foundation Punch Recipe

12 Oranges, peeled and quartered
6-8 Lemons, peeled and quartered
4 Qts. Water
1 cup Honey

Makes approximately 5 quarts.
Adding to the liquid a few
Oranges and Lemons at a time,
blend at (H) speed until
well liquefied.

Tea Punch

One part lemonade and two parts unsweetened silicon or mint tea.

Grape Punch

One part foundation punch and two parts unsweetened bottled or fresh Concord Grape Juice.

Strawberry Punch

One part foundation punch and two parts fresh Strawberry Juice which has been squeezed through a loosely woven muslin bag.

Raspberry Punch

One part foundation punch and three parts Raspberry Juice prepared the same as Strawberry Juice.

Mint Punch

One part foundation punch and one dozen sprigs of fresh mint. Chill for 1 hour.

Lemon Mint Punch

6 sprigs fresh Mint
2 cups Water
1 cup Honey
2 cups Lemon Juice
1 pinch of Sea Salt
1 Qt. Grape Juice, unsweetened

Blend Mint, Water and Honey on (H) speed. Simmer 5 minutes, and then strain. Add Lemon Juice, and Salt and chill thoroughly. Mix gently with Grape Juice and serve chilled. Makes about 16-18 servings.

Pineapple Beet "Pick-me-up"

2 cups unsweetened Pineapple juice chilled
1 cup raw Beets, diced
1 tbsp. Lecithin Liquid or granules

Blend thoroughly all together in blender at (H) speed. If desired can add other health producing ingredients such as wheat germ or rice polishings. See list on page
(3 servings.)

Pineapple Carrot Delight

2 cups chilled Pineapple Juice
1 Orange peeled and quartered
1 med. Carrot, sliced
1 tbsp. Honey
1 tbsp. Lecithin Granules or liquid

Blend all together at (H) speed until very smooth. Serve well chilled. Add chipped or cubed ice when serving, if desired.
(3-4 servings.)

3 O'clock Cocktail

2 cups unsweetened Pineapple juice, chilled
1 med. Carrot, cut in 1" pieces
1 stalk Celery, cut in 1" pieces
½ Cucumber, cubed
1 slice Lemon, or 1 tbsp. lemon juice
1 tbsp. Lecithin Granules
½ tsp. Rice Polishings

Blend all together until very smooth. If colder drink is desired, add some crushed ice, or pour mixture over ice cubes.

Vegetable Cocktail with a Zing

3 cups chilled Tomato Juice or whole tomatoes may be used
2 tbsps. Lemon Juice
1 med. Carrot cut in 1" pieces
1 large stalk Celery, cut in 1" pieces
1 med. slice Onion
Shake Cayenne Pepper
½ tsp. Sea Salt or Vegetable Seasoning
1 cup Chipped Ice

Blend first 7 items on (H) speed until smooth. Then add chipped ice and blend until ice is melted. If preferred, can put chipped ice in serving glasses.

This cocktail can also be heated and served as part of meal.
(4-5 servings.)

Pomegranate Juice and Goat Whey

1 large Pomegranate   1 cup Whey

Peel Pomegranate and put pith, seeds, and whey into liquefier.
Run blender just 2 to 3 seconds to remove juice without crushing
seeds too much--these can be very bitter. Strain.   (M)

Fresh Apple Cocktail

1/4 cup water   1 large eating Apple, chopped
1 tablespoon Lemon Juice   with core
1 tsp. Raw Sugar or Honey   1/2 cup cracked ice.

Blend until apple is liquefied. You may need to vary the lemon
juice and sweetening to suit taste. (H)

Prune and Apple Drink

1 cup revived Prunes, with   1 cup Apple Juice
    juice (pit before blending)   1 Tbsp. Lemon Juice

Blend until smooth. Add more apple juice if too thick.
    (H) speed

MILK DRINKS AND FROSTED SMOOTHIES

Banana Milk

1 cup Milk   1 Tbsp. Fruit Concentrate
1 ripe Banana

Liquefy.   (H)   1 serving

Date Milk Drink

5 Pitted Dates   1 tsp. Powdered Coconut
1 cup Milk and Cream   1 tsp. Nuts

Blend till creamy. (H)

Carrot Milk

1 cup Milk
1 medium-sized Carrot, chopped

Blend until very fine and smooth. (H) speed

Banana Fig Milk Shake

1/2 cup thick Soy Milk   1 very ripe Banana
1/2 cup Fig Juice   Carob to flavor, if desired
1 tsp. Rice Polishings   Run Blender until thick and creamy. (H)

– – –

Tahini Milk Shake

1 cup favorite Herb Tea   1 Tbsp. Honey
4 Tbsps. Milk Powder   1 Tbsp. Tahini (Sesame Butter)

Blend smooth and creamy. (H)

– – –

Spiced Milk

1/2 Tbsp. Honey   )
1 cup Milk   )   Blend till nice
Cinnamon to taste   )   and frothy (H)
1/4 tsp. Pure Vanilla)

Serve in tall glasses, grating a little nutmeg on top. Serve hot
or cold.   1-2 servings

– – –

Dates and Buttermilk

Soak Dates and liquefy in
   Buttermilk
(H) speed

Orange Buttermilk

1/2 cup Orange Juice
2 Tbsps. Honey
Piece Orange Rind
1-1/2 cups Buttermilk

Blend until creamy   (H)
 2-3 servings

Carrot Banana Milk Shake

1/2 cup Milk
1/2 cup Carrot Juice
1 very ripe Banana
1 tsp. Sunflower Seeds (optional)

Run in blender until very smooth
and creamy. (H)

– – –

Frosted Banana

1 cup Milk   1 large scoop Health Ice
1 Banana   Cream

(H) speed
Begin blending milk and ice cream, then remove lid and slice in
banana with motor still running. Try other soft fruits, or revived
dried fruits. Soy or nut milks may replace milk.   1-2 servings

Strawberry-Buttermilk Whizz

2 cups chilled Buttermilk
3 cups Fresh Strawberries or
    1-10 oz. Frozen berries
2 tbsp. Honey
2 cups Health Strawberry Ice
    Cream (see page 228)

Blend first 3 ingredients
together on (H) speed until
smooth. Serve in glasses and
top with one scoop Ice Cream.
Makes 6-8 servings.

Nutritious Eggnog

2 Eggs
1 tbsp. Honey

2 cups Milk
1 tbsp. Lecithin Granules
1 dash Sea Salt
$\frac{1}{2}$ tsp. True Vanilla Flavoring
$\frac{1}{2}$ cup Pineapple Juice

Place all ingredients in
blender and turn to (L) speed.
Blend until well mixed.
Sprinkle a little nutmeg on
the top of each drink if
desired. Makes about 4 servings.

Buttermilk Whirl

1 cup chilled Pineapple Juice
$\frac{1}{2}$ Lemon Slice, rind included
2 cups Buttermilk
1 tbsp. Honey
1 tbsp. Lecithin Liquid

Blend on (H) speed until
smooth. Makes about 3-4
servings.

Fruity Nut Milk Whiz

2 cups Cold Milk
1 cup Fresh or Frozen Peaches
1 cup Apricots (revived-see page
    49)
1 ripe Banana, peeled and
    quartered
3 pitted dates
2 tbsp. Almond Nuts (best if
    soaked several hours or over-
    night)

Put Almond Nuts in blender and
grind on (L) speed, then on (H)
speed until finely ground. Add
the rest of the ingredients and
blend on (H) until smooth. Chill
to serve. Makes about 4-5 servings.

Soft-as-a-Breeze Milk Shake

3 cups chilled Milk
3 cups Fresh Fruit of any kind,
    as Peaches, Pineapple, Straw-
    berries
2 tbsp. Lecithin Liquid

Put all ingredients in blender
container, and blend on (H) speed
until smooth. If colder drink is
desired, add a scoop of Health
Ice Cream to the top of each
drink. Makes about 8 servings.

Chilly Apricot Whirl

2 cups cold Milk
3/4 cup Revived Apricots (see
    page 49)
1 tbsp. Honey

Mix all ingredients in blender at
(H) speed until smooth. Chill
and serve. Top with Apricot Halves.
Makes about 3 servings.

Apricot Milk Shake

1 cup Apricots, revived (see
  page   for instructions)
1 cup Milk
½ pt. Health Vanilla Ice Cream
  (see recipe page 228)
A Few drops Almond extract.

Blend on (H) speed until fluffy.
This recipe can be made without
Ice Cream by adding 1 tbsp.
Honey and 1 tbsp. Lecithin
Granules. Makes 2-3 servings.

Purple and White Fizz

2 Egg Whites
½ Lemon juiced, or
  2 tbsp.
1 tbsp. Honey
1 cup Crushed Ice

Blend on (H) speed until
frothy. Pour into glasses
and add 2 tbsp. unsweetened
Grape Juice to each glass.
3-4 servings

"Honey-of-a-Banana" Milk Shake

1 cup Cold Milk
1 Banana, peeled and quartered
1 tbsp. Honey
1 cup Chipped Ice
1 tbsp. Lecithin Liquid

Blend on (H) speed until very
smooth. This is a real healthful drink. See page   for
additional food supplements
which may be added. Makes about
3 servings.

Pineapple Sunny Whiz

2 cups unsweetened Pineapple
  Juice, chilled
1 Orange, peeled and quartered
1 medium sized Carrot
1 tbsp. Lecithin Granules
1 tbsp. Yeast Powder

Blend all together on (H) speed
until very smooth. Makes about
2-3 servings.

Pineapple-Mint Fizz

1 cup unsweetened Pineapple chunks
  if not available use 1 cup
  unsweetened juice.
2 cups Cold Milk
1 sprig Fresh Mint
1 tbsp. Lecithin Liquid

Blend thoroughly at (H) speed
until nice consistency for
drinks. Makes 3-4 servings.

Vanilla-Cherry Supreme

2 cups Red Cherries or Bing
  Cherries if desired
1 Qt. Cold Milk
1 pt. Health Ice Cream (page 228)

Blend at (H) speed until real
creamy. Serve in tall glasses
and top with extra Ice Cream
and a Cherry.

Strawberry Milk Shake Supreme

3 cups Chilled Milk
3 cups Fresh Strawberries or
   1-10 oz. package Frozen Strawberries partially thawed
2 tbsp. Honey
1 tbsp. Lecithin Liquid
1 pt. Health Strawberry Ice Cream
   (see recipe on page 228)

Blend on (H) speed first four
ingredients until thoroughly
blended. Serve in glasses and
top with Ice Cream. Makes 7-8
servings.

Pineapple Delight

1 Qt. Pineapple Juice, chilled,
   unsweetened
4 large ripe Bananas

Blend together at (H) speed until
well blended. Makes 7-8 servings.

Pineapple and Banana Whip
a la Mode

6 cups Pineapple juice, chilled
4 ripe Bananas, peeled and
   quartered
Ice Cream (see recipe page 228)
1 tbsp. Lecithin Liquid

Put all ingredients into blender
and blend on (H) speed until
creamy. If preferred, Ice Cream
can be served on top of the drink
instead of blending together.
Makes a delicious drink to serve
those Drop-in-Guests. Serves
about 7-8.

Banana Whip

2 cups Cold Milk
½ cup Orange Juice
4 tbsp. Honey
1 tbsp. Lecithin Liquid
2 ripe Bananas, peeled and cut
   into 4 or 5 pieces

Put into blender in order given.
Blend at (H) speed until fairly
smooth. Then add the Lecithin
Liquid and blend until smooth.
Makes about 4-5 servings.

Heavenly Magic Banana Whirl

2 cups Chilled Pineapple Juice
2 ripe Bananas, peeled and
   quartered
3 cups Milk (any type as listed
   in front of book, page 122)
1 tbsp. Honey
1 tsp. Vanilla
2 tbsp. Lecithin Granules

Blend all together at (H) speed
until smooth. A little crushed
ice may be added if colder
drink is desired. Makes about
6-7 servings.

Date Milk Drink

5 Dates pitted and cut in half
1 glass of Milk and Cream
1 tsp. Powdered Coconut
1 tsp. Mal-ba Nuts

Put all in blender and run on
(H) speed. Serve immediately.
If desired Sesame or Sunflower
Seeds may be used in place of
nuts.

Cherry Whip

2 cups unsweetened Pineapple
  Juice
1 cup Fresh Tart Cherries or
  Bing Cherries if desired
1 slice Lemon or Lime
1 tbsp. Lecithin Granules

Blend together at (H) speed
until smooth. Serves 3-4.

Frosty Strawberry Delight

1 cup Fresh or Frozen Strawberries
1 cup Orange Juice
1 tbsp. Honey
1 cup Cracked Ice
1 tbsp. Lecithin Granules

Blend all ingredients at (H)
speed until smooth. Makes
about 3 servings.

Reducer's Special

2 cups chilled unsweetened
  Pineapple Juice
1 bunch Watercress
1 cup crushed Ice, or 3 Ice
  Cubes

Blend all together at (H)
speed until well blended.

Pineapple-Banana a la Mode

5 cups chilled Pineapple Juice
4 ripe Bananas, peeled and
  quartered
5 scoops Health Ice Cream

Pineapple-Banana a la Mode (Con't)

Put Pineapple Juice in blender and
add Bananas. Blend until smooth.
Add Ice Cream and blend a few seconds
longer. Makes about 7-8.servings.

Peach Almond Refresher

1 cup chilled Fresh Peaches or
  partially thawed Frozen Peaches
1 cup Milk
4 drops Almond Extract (True)
1 cup Vanilla Ice Cream (see page 228)
1 tbsp. Lemon Juice

Blend all together with the exception
of Ice Cream. Use (H) speed. Then add
Ice Cream and blend on (L) speed until
smooth.(In place of Ice Cream, 1 tbsp.
Heavy Cream and 1 tbsp. Lecithin Liquid)
Serve at once and garnish with thin
slices of peaches and sprigs of mint
if available. Makes 3 servings.

Sunset Orange Glow

1 cup cold Milk
½ cup Orange Juice
1 Orange, peeled and quartered
1 Lemon, peeled and quartered
1 tbsp. Honey
1 cup crushed Ice

Blend all together on (H) speed until
smooth. Makes 2-3 servings.

Banana Orange Frappé

1 ripe Banana
1 Orange, peeled and quartered
1 cup Milk
1 piece Orange Rind about 1"
   square
2 drops Almond Extract
1 tbsp. Honey
1 tbsp. Lecithin Granules

Put all ingredients into
blender and run on (L)
for a few seconds, then turn
to (H) until very smooth.
Pour into a freezing tray and
freeze to a mushy consistency.
Should be served partially
frozen. Garnish with sections
of Orange. Makes 3 servings.

Apricot-Pineapple Frosty Drink

1 Qt. chilled Pineapple Juice
2 cups revived Apricots (see
   page 22)
2 tbsp. Honey
1 tbsp. Lemon Juice
2 cups chilled Apricot Juice from
   reviving process

Blend all together on (H) until
smooth and frosty. Makes 7-8
servings.

Molasses Milk Whirl

1 cup cold Milk
1 tbsp. Molasses (unsulphured)
1 tbsp. Lecithin Granules

Blend until very smooth at (H)
speed. Makes 1 serving.

Peach Golden Dawn

1-$\frac{1}{2}$ pts. Fresh or Frozen Peaches
2 tbsp. Honey
2 tbsp. Lemon Juice
1 pt. Health Vanilla Ice Cream (see
   page 228 for recipe)

Blend all together at (H) speed until
smooth. Makes about 8 servings.

Raspberry Delight

1 cup Fresh or Frozen Raspberries
1-$\frac{1}{2}$ cups chilled Pineapple Juice
2 tbsp. Lemon Juice
2 tbsp. Honey
2 cups chipped Ice
1 tbsp. Lecithin Liquid

Put Pineapple Juice and Raspberries
into blender. Use (H) speed.
Strain to remove seeds. Return to
blender and add Lemon Juice, Honey,
and chipped Ice. Run at (H) speed
until smooth. Delightfully
refreshing and a healthful drink.
Makes about 3-4 servings.

Heavenly Bliss

$\frac{1}{4}$ cup hot Water
2 tbsp. Lecithin Granules
2 tbsp. Honey
2 tbsp. Carob Powder
3 cups hot Milk

Put first 4 items in blender and
blend on (H) until smooth. Turn
on (L) and gradually add the hot
Milk. This is a good "Nightcap"
drink. Makes about 4-5 servings.

"Goodnight" Snack

1 cup Milk
1 tbsp. Molasses
1 tbsp. Lecithin Granules

Blend all together using (H)
speed. Then warm to comfortable drinking temperature.
(This helps those with sleeping
 problems. It helps to relax).
Makes 1 serving.

Golden Daybreak Milk Shake

2-3 cups Milk
3-4 medium sized Carrots
    cut in 1" pieces
2 tbsp. Honey
2 tbsp. Sunflower Seeds

Put Sunflower Seeds in blender,
blend on (H) speed until finely
pulverized. Add rest of ingredients and blend on (H) until
smooth. This is a very nourishing drink for children and
convalescents and can be
served at any time during the
day. Makes 4 servings.

Apricot Smoothie

1 cup fresh, stewed, or revived apricots (see page 22)
Honey to taste, if desired
1 cup Milk
1 cup cracked ice

Blend until smooth and a creamy mixture is arrived at. Most other fruits can be used similarly for "smoothies"--even vegetables like carrot, tomato and spinach. (H)

Soy, sesame or nut milks may be used also.

Use honey, maple syrup or molasses if any sweetening is necessary.

— — —

Pineapple Banana Cream

1-1/2 cups Pineapple Juice, unsweetened
1/2 cup Milk Powder
1 ripe Banana, sliced
(H)
Blend, then add: 2 scoops Vanilla Health Ice Cream or Pineapple sherbet. (See recipe for Ice Cream page 228)

Pour into two tall glasses.

— — —

COCONUT MILK DRINKS

These can also be made with soy milk, raw milk, nut or seed milks. If necessary, add extra natural sweetening or flavoring.

Coconut Juice or Milk

Liquefy: (H)1 cup unsweetened shredded Coconut, or fresh, diced and ground dry in blender.
3 cups hot water

Blend half the quantity at a time if too full. Strain while hot through cloth bag of a juice press, or squeeze through a heavy cloth by hand. Chill.

Delightful addition to any milk or milk drink, including soy milk.

Apricot Coconut Fluff

1-1/2 cups Shredded Coconut   1-1/2 cups Oatstraw tea *or
                                     water *(see recipe page 20)

Blend till fine, then strain through fine strainer or cheesecloth.
Return juice to container and add: (H)

3/4 cup Juice from *Revived Apricots   1 Egg White
2 Tbsps. Lemon Juice   *(see page 22) 1/2 cup cracked ice

Blend till smooth and fluffy. (H)   3-4 servings

Favorite Fruit Shake

1 cup Fruit Juice--Orange Apple and Pineapple
1 good slice Papaya   1/2 cup Coconut Juice or
                                1 Tbsp. Cream

Blend ingredients in liquefier about 1/2 minute or till frothy. (H)

Carrot Coconut Milk

1/2 cup Hot Water   1 Tbsp. fresh Coconut, blender
                                grated
Liquefy, and when blended add:
(H)   1/2 cup fresh Carrot Juice

Coconut Pineapple Froth

2 Tbsps. Coconut Milk Powder   1 to 2 Tbsps. Pineapple, or more
1 to 2 tsps. Honey   1 cup boiling water
1 tsp. Gelatin   1 Egg White

Blend till frothy. (H)

Papaya Coconut Shake

1 cup Coconut Juice   1 good slice Papaya
   Dates, or other sweetener, if desired.

Blend to make a smooth "shake". (H)

Carrot and Coconut Cocktail

1/2 cup Coconut Juice   1 small Carrot, chopped
Liquefy. (H)

Sapote Flip

1 cup Coconut **or** Nut Milk
1 large Sapote- -remove seeds
1 dash of Pure Vanilla
1 tsp. fresh Coconut
1 tsp. Honey

Liquefy (H)

Prune Milk

$\frac{1}{4}$ cup revived Pitted Prunes
1 cup Coconut Milk or
  Sesame Milk
Few drops Pure Vanilla or a
sprinkle of Cinnamon

Blend until very fine and
smooth. (H)

MOCK-CHOC DRINKS

"Mock-Choc Milk

1 heaped tbsp. Soy Milk Powder
$\frac{1}{2}$ tbsp. Carob Powder
1 tbsp. Honey
1 cup Water

Blend until smooth and
creamy. (H)

"Mock-Choc" Drink, Hot or Cold

1 cup hot Milk
1 tbsp. Carob Powder
1 tsp. Whey Powder
1 tsp. Rice Polishings
1 tsp. Soy Milk Powder
Honey to sweeten
$\frac{1}{4}$ tsp. Pure Vanilla

Blend to a foamy drink.(H) Speed
Serve with a dash of cream on
top. (Makes a delicious cold
drink also.)

Iced Mint "Mock-Choc"

4 Tbsps. Carob Sauce
$\frac{1}{2}$ cup Water
$\frac{1}{2}$ cup Honey
$\frac{1}{4}$ tsp. Vegetable Seasoning
2 cups thick Soy Milk
1 tbsp. Whey Powder
$\frac{1}{4}$ tsp. Pure Vanilla
4-5 sprigs fresh Mint
1 cup cracked ice

Mix in blender until nice and
creamy. (H)

"Mock-Choc" Banana Shake

2 cups Milk or Nut Milk
1 Egg
1 Banana, sliced
$\frac{1}{4}$ cup Carob Sauce*(see recipe page 205
1 dash of Vegetable Seasoning

Blend to make smooth and creamy. (H)
2-3 servings

"Mock-Choc Sesame Milk

$\frac{1}{4}$ cup Carob Powder
$\frac{1}{2}$ cup Water
1/3 cup Raw Sugar
  (Cont'd)

"Mock-Choc"Sesame Milk (cont'd)

Simmer 5 minutes, stirring occasionally. Use a good table-
spoonful of this mixture to each cup sesame milk. Add a few
drops of pure vanilla.

Blend to a frothy drink. (H)

Enriched "Mock-Choc" Drink

1-1/2 cups Milk   1 Tbsp. Sunflower Seed Meal
1 Egg Yolk   1 Tbsp. Whey Powder
1 Tbsp. Rice Polishings   1/2 tsp. Vegetable Seasoning
2 Tbsps. Carob Powder

Blend Smooth. Cook over hot, not boiling, water, stirring
until thickened slightly. Add and blend till nice and frothy: (H)

1 Tbsp. Cream   1-1/2 tsp. Pure Vanilla
2 Tbsps. Honey   1 Egg White

Serve hot, or chill.   3-4 servings

"Mock-Choc" Nut Drink

1 cup Milk   1 Tbsp. Carob Sauce
1 Tbsp. Raw Nuts   Few drops Pure Vanilla
          (H)

Blend smooth, then heat in a double boiler, being careful not to
heat too much. Pour into a hot cup. Top with a spoonful of
whipped cream and dust with cinnamon.

Mocha Shake

1/2 tsp. Dandelion Root "Coffee"
1 cup Water

Prepare as regular coffee.

2 tsp. Carob Powder   )
1 tsp. Rice Polishings   )   Mix together
2 tsps. Honey   )   in blender.
Few drops Pure Vanilla   )

Pour in "coffee" and blend till foamy. Serve with sweet whipped
cream.   (H)

113

THERMOS DRINKS

"Vita" Broth

1 tsp. Vegetable Seasoning
1 cup Hot Water
Parsley
Watercress
Other green leaves to suit

Blend until very smooth.
Pour into preheated thermos
and take to work. (H)

Health Drink

1 tsp. Vegetable Seasoning
1 cup Hot Water
1 Tbsp. Whey Powder
1/4 tsp. Dulse
Cream to taste

Blend for a really delicious
drink. Pour into preheated
thermos. (H)

Lunch in a Thermos

1 cup Apple or Pineapple Juice
1/2 cup Orange Juice
1 tsp. Raisins
3/4 cup Cashews or Almonds
1 small Celery stalk, diced
1/2 cup Carrots, diced

2 sprigs Parsley
2 leaves Spinach or Romaine
    Lettuce
1/2 cup Fresh Fruit
1 small piece Banana
1 Egg
2 tsp. Wheat Germ

1 tsp. Rice Polishings

Blend all the ingredients for 3 minutes. Add 1 cup crushed ice
and pour into thermos. (H)

This makes a "complete meal". Sip it very slowly and enjoy
the full savor.

PROTEIN AND STARCH DRINKS

Protein Drinks

(1)   1 cup Buttermilk
       1 Egg Yolk
       1 tsp. Brewer's Yeast
       2 Tbsps. Wheat Germ
       1 tsp. Vegetable Seasoning
       1 Tbsp. Gelatin
       A few drops Lemon Juice

(2)   1 cup Papaya Tea
       3 Tbsps. Sunflower Seeds
       4 Tbsps. Cottage Cheese
       4 Dates

(3)   1 cup Carrot Juice
       1-1/2 tsp. Vegetable
          Seasoning
       3-1/2 slices "Nuttose",
          "Protose", etc.
       2 tsps. Dried Egg Powder
       1-1/2 tsps. Soy Sauce

       (Cont'd.)

(4) 1 cup Milk
     2 Tbsps. Skim Milk Powder
     1 tsp. Rice Polishings
     1/4 tsp. Dulse
     1 Tbsp. Black Walnut Butter
     1/3 tsp. Molasses
     3 revived Apricots

"Special Protein Cocktail"

1 cup cold Milk
1 Egg Yolk
1/2 cup Cheddar Cheese, diced
1 Tbsp. Flaxseed
1 Tbsp. Lecithin Granules
1 Tbsp. Wheat Germ
1 Tbsp. Rice Polishings

Put flaxseed in blender and
blend on (H) until finely ground.
Then add rest of ingredients
in order given. Blend all
together on (H) until smooth.
(This makes a delicious tasting
and nourishing protein snack.)
Makes 2-3 servings.

Try These Protein Drinks

The easiest, quickest way to
supply your system with protein
is to enjoy drinks made of foods
known to contain quantities of
this vital substance. We
give you four such drinks. You
will find these ingredients
available at all good Health
Food Stores.

Recipe #1

1 Tbsp. Soy Milk Powder
1 Tbsp. Gelatin
1 Egg Yolk
1 Glass Grape Concentrate
   (Makes 1 serving)

(5) Hot "Mock-Choc"
     2 Tbsps. Carob Sauce
     3/4 cup Hot Nut Milk
     2 Tbsps. Skim Milk Powder

     Use (H) speed for blending
     these recipes.

Recipe #2

Glass Raw Milk
1 Tbsp. Wheat Oil
1 Tbsp. Lecithin Granules
1 tsp. Vegetable Broth Powder
   (Makes 1 serving)

Recipe #3

1 Tbsp. Brewer's Yeast
3/4 glass Pineapple Juice
1/4 glass Skim Milk

Recipe #4

1 glass Tomato Juice
1 Tbsp. Wheat Germ Oil
1 Tbsp. Gelatin
1 Tbsp. Brewer's Yeast
   (Makes 1 serving)

Liquefied Drinks

Drink #1

1 cup Black Cherry Juice
2 cups unsweetened Pineapple Juice
2 Tbsps. Honey
1 Banana
2 Tbsps. Soyalac
1 Egg Yolk
1 Tbsp. Wheat Germ
1 tsp. Rice Polishings
   (Makes 3-4 servings)

Drink #2

Dates, just a few
1 cup Soy Milk
1 tsp. Bone Meal
   (Makes 1 serving)

Drink #3

1 Banana
2 Tbsps. Soyalac
1/2 cup chopped Parsley
1 cup Papaya Juice
2 Tbsps. Apple Concentrate
   (Makes 1 serving)

Drink #4

2 cups Pineapple Juice
1 cup Milk
1 Banana
3 Tbsps. Shad Roe
Small can Pimentos
   (Makes 3-4 servings)

Starch Drinks

(1) 1 cup Soy Milk
     4 Tbsps. Cooked Cereal
     1/4 tsp. Dulse
     Honey to sweeten
     Few drops Lemon or Vanilla

(2) 1 cup Flaxseed Tea
     2 Tbsps. Arrowroot
     1-1/2 Tbsps. Raisins or
           other Dried Fruit
     1 Tbsp. Whey Powder
     1/2 tsp. Pure Vanilla
     Pinch Nutmeg

(3) 1 cup Rice Water
     1/2 cup Cooked Potatoes
     Vegetable Seasoning
     Powdered Clove - mere shake
     1 clove Garlic
     1 sprig Marjoram
     1 small Green Onion

Drink #5

1 cup Blackberry Juice
1 cup Pineapple Juice and
   Crushed Pineapple
1 Banana
1 Egg Yolk
2 Tbsps. Soyalac
1 Tbsp. Honey

Blend together and serve with shredded coconut. Makes 3 servings

These Drinks are very tasty, yet nutritious drinks. Try serving them to your drop-in guests.

----

(4) 1 cup Huckleberry Tea
     2 tsps. Flaxseed Meal
     1 Banana
     2 tsps. Apple Concentrate

(5) 1 cup Carrot Juice
     1/2 cup Corn, off cob
     Piece of Celery
     Vegetable Seasoning to taste

     After blending on (H) this can be sieved. Add a little Sweet Raw Cream.

Note: Sweet Potatoes or Yams also make a very good starch base for drinks.

Yam Delight

3   cups Water
2   cups Steamed Yams
1   Tbsp. Vegetable Seasoning
1   Tbsp. Brewer's Yeast
1   Tbsp. Rice Polishings

Put in blender and blend on
(H) until smooth. Add 1
Tbsp. Lecithin granules or
liquid and blend a few seconds
longer. If too thick add extra
water or milk. Serve either
warm or cold. Makes 3-4
servings.

Lima Bean Drink

2   cups Vegetable Broth
    (see page 141)
1   cup Lima Beans, cooked
1   Tbsp. Vegetable Seasoning
1   Tbsp. Brewer's Yeast
1   Tbsp. Whey Powder
1 · Tbsp. Honey

Blend together on (H) until
smooth. Add 2 Tbsps. Cream
and blend a few seconds longer.
Season to **taste.** Serve
warm or cold. Makes 3-4
servings.

Nut & Seed
DRINKS

The blender will chop nuts in 3 to 5 seconds, grind them to a powder in a little more time, or reduce them to a butter. Quick switches to on and off at high speed, and a rubber scraper to scrape off the sides accomplish this. The longer you blend, the finer the butter.

By using a liquid with your nuts and seeds, you can whip up nutritious milk-substitute drinks in no time. Liquefied nuts can be handled very nicely in the intestinal tract.

Almond Nut Milk

Use blanched or unblanched almonds (or other nuts). Soak overnight in pineapple juice, apple juice, or honey water. This softens the structure of the nut meats. Then put 3 ounces of soaked nuts into 5 ounces of water and blend for two to three minutes. Flavor with honey, any kind of fruit, concentrate of apple or cherry juice, strawberry juice, carob flour, dates or bananas. Any of the vegetable juices are also good with nut milks.

Nut milks can also be used with soups and vegetarian roasts as a flavoring, or over cereals. Almond milk makes a very alkaline drink, high in protein and easy to assimilate and absorb.

Seeds and Sprouts

Seeds and sprouts are going to be the foods of the future. We have found that many of the seeds have the hormone values of male and female glands. Seeds carry the life force for many years, as long

as they are enclosed by the hull. Seeds found in tombs, and
known to be thousands of years old, have grown when planted.
To get these seeds into our bodies in the form of a drink gives
us the finest nutrition.

Flaxseed and sunflower seeds, sesame seeds, apricot kernels,
dry melon seeds, etc. grind dry in the liquefier very well. As
these deteriorate quickly, keep your blender handy and grind
them as often as needed.

Cantaloupe Seed Drink

Instead of throwing away the seeds and pulp from the inside of
the cantaloupe, blend these thoroughly with a little pineapple
juice or oatstraw tea sweetened with honey; strain to remove
the seed hulls, and serve as a delicious "nut" milk drink,
rich in the vital elements of seeds.

Variation: Squash seeds may be similarly treated in a suitable
liquid, flavored with honey or maple syrup and a few dates or
sliced fresh fruit.

Also: Pepitoria Seeds (from Guatamala) . . . very high in
protein.

Sesame Seed Milk

I believe that sesame seed milk is one of our best. It is a wonderful drink for gaining weight and for lubricating the intestinal
tract. Its nutritional value is beyond compare, as it is high in
protein and minerals. This is the seed that is used so much as
a basic food in Arabia and East India.

> 2 cups water
> 1/4 cup Sesame Seed
> 2 Tbsps. Soy Milk Powder

Blend for 1-1/2 minutes to make very smooth. Strain if desired
through a fine wire strainer or three or four layers of cheesecloth. This removes the hulls.

Variations:

> 1 Tbsp. Carob Powder
> 6 to 8 Dates

Blend in for flavor and added nutritional value any one of the
following:

(Cont'd.)

119

Banana	Stewed Raisins
Apple Concentrate	Cherry Concentrate
Date Powder	Grape Sugar

After any addition, always blend to mix. (H) speed

This drink can also be made from raw milk or goat's milk if the doctor advises, in place of the water.

Other Uses for Sesame Seed Milk:

Salad Dressings
Added to Fruits
For after-school snacks
Added to Vegetable Broth
Used on Cereals for
   breakfast

Mixed with any kind of Nut Butter
Twice daily with Bananas to gain
   weight
Added to Whey Drinks to adjust
   intestinal sluggishness
With supplements, such as
   Flaxseed or Rice Polishings

Sunflower Seed Milk (The vegetarian's best protein--Sunflower Seeds)

The same principle as is used for making nut milks can be employed to make sunflower seed milk; i. e., soaking overnight, liquefying, and flavoring with fruits and juices. Use in the diet the same way as the almond nut milk. It is best to use whole sunflower seeds, and blend them yourself. If you do not have a liquefier, the sunflower seed meal can be used.

Soy Milk and Soy Cream

Soy milk powder is universal in every health food store.

For soy milk add 2 Tbsps. of soy milk powder to one pint of water. Sweeten with raw sugar, honey or molasses and add a pinch of vegetable seasoning. For flavor, you can add any kind of fruit, apple or cherry concentrate, carob powder, dates and bananas. You can add any other natural sweetener.

Keep in refrigerator. Use this milk in any recipe as you would regular cow's milk. It closely resembles the taste and composition of cow's milk and will sour just as quickly, so it should not be made too far ahead of time.

Soy Cream

1 cup water
1/2 tsp. Pure Vanilla

1/2 cup Soy Milk Powder
Honey if desired

(Cont'd.)

Soy Cream (Cont'd.)

Begin blending and gradually add: 1 cup Soy or Safflower Oil

Chill.

NUT DRINKS

Teas can be substituted for water in the following drinks; e.g., oatstraw tea, strawberry tea, peach leaf tea, and golden seal tea.

Nut-Cream or Nut-Milk

Soak seeds or nuts overnight. Do not wash after soaking. Excellent choices are: almonds (blanched after soaking if desired), sunflower seeds, sesame seeds, millet or any other nuts.

Liquefy until smooth: (H)

1-1/4 cups Soaked Seeds or
   Nuts
1 cup pure water

For Nut-Milk add more water.
days.

Add and blend well:

2 Tbsps. Honey
2 Tbsps. Sesame Oil
Vegetable Seasoning (opt.)

Refrigerate. This keeps several

Nut Milk Drink

5 Tbsps. Nut Butter
5 cups warm water
2 Tbsps. Honey

Blend. (H)

Almond Nut Milk

1 Tbsp. raw Almond Butter
1 cup warm water.

Blend. (H)

Orange Almond Milk

1 tsp. Almond Butter
1 cup fresh Orange Juice,
   Apple, Grape, or
   Pineapple Juice

Blend. (H)

Maple Nut Fruit Nectar

1 tsp. pure Maple Syrup
3 Tbsps. Raw Nuts
1 cup Fruit Juice

Blend. (H)

Maple Nut Banana Cream

1 Tbsp. Maple Syrup
2 Tbsps. Nuts
1 cup Milk
1 Tbsp. Sweet Raw Cream
1 ripe Banana, sliced

Blend nice and creamy. Serve
   cold or even warmed. (H)

Jumbo Fruit-Nut Drink

1 cup Pineapple Juice
1/2 cup Black Cherry Juice
2 Tbsps. Soy Milk Powder
1 Tbsp. Coconut
6 pitted Dates

1 Tbsp. Honey
1/4 cup Black Walnuts
1 Egg
1 Banana, sliced

Makes three to four drinks when blended. (H)

Pecan Apple Fruit Drink

6 Pecans, soaked
1 Apple, diced
3 tsps. Raisins

1 Banana, sliced
1 cup Pineapple Juice

Blend. (H)

SESAME SEED SUGGESTIONS

Sesame-Banana Milk Shake

1 cup Sesame Milk
1 sliced Banana
3 to 4 chopped pitted Dates

Liquefy and serve. (H)

Sesame Fruit Shake

1 cup Sesame Seed Milk
1/2 Banana, chopped
2 to 3 chopped Dates
Small slice Papaya

Blend Smooth. (H)

Sesame Nut Drink

Beat together 1 cup sesame milk
and 1 Tbsp. nut butter for a
rich protein drink. Maple
syrup, raisins, or honey may
be added for sweetening.

Sesame Supplement Cream

1 cup Sesame Milk (Cont'd.)

Sesame Supplement Cream
(Cont'd.)

1 tsp. Rice Polishings
1 tsp. Flaxseed Meal
1 Tbsp. Sunflower Seed Meal
1 Tbsp. Wheat Germ
3 or 4 Dates, chopped, or
    Raisins, Figs, or Papaya
    to flavor.

Blend well and use on break-
    fast cereal or over fruit.
    (H)

Sesame Nut Cream

1 cup Sesame Milk
1/2 cup Nut Butter
6 pitted Dates, chopped

Blend well and serve over
    breakfast fruit, or as a sweet
    dressing for salads. (H)

Tahini Shake

1/2 cup Tahini
1 cup water
1 Tbsp. Honey -- Blend. (H)

Sesame Tomato Cocktail

1-1/2 cups Tomato Juice
1/2 cup thick Sesame Milk
1/4 tsp. Celery Powder
1/4 tsp. Vegetable Seasoning
1/2 cup cracked ice

Blend until smooth.(H)
   3-4 servings

Sesame Broth

Stir 1 tsp. of Vegetable Seasoning into a cup of sesame milk and
heat just to boiling point. Add
a knob of sweet butter and some
chopped parsley. A nice broth
for one.

Sesame Seed Dressing

1 cup boiling water
1 cup Sesame Seed or Meal
1 cup cold-pressed Oil
4 tsps. Vegetable Seasoning
   and Lemon Juice to taste

Blend the sesame in the water
   smooth first, then add the
   oil, seasoning and lemon
   juice and blend to make a
   thick, creamy dressing. (H)

Thin or change to suit taste.

Dr's Drink: 1 tbsp. any good
brand of Sesame seed meal or
butter: 1 glass liquid (may
be fruit juice, vegetable juice,
soy milk, or broth and water):
1/4 avocado; 1 tsp. honey, or to
taste. Blend 1/2 minute.

NUT BUTTERS

You can make nut butter without the addition of oil, as nuts furnish their own, but it takes longer, requires a lot of stopping
and starting of the machine and scraping with a rubber spatula.
A little oil hastens the process considerably--2 tablespoons to
1 cup of nuts.

Nut Butter in a Jiffy

2 cups Nuts such as Pecans, Almonds, Walnuts, or Cashews
  (Best to soak overnight)
$\frac{1}{2}$ cup good salad oil

Put soaked nuts and oil in blender. Begin on (L) speed for a few
seconds, then turn on (H) and continue blending until mixture is
of desired consistency.

- - - - - -

Cashew Nut Butter

1 cup Cashew Nuts

Blend on (L) until finely chopped, then turn to (H) to make
finished butter. (Can use any other type of nuts but it will
be necessary to add 1 tbsp. salad oil when using other kind)
Peanuts can be used, if desired, with no oil required.

- - - - - - -

Jiffy Made Butters

Butter base is made as follows:

2 tbsp. Cream or Milk
$\frac{1}{2}$ cup Butter or Margarine (room temperature)

Method: Turn motor to (L) speed until well mixed. Stop motor
from time to time to push mixture into blade section with
spatula. Proceed with any of the following suggestions.

Cheese Butter: Add $\frac{1}{2}$ cup cheddar cheese, which could be made
beforehand, by cutting into cubes 1" in size and placing in
blender container. Turn to (L) speed and run until desired
fineness is obtained.

Honey Butter: Add 2/3 cup honey to the butter base. Delicious used as a spread on rye or other health bread or toast.

Onion Butter: Add 1 medium green onion, cut in $\frac{1}{2}$" slices.
Finely chopped parsley or watercress can also be added. This
is nice served with slices of beef or on vegetables.

Caper Butter: Add 3 tbsp. capers to butter base and a dash of
lemon juice. Nice to use with fish.

Cinnamon Butter: Add $\frac{1}{2}$ tsp. cinnamon and 2 tbsp. honey to butter base. This is delicious as a spread on your favorite toast or waffles.

Herb Butter: Add to your butter base 3 sprigs of parsley, leaves only, $\frac{1}{2}$ thin slice of onion. Shake sea salt, $\frac{1}{2}$ tsp. dill, marjoram, savory or oregano. This spread is a tasty addition to your casserole dishes. Just spread over top after removed from oven, or a little added on top of each serving can add zest to any simple dish.

Lemon Parsley Butter: Add 4 springs parsley (stems removed), 3 tbsp. lemon juice, $\frac{1}{2}$" square of lemon rind, and a shake of cayenne. Tasty with fish.

Garlic Butter: Add $\frac{1}{2}$ clove garlic and 4 springs parsley, finely ground, to butter base. Makes a fine spread for toasted rye or other health breads.

- - - - - -

Freshly Churned Butter

$1\frac{1}{2}$ cups Heavy Cream
$\frac{1}{4}$ cup Ice Water

Turn blender on (L) speed until cream is stiff. Now, pour ice water through opening in lid and blend on (M) until butter forms. Drain water off and pack into jar to use as desired. Can make balls with melon-ball cutter. (If garlic flavor is desired, simply put 1 small clove garlic into blender with the cream.) Lemon flavor can be made by adding 2 tbsp. lemon juice to the butter after it is made. Add pinch of sea salt, if desired.

Use fresh, raw, unsalted nuts and keep the finished butter in the refrigerator to prevent deterioration. Use cold pressed oils, such as almond, sesame, or sunflower seed, matching the oil to the nut used if possible; e.g., sunflower seed, sunflower seed oil; etc. If you must have your nut butter salted, add a little vegetable seasoning while grinding.

Sample Recipe -

Black Walnut Butter

1 cup Black Walnuts   Vegetable Seasoning, if
2 Tbsps. Safflower Oil   desired

Use fresh raw nuts and grind in liquefier until a good creamy nut butter consistency is reached. (L)

SOUPS

There is nothing quite like a homemade broth or soup, and with the blender to aid you, there are simply thousands to create. Broths are healthful and can be served at any meal. Do not use meat stock except in special broths for specific conditions. Use vegetable stock, herb teas or bran water. A broth may be made from any vegetable or combination of vegetables with vegetable powder seasoning instead of common salt.

Do not use flour for thickening; use potato, rice, barley, or extra vegetables. Try adding wheat germ or flaxseed meal after cooking to thicken.

Milk, cream, or butter should be added just before serving so they are not cooked. Parsley added to soups can never be wrong. Chop carrot tops finely and add instead of parsley for a change. Use herbs generously for flavor; garlic and onions also; or green peppers or paprika.

Do not serve soup too hot.

You can make tasty soups in your blender from odds and ends of left-over cooked vegetables and their juices. Add an onion and some broth made of vegetable seasoning for extra appeal. Do not re-cook. Just heat through and serve.

Basic Vegetable Soup

1/4 small Onion
1/2 cup Vegetable Broth

Blend 5 seconds on (H) then to (M)

1/2 cup cooked Potato
1 cup cooked Vegetables
1/4 cup Parsley
1/2 tsp. Celery Salt

Add all remaining ingredients after having blended the first two for 5 seconds, and blend till pureed. Remove cap while motor is running and add gradually:

1 cup Cream

Heat to serving point over hot water. Delicious served cold. (A good way to use left-over vegetables.)

Minestrone

1/2 cup Bran Water (page 48)
1 clove Garlic
1/4 cup parsley
1 sliced medium sized Onion
(L) speed

1 cup Celery, cut up
1/4 tsp. Oregano
1/8 tsp. Red Pepper

Blend briefly, put in saucepan with 1-1/2 cups vegetable broth, cover and simmer 15 minutes. Then add:

2 medium Tomatoes, blend 5 seconds. Add:

1-1/2 cups roughly sliced cabbage. Blend another 5 seconds(H)

Add to saucepan with:
1 cup Chick Peas, cooked and drained   (Cont'd.)

127

Minestrone (Cont'd.)

1 cup cooked, whole wheat Macaroni
1-1/2 cups Vegetable Broth

Simmer all ingredients in saucepan another 10 minutes, tasting for seasoning. Serve with grated Parmesan cheese. 3-4 servings

Herb Soup

1/2 cup Bran Water (page 48)   1/4 tsp. Basil
2 medium Tomatoes, sliced   1/4 tsp. Tarragon
1/2 small Onion   1/2 tsp. Vegetable Seasoning
1 Carrot, cut up   Dash Paprika
1 stalk Celery and Leaves, cut up
(H) speed
Blend until fine. Put in saucepan, adding 1-1/2 cups vegetable broth. Put lid on and cook very slowly about 15 minutes. Add chopped parsley and serve. May also be served cold.

Tomato-Green Soup

4 Tomatoes, sliced   4 tsps. Nut Butter
1/2 cup Alfalfa Leaves   1/2 cup or more Raw Milk
1/2 tsp. Dulse   2 Tbsps. Sweet or Sour Cream
3 tsps. Vegetable Seasoning   1 Tbsp. Chopped Onion
Sprig Mint   Clove Garlic

Blend in liquefier till very fine and smooth. Heat gently in double boiler till just hot. Serve immediately. (H) speed.

Variation: A dash of nutmeg, mace or cloves for a different flavor.

Swiss Chard Soup

1 cup steamed Swiss Chard   1 or 2 leaves Fresh Herbs
2 tsps. Vegetable Seasoning   1/2 cup Mint Tea (or other)
1 tsp. Kelp Powder   2 cups raw Milk
1/2 Onion, sliced   1/2 cup Cream
1/2 Green Pepper, sliced   1/2 cup Health French Dressing

Blend to smooth consistency in liquefier. Heat in double boiler to serving temperature. Stir in 2 tablespoons grated Romano cheese and serve. (H) speed   4-5 servings

Extra cheese sprinkled over the soup makes a nice garnish.

Tomato Okra Soup

1 cup Okra   )   Blend a few moments to chop. (L)
1/2 cup water   )   (Cont'd.)
                    Steam till tender

128

Tomato Okra Soup   (Cont'd.)

1 qt. Tomatoes   )
1 pint thick Nut Milk)   Blend 3 seconds.(H) speed
Vegetable Seasoning   )

Add to okra, heat.   Add knob of butter and serve. 5-6 servings

Beet-Potato Soup

1 cup sliced, cooked Beets
1/2 small Onion
1 tsp. Vegetable Seasoning
1/4 tsp. Paprika

2 Tbsps. Lemon Juice
1 medium Potato, unpeeled,
   cooked
Blend, and with motor running,
   add: (H)

1 cup Vegetable Broth
1 cup Sour Cream
1 cup cracked ice

When thoroughly blended, add
   fresh chopped Dill and
   serve cold.

Onion Consommé

6 large Onions
4 cups water
(H)
Blend to finely chop onion.
Simmer till cooked.   Strain
out onion.

1/4 cup Vegetable Seasoning
Sweet Butter to taste

Add to broth and serve.
Garnish with parsley.
3-4 servings

Tomato-Avocado Soup

1 qt. Tomato Juice
Vegetable Salt to taste
1 Avocado   (Cont'd.)

Tomato Avocado Soup (Cont'd.)

1/2 cup Milk or Soy Milk

Blend till smooth.   Heat.
Serve with Chopped Chives. (H)

Potato and Parsley Broth

2 cups diced, unpeeled Potatoes
1 cup Parsley
1 cup Oatstraw Tea*(see page 20)
1 to 2 tsps. Vegetable Seasoning
(H)
Blend smooth. Simmer a few
minutes to cook, add milk to
make right consistency. Just
before serving add a little
butter.

Mushroom Soup

1/2 cup Water
1-1/2 cups Mushrooms, sliced
1/2 small Onion, sliced
2 cloves Garlic
2 tsps. Vegetable Seasoning
1/2 tsp. Paprika

Cook gently until tender.   Add
and blend till smooth: (H)

1/2 cup Raw Cream
1/2 cup Raw Milk

Heat in double boiler till warm.
Serve.   3-4 servings

Smooth, Creamy, Vegetable Soup

2 cups chicken broth
1 cup diced raw Carrots
½ cup diced Green Peppers
¼ cup raw Peas
½ cup diced Celery
1 tsp. Vegetable Seasoning
Shake Cayenne Pepper
2 tbsps. Lecithin Granules
1 cup Milk
Simmer vegetables in chicken
broth until tender. cool slightly,
put in blender and mix on (H)
speed until very smooth. Add milk
and granules and run on (L) speed
until well blended. (This can be
served hot or cold and can be made
more attractive when serving by
sprinkling with finely chopped
chives, parsley, or watercress.
(4-5 servings.)

Sunny Carrot Soup

1 cup Sunflower Seeds ground fine
   on (H) speed until quite fine
Then add the following:
3 cups Milk
1½ cups fresh or cooked Carrots
   cut into 1" pieces
¼ tsp. Sea Salt
Shake Cayenne Pepper
1 tbsp. Lecithin Granules or
   liquid
Blend all together until very
smooth. If thinner consistency
desired, add more milk. Heat to
serve and garnish with finely
chopped parsley or watercress.
(4 servings.)

Quick Bean or Pea Soup

Dried Peas or Beans can be
soaked overnight for using to
make soup in blender, but can
also be done as follows, and
this takes considerably less
time:
Put 2 cups Water to each cup
of Peas or Beans. Blend on (H)
speed until well pureed.
(Cooks in half the time of regular soup made with dried peas
or beans.) Make soup as desired, using this puree in
place of whole peas or beans.

Barley Soup

2 cups whole unpearled Barley.
Soak overnight. Next day cook
in same water for 2 hours.

1 cup Celery
1 large Onion
1/2 cup Parsley
3/4 cup Water (from Barley)
2 tsps. Vegetable Seasoning

Blend to chop vegetables. Then
add to barley and cook until
tender. Serves 3-4.

Sweet Potato Soup

2 cooked Sweet Potatoes
1 cup Milk or Cream

Blend together on (L). Heat for
serving without boiling. Garnish
with chopped chives.

Peppermint Soup

1 cup unsweetened Pineapple
    Juice
1 cup strong Mint Tea
2 tsps. Dr. Jensen's Gelatin
1/4 cup Peppermint Leaves
1 Banana, very ripe
1 Tbsp. Apple Concentrate

Blend in liquefier till fine
and smooth. Serve cool with
leaf of mint in each bowl.

Cool Avocado Soup

1 large Avocado
1-1/2 cups Vegetable Broth
1 clove Garlic   (see page 141)
1/8 tsp. Capsicum Pepper
1 tsp. Vegetable Seasoning

Blend, and with blender still
running add:

1-1/2 cups Cracked Ice
1/2 cup Milk or Cream

If too thick, add a little more
cream. Serve with chopped
chives, dill or parsley.

Cool Cucumber Soup

Blend to chop vegetables:

2 cups cold Mint Tea or Water
2 cloves Garlic, chopped fine
Juice and rind 1 Lemon
2 tsps. Vegetable Seasoning
1 Cucumber, sliced
1/2 cup Mint Leaves

2 Tbsps Olive Oil) Blend
2 cups Yogurt   ) in

1/2 cup Currants - stir in

Chill. Serve with garnish
of Paprika.

Cool Apple Soup

2 cups Nut Milk
2 Apples, washed and chopped
2 tsps. Gelatin
Honey to taste
1 Tbsp. Grape Concentrate, juice
    rind of 1 Lemon

Blend till smooth. Serve cold.
Garnish each dish with a shake
of ground Cloves.

Fresh Pea Soup

1/2 cup fresh ,tender   (uncooked)
    Peas
1 cup Vegetable Broth or Water
1 sprig of Mint
1 tsp. Vegetable Seasoning
1/2 tsp. Raw Sugar
2 Tbsps. Raw Cream

Liquefy till very smooth. Serve
cold or heat over boiling water
to serving point if desired.

Variation: Add small piece of
Celery.

Spanish Soup

1/2 small Onion
1 clove Garlic
1/2 Green Pepper
3 ripe Tomatoes
1 small Cucumber, unpeeled
1 tsp. Vegetable Seasoning
1/4 tsp. Capsicum Pepper
2 Tbsps. Olive Oil
3 Tbsps. Lemon Juice
1/2 cup Ice Water

Blend until all of cucumber is
blended. Chill. Serve with
croutons of rye bread.

Pink "Dandy" Soup or Puree

½ cup Sunflower Seeds
4 cups Water or Milk
4 med. Carrots cut in 1" pieces
1 med. Beet cut in 1" pieces
½ tsp. Sea Salt
1 tbsp. Lecithin Liquid or
   Granules
2 tbsps. Wheat Germ Flakes
1 tbsp. Rice Polishings
Put sunflower seeds in blender
and blend on (H) until quite
fine. Then add rest of ingredients and blend on (H) until
smooth. (This can be served
as either a warm or a cold
soup. If too thick, add more
liquid. If puree is desired,
use less lighid.) (4-5 servings.)

Potato Corn Chowder

2 cups Milk
1½ cups Fresh or Frozen Corn
1 small Potato
1 Egg Yolk
1 medium sliced Onion
½ tsp. Sea Salt
1 tsp. Celery Seeds
1 cup Cheese, cubed
1 tbsp. Lecithin Granules
Shake Cayenne Pepper
Put milk in blender, add remaining ingredients in order
losted. Blend until very smooth
using (H) speed. Heat to serve.
Garnish with finely chopped
parsley. 3-4 servings

Nutritious Tomato Soup

½ cup Sunflower Seeds
1 qt. Tomatoes or Tomato juice
2-3 cups Milk
½ tsp. Vegetized or Sea Salt
2 tbsps. Lecithin Liquid or
   Granules
Shake of Cayenne Pepper
1 tsp. Celery Seeds
1 tbsp. Rice Polishings
1 tbsp. Yeast Powder
Put sunflower seeds in blender
and blend on (H) until finely
ground. Add other ingredients
and blend on (H) until smooth.
2 tbsps. Wheat Germ nay be added when serving, if desired.
(This makes a very nutritious
soup for children's lunch and
could be taken to school in a
thermos as a warm noon-day
meal.) May have to be done in
two lots. 3-4 servings

"The Weightwatchers' Soup"

3 cups Chicken Broth, or can
   use 2 cups Water, 2 tbsps.
   Vegetable Seasoning
Few Springs Watercress
3 tbsps. Sesame Seeds
1 tsp. Rice Polishings
¼ tsp. Sea Salt
Put Sesame seeds in blender and
grind on (H) speed until finely
ground. Add rest of ingredient
and blend on (H) until smooth.
Serve with watercress, finely
chopped. 4-5 servings

Asparagus Soup au Gratin

1 lb. fresh Asparagus, washed,
    trimmed and cut into 1 in.
    pieces. Simmer in 3/4 cup
    water until tender (about
    8 minutes).
Proceed as follows:
Place in blender container
3-1" cubes Cheddar Cheese
    grated on (L) speed until
    finely grated.
Add: (H) speed
3 cups Milk
2 tbsps. Butter or Margarine
½ tsp. Sea Salt
½ tsp celery seeds
3 tbsps. Soy Flour
1 tbsp. Lecithin Granules
Blend all together until
smooth, then heat to serve,
stirring constantly. Sprinkle
with finely chopped parsley or
watercress when serving.
4-5 servings

Beet Borsch au Gratin

3 cups cooked or raw Beets
2 cups Water
1 cup sliced Carrots
1 slice Onion
1 tsp. Sea Salt
1 tbsp. Lecithin Granules
1 cup Sout Cream (if not avail-
    able, use Fresh Cream and add
    1 tbsp. lemon juice.)
Blend all together until smooth.
Heat to serve, garnish with a
little heavy cream and sprinkle
with finely chopped ;arsley or
watercress. (7-8 servings.)

Carrot Soup

½ cup Sunflower Seeds
3 cups Water; 1 cup Milk
6 medium sized Carrots
4 tbsps. Wheat Germ
2 tbsps. Lecithin Liquid or
    Granules
½ tsp. Vegetable Seasoning or
    Sea Salt
1 tbsp. Yeast Powder
Blend thoroughly on (H) speed
until smooth. Heat to serve.
(Can use all milk in place of
water, if desired.)
This is especially good for
children and elderly folk.)
If desired, one or two egg
yolks may be added, and this
will make a "meal in itself".
(4 servings)

Special Luncheon Soup

2 medium or 1 large Avocado,
    peeled and sliced
1 tsp. Vegetable seasoning
1 tbsp. Lecithin Liquid or
    Granules
1 tbsp. Lemon Juice
Shake of Cayenne Pepper
1 cup Milk
Blend all together until very
smooth, using (H) speed.
(Can use as a puree or soup by
adding more or less milk.)
Top with tsp. Heavy Cream and
sprinkle with finely chopped
Parsley. (2-3 servings.)

RAW SOUPS

The blender makes possible a new area of health soups--the raw soup. Just blend the raw vegetables with a suitable liquid and seasoning and serve as a chilled soup, or just heat to serving point.

Vegetable Broth Delight

1 cup Okra
1 cup String Beans
1 clove Garlic
1/2 cup Celery
1/2 cup Carrots
1 large Onion
2 cups diced Turnips
1 pint Tomato Juice
1 Tbsp. Vegetable Seasoning
1/2 cup Peas

(M) speed
Cut vegetables up roughly before putting in small quantities in liquefier. Run till finely chopped. (Save peas out). Add peas, steam till tender. May be re-blended for a smoother soup. A little cream may be added at the table if desired.
3-4 servings

Chilled Raspberry Soup de Luxe

6 cups fresh Raspberries or
   1 - 10oz. package frozen
   berries (thawed).
1 cup Water
1 tsp. Lemon Juice
1 tbsp. Lecithin Granules
Heavy Cream
Put water, berries and lemon juice in blender, using (H) speed until smooth. Put through sieve to remove seeds. Chill, serve in goblet or sherbet glasses. Pour little heavy cream over each serving. Can top with fresh berry, if desired. (3-4 servings.)

Cucumber and Tomato Soup

2 cups finely pureed fresh
   Tomato
1/2 small Onion or Green
   Onions
6 sprigs Parsley
1 tsp. Vegetable Seasoning
1/2 cup Sour or Fresh Cream
1/2 unpeeled Cucumber
(H) speed
Blend till smooth, thinning with milk if necessary. Chill
3-4 servings

Fresh Corn Soup

1-1/2 cups Corn-off-cob
2 or 3 leaves Basil
1-1/2 tsp. Vegetable Seasoning
1-1/2 cups Cream or Half and
   Half
Blend in liquefier until very smooth. This is excellent for bland diets when strained. Serve warm, if desired. (H) speed
3-4 servings

Beet Borsch Soup

1 cup clean diced raw Beets
3/4 cup diced raw carrot
1/4 cup diced Cucumber
1 small Onion, sliced
1 cup diluted fresh Beet Juice
   or Vegetable Broth

1 Tbsp. Lemon Juice
1 tsp. Raw Sugar
Dash Celery Salt
A little Dill
1 tsp. Vegetable Seasoning

(M)
Blend in liquefier, adding more liquid if necessary. Check seasoning.
Serve cold, garnishing with additional slices of cucumber and dill,
plus spoonsful of sour cream or yogurt.

Carrot-Milk Soup

3/4 cup chopped Carrot
1-1/2 cups Raw Milk
3 tsps. Vegetable Seasoning
Shake of Cinnamon or Nutmeg

Blend to a smooth cream. Add
a little parsley and blend briefly
or chop. (H)

Buttermilk Soup

2 cups Buttermilk
1 Egg
2 Tbsps. Raw Sugar
1/2 tsp. Pure Vanilla
Juice of 1/2 Lemon

Blend a few seconds and serve
    cold. (H)

CREAMED SOUPS

Variety Cream Soups

Place in container and blend until smooth: (H) speed

2 cups Milk, or part Cream, stock or Vegetable Broth. . Also:
2 Tbsps. Arrowroot
2 Tbsps. soft Butter
1 tsp. Vegetable Seasoning

1 thin slice Onion
3 sprigs Parsley
1/4 cup Celery Leaves

Add one of these:
2/3 cup Asparagus   or
1 cup Corn   or
2 cups raw unpeeled Cucumber or
6 - 8 Mushrooms, sauteed--include caps and stems   or
2 cups tightly packed greens. (If peas are used, cut arrowroot
   to 1 Tbsp.) 4-5 servings

Stir and cook over low heat until soup simmers--for about 5
   minutes.

"Odds and Ends" Soup

1½ cups Milk
1 cup any left-over vegetables
  such as Broccoli, Carrots,
  Green Beans, etc., or can use
  combination of vegetables.
½ cup Sunflower Seeds
1 tbsp. Soy Milk Powder
2 tbsps. Butter
1 tsp. veg. Broth Powder
½ tsp. Sea Salt
1 tbsp. Wheat Germ
1 tbsp. Yeast Powder
Put sunflower seeds in blender
using (H) speed until finely
ground. Add rest of ingredients,
and blend until smooth, and heat
to serve. A shake of Cayenne
pepper gives this soup a zing.
(4 servings.)

Cream of Avocado Soup

1 cup Chicken Broth
1 cup Whipped Cream
2 med. size Avocados, peeled and
  cubed
2 tbsps. Lemon Juice
½ tsp. Sea Salt
Pinch Cayenne Pepper if desired.
Put first 3 items in blender and
blend on (L) speed until smooth.
Add remaining ingredients and .
blend a few seconds more on (H).
Chill before serving. Suggestion:
Put little Yogurt or Cottage
Cheese on top, with sprigg of
parsley, for added interest.

  3-4 servings

Liquefied Soups (Avocado)

1 med. size Avocado
2 cups warm, sweet Milk
Few sprigs parsley
1 stalk celery cut into
  1" pieces
3/4 cup brown rice or barley,
  cooked
Blend all together on (H)speed
until smooth. (3-4 servings.)
Soup stock can be substituted
for the base of this soup.
Corn, carrot, asparagus, spinach or or mushroom may be
used instead of avocado.
Rice flour may be added for
thickening.
Other combinations may be
made by using a little butter,
beet greens, endive or some
tomato.

Quick Creamed Vegetable Soup

4 cups Milk
2 tbsps. Butter or Margarine
1 tbsp. Soy Flour
½ tsp. Sea Salt
1 tsp. Celery Seeds
1 cup each of the following:
Carrots, Celery, Asparagus
  (cooked)
1 tbsp. Liquid Lecithin Granules
Put 2 cups Milk in blender, add
butter or margarine, Soy Flour,
salt, vegetable seasoning and
cooked vegetables. Blend on
(H) until smooth. Pour into
saucepan and add remaining
milk. Heat to serve.
(Soups best not eaten too hot.)
(4-5 servings.)

Cream of Carrot Soup

1/2 cup diced, hard Cheddar Cheese, blender grated. Set aside.

2 cups Milk	) Blend till Carrots are finely
1 slice medium sized Onion	) chopped. Put in saucepan.
4 medium carrots, cut up	) Bring to boil and simmer
5 sprigs Parsley	) 2 minutes. Remove from
1-1/2 tsps. Vegetable Seasoning	) heat. (H)
1/4 tsp. Red Pepper	)

Add:

3 Tbsps. Butter and the Grated Cheese mentioned above. Add
a little more milk if thinning is necessary. Garnish with parsley.

3-4 servings

Cream of Mushroom-Egg Soup

1/2 lb. fresh Mushrooms. Steam in a little Vegetable Broth 5
minutes.

2 cups Vegetable Stock blended with mushrooms till coarsely chopped.
Add:

3 Egg Yolks. Blend briefly. (L)

Cook very gently over water till thickened. Add:

1 cup Cream. Check for seasoning. Serve.

Cauliflower Soup

1 Cauliflower, or 1 package frozen	1/8 tsp. Nutmeg
1 cup boiling Vegetable Broth*	1/2 medium sliced Onion
1 Tbsp. Butter	1/4 tsp. Red Pepper
1/2 tsp. Vegetable Seasoning	

Simmer gently about 5 minutes. Place in blender. (M) speed

Add: 1/2 cup cooked Potato

Blend, and while running add:

1 cup Milk or Cream--or more until desired consistency is
   reached.

Delicious served chilled with parsley. Or heat to serving point,
sprinkle each serving with grated Swiss or Gruyere cheese and
put under broiler to melt cheese.

137

Spinach-Mushroom Soup

2 good cups fresh Spinach
1 cup sliced Mushrooms
1 small Onion, cut up
1/2 tsp. Vegetable Seasoning

1/2 cup Vegetable Broth or
   Herb Tea *
1/4 tsp. Nutmeg
Shake Paprika

Cook very gently for 5 minutes, then liquefy till smooth. (H)

2 cups Milk and Cream. Add last.

Serve cold if desired, but better served hot, stirring in 1 Tbsp. butter just before pouring out of saucepan.

Cream of Lentil Soup (or Split Pea)

1 small Onion)
1 clove Garlic)   Blend to chop fine. (L)
1 cup Water   )
1 cup Yellow or Green Lentils
Milk or Cream

Put all together in saucepan, adding more water or bran water. Cook till soft. Gradually blend in liquefier, using liquid and adding milk or cream to thin. Season with Vegetable Seasoning. Heat without boiling. A spoonful of butter and a handful of parsley can be added just before serving.

Cream of Mushroom Soup

Saute 1/2 lb. well-washed chopped mushrooms in 4 Tbsps. butter. Add:

1/2 cup chopped Celery
1/4 cup chopped Onion

1/8 cup chopped Parsley
1/8 cup finely sliced Carrots

Add 2 cups stock, bouillon, or water with 2 tsps. Vegetable Seasoning. Simmer 20 minutes. Liquefy and season to taste.
                        (H)   3-4 servings

Sweet Corn Cream Soup

1-1/2 cups Corn-off-Cob
2 cups Milk and Cream
       Dash of Paprika

1 slice Onion
1 tsp. Vegetable Seasoning

Blend until very smooth. Heat over boiling water to serving temperature. Add knob of butter and sprinkle with chopped parsley. (H) speed   3-4 servings

*For recipe for Vegetable Broth see Page 49

Creamed Split Pea Soup

Soak overnight in 2 quarts water: 1 lb. Split Peas.   Then simmer
1 hour with:

1 Bay Leaf   and   2 cloves Garlic

Skim water while cooling.   Remove Bay Leaf and add:

1/2 cup Onion, chopped   1/4 tsp. Thyme
1 cup Celery with leaves   3 Tbsps. Vegetable Seasoning
1 cup Carrots

Cook for 1/2 hour more.   Liquefy in blender (H) speed.
Add   8-10 servings
1 cup Heavy Cream.   Serve immediately.

Tomato Cream Soup

6 ripe Tomatoes   1/2 tsp. Vegetable Seasoning
3 sprigs Parsley   Dash Lemon Juice
1 tsp. Raw Sugar   Sprinkle of Cloves
2 slices Onion   Cream or Milk to thicken
                    (H)
Make very smooth in blender.   Heat over hot water and when
thoroughly hot add cream and milk to correct consistency.

Broccoli Cream Soup

1 small stalk Celery and Leaves,)
    chopped   )   Put in covered sauce-
1 medium sized Onion, chopped   )   pan and simmer for 10
1 medium Carrot   )   minutes.   Put in
1 clove Garlic   )   Liquefier. (M) speed
1/2 cup Oatstraw Tea (page 20)   )

2 cups cooked Broccoli, roughly cut   Pinch Capsicum Pepper
1 tsp. Vegetable Seasoning   1/2 cup cooked Whole
                                        Wheat Macaroni

Add to liquefier.   Turn on, adding: (L) speed

1 cup Vegetable Broth   and   1/2 cup Cream or Milk

Serve cold with a spoonful of cream dressing, or warm to
    serving temperature.

Vichyssoise

1 cup diced raw Potatoes,
   unpeeled
1/4 cup sliced Green Onions
1-1/2 cups Water
1-1/2 tsps. Vegetable Seasoning
1 cup raw Peas
1/4 cup diced Celery
1 cup Heavy Cream
  (H)

Mix together the vegetables,
water and seasoning and cook
until tender. Cool. Put in
blender and run until properly
smooth. Add cream and blend
again. Serve very cold with
chopped chives as a garnish.
3-4 servings

Sour Creamed Cucumber Soup

1 unpeeled Cucumber, chopped
1-3/4 cups very thick Almond
   Nut Milk
1 tsp. Celery Salt
Dash of Cayenne
1/2 tsp. Poultry Herbs
1 cup Sour Cream

Blend smooth. Serve chilled,
garnishing with chopped parsley
or chives. (H)
   3-4 servings

Watercress Soup - Creamed

1 bunch washed Watercress
1 Tbsp. Arrowroot
2 cups Vegetable Broth
1 cup Cream

Blend till watercress is finely
chopped. Put in saucepan to heat
to serving point, lastly stirring
in 1 cup cream. Garnish with
spoonful of whipped cream and
a sprinkling of paprika.
  (H)   3-4 servings

Cream of Lima Soup

1 package Baby Limas (green)
1/3 cup Green Onion or
   Scallions, chopped
A little Water

Cook gently until tender.

1/2 tsp. Marjoram, fresh or
   dried
4 sprigs Parsley
Shake Red Pepper
1/4 tsp. Vegetable Seasoning

Put in liquefier with beans
and liquid, blend till smooth.
Then gradually add: (H)

1/2 cup Milk or Cream

Blend for just a moment. Pour
into saucepan and add 1-1/2
cups vegetable broth. May
be served hot or cold. Garnish with chopped parsley
or chives. 3-4 servings

Soy Milk Creamed Greens

Heat Soy Milk in a double boiler
Into this, liquefy a few leaves
of spinach, kale and other
greens for 2 or 3 seconds.
Add a little oil and vegetable
seasoning. Serve straight
away while still hot. (H)

SPECIAL SOUPS

The following three soups are for specific conditions, taken from Dr. Jensen's "Vital Foods for Total Health", but they can also be used by anyone at any time.

Vital Broth

2 cups Carrot Tops
3 cups Celery Stalks
2 cups Beet Tops
2 cups Potato Peelings
  (Cut 1/2 inch thick)
2 cups Celery Tops
2 qts. Distilled Water
1/2 tsp. Vegetable Seasoning

Liquefy (H) in small amounts till vegetables are finely chopped. Add a carrot and an onion for flavor if desired. Bring slowly to a boil, simmer 20 minutes approximately. Strain and use.

        8-10 servings
Excellent for elimination.

Clam Consomme - An Iodine Special

2 cups unsalted Clam Juice
1/2 small Onion, sliced
1 thin slice lemon
1/2 tsp. Celery Salt
1 fresh Tomato, quartered
1 tsp. Vegetable Seasoning
Dash Paprika

Blend till smooth. (H) speed

Heat to serving point over
  hot water.

Veal Joint Broth

Use a clean, fresh, uncut Veal Joint and after washing in cold water, put in large cooking pot.

1-1/2 cups Apple Peelings,
  1/2-inch thick
2 cups Potato Peelings,
  1/2-inch thick
Small stalk Celery, cut
1/2 cup Okra, preferably fresh.
  If not fresh, use canned or
  1 tsp. Powdered Okra
1 large Parsnip, cut
1 Onion, chopped
2 Beets, chopped
1/2 cup Parsley
2-1/2 qts. Water or Oatstraw
  Tea   8-10 servings

Blend (H) in small amounts and add to veal joint. Simmer all together four to five hours; strain off liquid and discard solid ingredients. There should be about 1-1/2 qts. of liquid. Drink hot or warm. Keep in refrigerator.

This broth is rich in sodium. Excellent for glands, stomach, ligaments and digestive disorders. Helps to retain youth in body.

CHEESE SOUPS

When using cheese in soups, one must take into account the kind of cheese being used and alter the seasoning to suit. Onion, garlic and herbs can be added as desired.

Simple Cheese Soup

2 cups Vegetable Broth.
    boiling

1/2 Onion, sliced   )
1/2 clove Garlic, if desired)
2 tsps. Vegetable Seasoning)
Sprigs of Parsley   )
1-1/2 cups Cheese, cubed   )
(H)
Place these ingredients in pre-
    heated blender, add boiling
    broth and blend smooth. Pour
    into hot soup bowls and eat.
        3-4 servings

Variations on Above

The waters in which different
    vegetables have been cooked
    make an infinite variety of
    soups, using the above method.
    A little of the vegetable itself
    adds character. See following.

Pea-Cheese Soup

1 cup water from peas) Bring
1 cup Mint Tea   )   to
4 Tbsps. Peas   ) Boil

1/2 Onion, sliced
2 tsps. Vegetable Seasoning
1/2 tsp. Dulse Powder
1 cup cubed Cheese

Blend to a delicious cheese
    flavored pea soup. (H)

Mixed Vegetable Cheese Soup

2 cups Herb Tea   ) Bring
1 cup sliced Vegetables) to boil

2 tsps. Vegetable Seasoning
1/2 tsp. Dulse Powder
1 cup cubed Cheese   (Cont'd.)

Mixed Vegetable Cheese Soup (Cont'd.)

1/4 cup Oil

Place ingredients in pre-heated
blender and run on high speed
until very fine and smooth.
Pour into hot soup bowls and
serve immediately.

Suggestions:

Suitable vegetables are: Onion,
Celery, Carrots, Peas, Parsle
Zucchini. All vegetables are
used raw.

The rawest of raw soups can be
made very appetizing by using
vegetable juices for the base,
various cheeses with vegetable
seasoning, and herbs for flavor

Blend smooth, chill and serve
garnished with parsley or mint
leaves. Try Celery Juice with
Cheddar Cheese and a little
Dill Weed. Also Tomato Juice,
Cottage Cheese, and Basil,
Marjoram, or Oregano.

It is possible to blend with the
cold ingredients and then the
soup can be heated or cooked
in a double boiler to warm.

Using different cheeses alters
the flavor of the soups. For
Roquefort Cheese Soup

2 cups Herb Tea or Vegetable
    Broth--bring to boil.
1/2 Onion, sliced
4 Tbsps. crumbled Roquefort
(H)Begin blending with boiling
    tea then add - 4 Tbsps. Crea
Serve in hot bowls with dash of
    Paprika as garnish.

ottage Cheese Soup

cups Vegetable Broth or
Herb Tea--bring to boil

2 Onion, sliced
arden Cress, or favorite
rb to season and color
sps. Vegetable Seasoning
2 tsp. Dulse Powder
2 cup Cottage Cheese

end above with boiling tea.
)
little Cream may be added
if desired.   3-4 servings

rve in hot bowls.

eese Milk Soup

1/2 cups cubed Cheddar
cups very hot Milk
clove Garlic, chopped
sh of Nutmeg
sh of Paprika
sps. Vegetable Seasoning
Vegetable Bouillon Cube
Egg Yolk

end in pre-heated blender
until smooth and creamy.
Serve in hot soup bowls
with a sprinkle of wheat-
germ. A little chopped
parsley gives color.

Sopa de Queso

1/2 ripe Tomato, sliced and
    stewed over very gentle heat

1/2 sliced Onion
1/2 Bay Leaf

Add above and cook slowly a
    few minutes, lid on pan.

1/4 tsp. Paprika
1/4 tsp. Cinnamon
3 cups seasoned Vegetable
    Stock or Water

Add and cook 15 minutes.

Carefully pour off 2 cups clear
    broth into another saucepan.
    Add a handful of

Green Spinach Noodles

Return to fire to cook noodles.

1 Egg
1 Tbsp. Butter
1 Tbsp. Olive Oil
1/2 cup cubed Edam Cheese

Blend above in liquefier until
    custardy. (M)

Add thick soup (bay leaf removed)
    and blend till smooth. Pour
    into hot noodles. Serve
    immediately.

- - - - - - - - - - - - -

routed Legume Soups

ans and whole peas can be sprouted first for added value. Blend-
before cooking reduces cooking time to a fraction. Liquefy the
routs with a sliced leek and vegetable seasoning to taste. Use a
getable broth or herb tea for the base. Blend smooth and heat to
rving point in a double boiler. A little longer time will cook your
up, if desired. Add flaxseed meal or a little rice polishings to
cken if desired. Add butter or cream before serving. Liquefying
umes aids in their digestion.

Legume Soup

1/2 cup cooked Beans (or other Legume)
2 cups Vegetable Broth, Bean Liquor or Herb Tea
2 sprigs of mint--or other suitable herb.
Vegetable Seasoning to taste
1/2 tsp. Dulse Powder
1/2 Onion, sliced
 (H)
Blend very smooth, then heat to serving temperature; or have ingredients very hot before blending and serve straight from the container into hot soup dishes.

2 Tbsps. Butter or Cream-- stir in.

Chopped Parsley or Chives make a nice garnish. 3-4 servings

Sprouted Barley and Kale Soup

Liquefy sprouted barley with kale, adding a little Vegetable Seasoning. Heat to serving point, and if it is your desire to have the soup slightly thickened, add flaxseed meal or a little rice polishings. Just before serving add a knob of butter.

Nut Butter Soup

2 cups hot Milk
2 Tbsps. Raw Nut Butter
1/2 Apple, sliced
Juice of 1/2 Lemon
A little Lemon Rind
Pinch of Cinnamon and Nutmeg
Vegetable Seasoning to taste.

Pour milk in preheated blender. Add ingredients and blend well. Serve in hot bowls, no reheating. (H) speed   2-3 servings

Peanut Soup

1/3 cup Peanuts--blender chop (L) and set aside
1/2 cup Peanuts--grind fine in blender (L) increase to (H)

1 slice Onion
3 Tbsps. Butter or Oil
2-1/2 Tbsps. Arrowroot
Vegetable Seasoning to taste
3 cups hot Vegetable Stock

Add to fine peanuts in blender and blend smooth.(H)

Cook in double boiler, stirring till thick. Remove from heat.

Mix together well and stir in:

1 cup Heavy Cream
1 Egg Yolk

Serve garnished with chopped peanuts. 4-5 servings

Cream of Nut Soup

2 cups Almonds , blanched if desired. Blender grind.(L)

3-1/2 cups rich Vegetable Stock
Vegetable Seasoning to taste
1/2 small Onion, chopped.

Bring above to boil. Add to ground nuts in blender. Blend smooth. Cook gently in double boiler, stirring until thick. Return to blender and with motor still running add: (H)
4 Egg Yolks
1/2 tsp. Ground Coriander
1 cup Heavy Cream, warmed

Serve in hot soup bowls, garnished with minced chives and grated orange
*Try Cashew Nuts or Pecans.
               4-5 servings

144

Almond Soup

1/2 Onion, sliced
1/2 clove Garlic
1 fresh Bay Leaf
2 Tbsps. Almond Butter

1 Tbsp. Cream
1 Tbsp. Honey
1 tsp. Vegetable Seasoning

Place in preheated blender: (H)

2-1/2 cups Mint Tea or Water
4 very ripe Tomatoes, sliced
  (Blanch of desired)

For this recipe Cashews
or Pecans may also be
used for a slightly
different flavor.

Bring to boil. Pour quickly
  over ingredients in blender
  and blend very smooth. Pour
  into hot bowls and serve
  immediately.

3-4 servings

SALADS

SALADS

For small quantities, most vegetables for salads may be processed
in the liquefier instead of grating, and it is done in a wink!

But don't let the liquefier make you neglect the important quality
of crispness in salads by over-mincing. For tempting molded
salads and as a mixer of seasonings for an aspic, it is your trusted
friend. Try it for mashing avocado, grating cucumber, or blending parsley.

Remember the rules for abundant health--at least 60% of your food

145

should be raw; also, have at least four to six vegetables a day. Try to have two tops of vegetables each day, and your salad is the best place to put these as they are most beneficial uncooked. Fresh, raw vegetables are rich in certain vitamins and minerals which are essential to good health. Salads give you these precious elements.

LIQUEFIED SALADS

MAKE A SCOOP; SHAPE IN CUSTARD CUPS OR IN MOLDS OF VARIOUS FORMS

Spring Blend

2 leaves Dandelion, Parsley, Alfalfa
2 sprigs Celery Leaves
3 leaves fresh sweet Basil
A few Alfalfa Sprouts

Blend in 1/4 cup Pineapple Juice until very fine.(H) Stir in:

1 cup Cottage Cheese

Chill and stuff big tomatoes, arrange on pale Romaine leaves and garnish with Watercress and Scallions

Gold on Avocado

1/2 cup Buttermilk)
1/2 cup Chopped Carrot)
Slice of chopped Onion)

(H)
Blend above fine; add and blend:

1/2 cup yellow crumbly Cheese Chill to thicken.

Stuff Avocadoes. Arrange on a bed of shredded Zucchini (with skin). Garnish with sprigs of Watercress and Carrot flowers.

Pinked Peppers

1 cup Cottage Cheese
1/2 cup Yogurt   (Cont'd.)

Pinked Peppers (Cont'd.)

1/2 cup Sour Cream
4 tsps. Cherry Concentrate
1/4 cup finely ground Carrot
Pinch Sea Salt

Blend until smooth. Chill and stuff Green Peppers. Serve on a bed of Romaine. Garnish with sticks of Zucchini. (H)

Apple Ring Salad

Juice of 1 Orange
1 Apple, chopped
2 stalks Celery, chopped
1 Banana
1/4 cup Chopped, soaked Dates
(H)
Blend in order given. Stir in:

1/4 cup Rice Polishings
1/4 cup Sunflower Seeds

Chill. Spread on Apple Rings and place on a bed of leaf lettuce. Garnish with date halves. Add whipped cream.

Almond Celery Sticks

1/2 cup Salad Dressing
4 Tbsps. Almonds, chopped a little--coarse blend (L)
1/2 cup Cucumber chunks--add and blend a little, also
1 tsp. Vegetable Seasoning
2 Tbsps. Almond Nut Butter--stir in
Chill. Stuff Celery sticks.

Tangy Stuffed Celery

1/3 cup Lemon Juice
2 Tbsps. Honey
2 medium sized Beets, diced
1 small Apple, diced
1-1/2 tsps. Vegetable Seasoning
3/4 tsps. Dulse Powder

Blend until very smooth, scraping down sides of blender container frequently. (H)

1 cup Sour Cream--stir in. Chill.

Stuff Avocado halves or use to stuff Celery Stalks.

Sweet-Sour Beets

1/2 cup Lemon Juice
2 Tbsps. Honey
2 medium sized Beets, diced
1/2 Apple, diced
1-1/2 tsps. Vegetable Seasoning
3/4 tsp. Dulse Powder

Blend in liquefier, scraping down sides frequently until you have a smooth consistency.

1/2 cup Sour Cream--stir in. Chill.

Stuff tender young Celery Stalks, leaving some with delicate leaves on.

Carrot Salad

1 cup Carrot--chopped
1/4 cup Nuts
1/4 cup Raisins--soaked
1/4 cup Parsley

Liquefy in enough Pineapple Juice to blend smooth.

Liquefied Greens

2 Romaine leaves
Small bunch Alfalfa Sprouts
  (Remove seed hulls.)
Sprig of Mint
2 rings Green Pepper
1/2 Avocado
1/4 Baby Zucchini Squash, chop
Few Alfalfa leaves
1/2 stalk Celery, chop
2 tsp. Whey Powder
1 - 2 tsps. Honey
1 cup Nut Milk as base

Green Cheese Salad

Liquefy Alfalfa in Pineapple Juice (or other unsweetened fruit juice) long enough to make into a fine pulp.

Lightly stir into Cottage Cheese

Mold neatly onto a bed of purple-leafed lettuce with a shredded carrot border. Garnish with freshly shredded coconut.

Protein Liquid Salad

2 leaves Lettuce
1 leaf Beet
1 leaf Comfrey
1 leaf Turnip
1 leaf each fresh Herbs--Bay Rosemary, Basil
2 sprigs Parsley
1 stalk Celery, chopped
1/4 Carrot, chopped
2 tsps. Gelatin
1 Tbsp. Soy Milk Powder
1 Tbsp. Apple Concentrate
1 Egg Yolk
2 Tbsps. Cottage Cheese
2 tsps. Nut Butter
1 cup Mint Tea to Liquefy

Blend on (H) until well liquefied

Corn Salad

1 cup Corn-off-Cob
2 slices Onion
1 - 2 fresh leaves Sweet
   Basil
1-1/2 tsps. Vegetable Seasoning
1/4 tsp. Dulse
1-1/2 Tbsps. Sweet or Sour Cream
1 cup Celery Juice to blend
   Strain.   (H)

Carrot Slaw

2 Tbsps. Honey
Juice of 1/4 Lemon
4 Tbsps. Sour Cream
2 tsps. Vegetable Seasoning
1/4 Cabbage, roughly cut
1 cup Carrot, chopped

Place in blender in order given.
   Blend to "slaw" consistency,
   scraping down sides of container often while blending.
   Chill.   (L)

Scoop out onto Lettuce cups,
garnish with Olives and
Parsley.

Slaw with Cream Dressing

1 small head Cabbage
1/2 Green Pepper
1/2 medium sized Onion
1 Carrot

Put, some at a time, coarsely
   chopped into blender. Cover
   with water, blend to shred.(L)
   Drain. Repeat till all vegetables are chopped. Put dried
   ingredients into salad bowl.
   Toss lightly with Sour Cream
   Dressing (see "Dressing"
      Section)

Green Salad Blend

1/2 cup Yogurt   ) Coarse
1/2 cup Cashew Nuts) Blend
                         (L)
Add 1 cut Green Pepper and
   blend all together briefly.
   Then add and blend quickly,
   so as not to "mush", one
   small Avocado, cut up, with
   Garlic Salt to taste.

Chill. Scoop or shape onto
   Lettuce. Top with plenty of
   broken Cashews. Garnish with
   Parsley and Carrot Sticks.

Fruit Salad

1 small Apple
1/2 Banana
1 small Peach
2 Dates, soaked
2 Tbsps. Sunflower Seeds
1 tsp. Rice Polishings

Chop fruit. Use a suitable
   cream dressing in which to
   liquefy. (A scoop of Health
   Ice Cream could be added as
   a special treat.)   (M)

Coconut 'n Fruit

1/2 cup Herb Tea
1 small Apple, chopped
1 Carrot, chopped
      (H)
Blend very fine. Stir in:

1/3 cup Sour Cream
1/4 cup Coconut

Chill. Circle salad plate with
   delicate Bib Lettuce. Pile
   Coconut blend in center or
   shape in mold. Surround with
   slices of fresh Fruit. Garnish
   with a little extra Coconut.

Cabbage Slaw

1 head Cabbage, eith Red or White

Fill blender container to last cup markings, or 3/4 full.
Add just enough water to cover cabbage. Turn to (H) speed,
just until cabbage is chopped. Drain thoroughly in sieve or
collander. Empty on paper towel to absorb excess moisture.
It might be necessary to repeat process, until cabbage is
used up. Put in bowl and add sour cream dressing made as
follows:

1 cup Sour Cream (if necessary, sour fresh cream by adding little
    Lemon Juice)
1 tbsp Apple Cider Vinegar
1 tsp. Sea Salt
1 tsp. Celery Seeds

Put all in blender and turn on (M) speed until smooth.

For variations, use ½ green peper, 1 slice of onion and 1
raw carrot along with the white cabbage. Also a few sprigs of
parsley or watercress may be added. When serving, Lecithin
Granules may be sprinkled over the top for added nutrition.

Cabbage au Grautin

1 medium size Cabbage, white or red
½ cup Water
2 tbsp. Butter or margarine
½ tsp. Sea Salt
1 cup grated Cheese
½ cup Sour Cream
1 shake Cayenne

Fill blender container with cabbage and turn speed to (L).
Blend a couple of seconds, no more. Then drain in collander.
Put in large dish and repeat until desired amount of cabbage
is chopped. Mix balance of ingredients together and pour
over chopped cabbage. Toss lightly until cabbage is well
mixed with cheese dressing. Serve in lettuce cups or cups
made from curly cabbage leaves. Garnish with red radishes
made in tulip design, if desired.

Fruit-Nut Salads

Liquefy your fruit salads, adding soaked nuts for variety. Serve topped with whipped cream, yogurt or chopped nuts. (M)

All kinds of fruits may be pureed. Fruit juices make a good base, and oatstraw, peach leaf, or strawberry teas may also be used.

MOLDED GELATIN SALADS

Molded Asparagus Salad

2 cups Asparagus, diced and
   cooked. (Save water.)
1 Tbsp. plain Gelatin. Dissolve
   in 1/4 cup Cold Water

1 cup boiling liquor from
   Asparagus. Dissolve Gelatin
   mixture in this.

Put all in blender with:

1/2 tsp. Vegetable Seasoning
1 slice Onion
1 Pimento
1 Tbsp. Lemon Juice
1/2 cup diced Celery
(H)
Blend till finely chopped. Chill
   and when the salad begins to
   thicken add:

3 diced hard boiled Eggs
1 cup Mayonnaise
The cooked Asparagus

Turn into a mold; chill till
   firm and turn out onto crisp
   lettuce leaves, placing tomato
   wedges around. Serve with
   French Dressing.

Tomato Aspic

1 package Lemon Health Gelatin
1 cup hot Tomato Juice
   Blend. (L)　(Cont'd.)

Tomato Aspic (Cont'd.)

Add:

3/4 cups additional Tomato
   Juice
2 Tbsps. Lemon Juice
1 thin slice Onion
1 cup Celery, cut up
1/2 cup Stuffed Olives

Blend to chop fairly fine, then
   add for 2 to 3 seconds (L)

1 hard boiled Egg, cut a little

Put into molds and set. Serve
   on crisp greens.

Cucumber-Garlic Salad

2 cups Yogurt
1/2 clove Garlic
1 Tbsp. Lemon Juice
1 tsp. Vegetable Seasoning

With the blender running, add
   to above:　(H)

2 Cucumbers, chopped

Blend till smooth. In 1/4 cup
   of the above mixture dissolve

2 Tbsps. Gelatin

Mix to soften, heat to dissolve,
and add to mixture with blender
running. Mold and chill.

Easy Way to Dissolve Gelatin

A simple easy way to dissolve gelatin either plain or flavored is to put the gelatin and hot water or juice according to recipe in blender and turn to (L) speed and blend until gelatin is all dissolved. Add other ingredients as called for in recipe and blend as per instructions. This way saves time and extra bowls.

Golden Aspic

1 envelope Clear Gelatin
½ cup boiling Water

Blend on (L) speed until gelatin well dissolved. Then add the following ingredients:

1 tbsp. Honey
2 cups sliced fresh or frozen
 Peaches (thawed)
½ tsp. Sea Salt, if desired
1 small piece of Onion

Blend all together until smooth. Pour into loaf pan and allow to set. Slice when ready to serve.

Dark Eyed Susan Jellied Salad

½ cup hot Water
2 envelopes Clear Gelatin
1 tbsp. Lemon Juice
3-½ cups Pineapple Juice
4 medium Carrots cut in 1" pieces
1 cup Cheddar Cheese
1 cup Raisins

Put hot Water and Gelatin in blender. Turn on (L) speed until well dissolved. Add Pineapple Juice, Lemon Juice, and then add Carrots and ½ cup Cheddar Cheese.
(Con't.)

Dark Eyed Susan Jellied Salad (Con't)

Blend on (H) speed until Carrots are chopped finely. Last, add a few Raisins and put in refrigerator to set. Serve on Lettuce Leaf with a sprig of Parsley or Watercress and a small serving of cheese cut by a fancy slicer, if available.

Tomato and Olive Aspic

1 cup hot Tomato Juice
2 envelopes Clear Gelatin
1 Bay Leaf
3 Whole Cloves
½ tsp. Sea Salt
3 medium stalks Celery, cut in 1"
 pieces
1 Lemon, peeled and quartered
1 slice Lemon Peel about 1 inch long
3/4 cup sliced Olives
3 cups chilled Tomato Juice

Put hot Tomato Juice and gelatin into blender and run on (L) speed until gelatin is well dissolved. Add rest of ingredients with the exception of the Olive slices. Turn speed to (H) and blend until well pureed. Add sliced Olives and put in 1 Qt. pan. Chill until firm. Makes approximately 10 servings.

Jellied Beet Salad

1 package Lemon Health
   Gelatin
1 cup hot Beet Juice from
   cooking beets

Blend to dissolve Gelatin. Add:
       (H)
1/4 large Lemon
1 tsp. Vegetable Seasoning
1 Tbsp. fresh Horseradish,
   grated
1/2 small Onion
   (H)
Blend till all are liquefied, add:

2 cups cooked Beets and blend
   to chop. Turn into ring
   mold.

Now blend separately: (L)

1/2 cup Water
2 sliced Carrots
2 Celery Tops, cut up

When chopped, add to beets in
   ring mold. Stir to mix.
   Chill to set. Curly endive
   makes an attractive garnish.

Molded Avocado Salad

1/2 cup Hot Water
1 envelope Plain Gelatin
Blend fast about 1/2 minute, add:
(H) speed
1 cup Sour Cream
1 Tbsp. Lemon Juice
1/2 tsp. Vegetable Seasoning
1 thin slice Onion (or 1/2 tsp.
   Onion Powder)
Dash Capsicum Pepper
1 medium Avocado

Blend about a minute, pour
   into mold. Chill. Can be
   served with fish salad.

Egg Salad Aspic

1 envelope Gelatin, plain
1/2 cup Boiling Oatstraw Tea

Blend fast about 1/2 minute, add

1 slice Onion, medium sized
1 tsp. Soy Sauce
2 Tbsps. Lemon Juice
1-1/2 tsps. Vegetable Seasoning
1/8 tsp. Cayenne
3/4 cup Health Mayonnaise
1/2 cup Celery, cut
1/2 cup Green Pepper, cut
2 Pimentos (or canned)

Blend on (L) speed, dropping
in one at a time, four hard
boiled eggs
Pour into mold and chill.

Garden Green Pea Mold

1 envelope Plain Gelatin
1 cup Green Pea water, boiling
Blend 1/2 minute, (H) speed.
Then add:
2 cups very lightly steamed
   peas, fresh or frozen
1/2 tsp. Vegetable Seasoning
1/8 tsp. Paprika

Blend again, then with liquefier still running, add:

1 cup Sour Cream. (M)

Mold, chill, and use as base
   for such other salads as fish,
  *Pineapple-Carrot Salad, etc.

  * See following page for
    recipe.

Pineapple-Carrot Salad

1 package Lemon Flavored Health Gelatin
1 cup hot unsweetened Pineapple Juice
1 Orange, peeled and quartered

Blend at (H) speed a quarter minute. Add:

> 2 chopped medium sized Carrots
> 1 cup Crushed Pineapple
> 1/4 cup Honey

Blend very briefly, just to finely chop Carrots. Oil a salad mold, pour in, and when chilled serve on crisp salad greens.

— — — — — — — — — — — — — —

SALAD DRESSINGS, DIPS AND SPREADS

SALAD DRESSINGS

Salad dressings of all types are turned out with speed and ease in your blender. All sorts of additional health ingredients may be added without their being detected.

Parsley and watercress whiz away, leaving only an attractive shade of green behind. Garlic disappears to a mere provocative tang. Therapeutic teas and juices can be used as bases, without detracting from the tastiness.

153

Ground nuts and nut butters (liquefier prepared) make protein-rich nut dressings.

Instead of using just lemon juice, add some of the whole sliced lemon with the rind, so as to get the bioflavinoids in the peel. If vinegar is used, it should be aged apple cider vinegar, not the distilled varieties.

Soy Mayonnaise

1/2 cup thick Soy Milk)
1 Tbsp. chopped Carrot) Blend
   for color   ) (H)
1 tsp. Onion   )

Add:
1 tsp. Vegetable Seasoning
1/4 tsp. Celery Salt
1 tsp. Honey

Add gradually: (L)
3/4 cup Safflower Oil
2 or 3 Tbsps. Lemon Juice
   for additional flavor

Mayonnaise Dressing

1 whole Egg
2 Tbsps. Lemon Juice
1/2 tsp. Dry Mustard
1/2 tsp. Vegetable Seasoning
1 cup Vegetable Oil

Blend all ingredients with
   1/4 cup of the oil. Add remaining oil gradually while
   still blending. (L)

Tahini Mayonnaise

1 cup Tahini (Sesame Nut
   Butter)
1 cup Water
1/2 cup Lemon Juice or part of
   Sliced Lemon
Vegetable Seasoning
Garlic Powder to taste.

Blend to make a smooth dressing.
(H)

Health Salad Dressing

1/2 cup boiling Water or
   1/2 cup your favorite Herb
   Tea. Place in preheated
   blender. Quickly add:

1 Tbsp. Rice Polishings
1 Tbsp. Milk Powder
1 tsp. Vegetable Seasoning
1/2 tsp. Dulse Powder
Herbs if desired
(H) speed
Blend smooth, and with blender
   still running, add:

1 Tbsp. Cream
1 Tbsp. Oil

A little Lemon Juice may be
   added for variation.

Roquefort Dressing

2 Egg Yolks
2 cups Olive Oil
1/4 tsp. Caraway Seed
Pinch Dry Mustard
1/2 Tbsp. Vegetable Seasoning
Juice of 1 Lemon
1 cup Buttermilk
4 ounces Blue Cheese
   (L)
Blend Egg, Oil, Caraway Seed,
   Mustard, Seasoning and Juice
   of Lemon. Gradually add:

1 cup Buttermilk and Blue Cheese,
   running blender just to crumble
   cheese. (L)

Dr. Jensen's Favorite Dressing

1/2 cup Yogurt
1 Tbsp. Roquefort or any hard cheese

Blend briefly to crumble cheese. (L)

French Dressing

1 cup Oil
3 Tbsps. Lemon Juice
1 tsp. Honey
1 tsp. Vegetable Seasoning
2 tsps. Paprika
1/2 small White Onion
1 tsp. Dry Mustard
1/8 clove Garlic (optional)

Place all ingredients in the
    container in order indicated.
    Blend till smooth. (M)

Simple French Dressing

1 cup Olive Oil
1/8 cup Lemon Juice
1 tsp. Vegetable Seasoning
1 tsp. Honey

Blend to a smooth dressing.
    (M) speed

Variations of Above

(a) Mint Dressing

6 sprigs Fresh Mint
1 cup French Dressing

Blend until mint is in very
    fine particles. If for
    fruit salads, add a teaspoon
    of honey.

(b) Pecan Dressing

1/4 cup Pecans, soaked
1 cup French Dressing

Blend. Serve on mixed greens.
    (M)

Herbed Dressing

Blend: (H) speed
1 cup French Dressing
1/4 cup Parsley
1/2 tsp. of your favorite
    herb, Marjoram, Dill,
    Oregano, or Tarragon.
    Use fresh Tarragon, Dill,
    or Sweet Basil when avail-
    able. Remember discretion!

Pimento Salad Dressing

1 4-ounce can Pimentos, in-
    cluding juice
2 Tbsps. Blue Cheese
1/3 cup Salad Oil
1/4 cup Cider Vinegar
1-1/2 tsp. Sugar, Raw (or
    honey)
1/2 tsp. Vegetable Seasoning
Thin slice Small Onion

Blend just a few seconds until
    smooth. Good on vegetable
    salads, citrus salads.
    (M)

Parsley Dressing

1 cup Safflower Oil
3 Tbsps. Lemon Juice
1 tsp. Honey
1 tsp. Vegetable Seasoning
2 tsps. Paprika
1/2 small White Onion
1 loosely packed cup raw Parsley

Place all ingredients in the
    container in order indicated.
    Blend till smooth. (H)

Carrot Dressing

3/4 cup Carrot Juice
1/4 tsp. Vegetable Seasoning
1 Avocado, peeled and stoned

Blend till creamy   (M)

Cucumber Dressing

1 cup Health Mayonnaise
1 tsp. Chili Powder
1 Tbsp. Apple Cider Vinegar
1/2 tsp. Vegetable Seasoning
6 pitted Green or Stuffed Olives
1 stalk Celery, cut up,
   with tops
1 Cucumber, unpared, cut up
Juice of 1/2 Lemon
 (L) speed
Blend until solid ingredients
   are fairly fine (not a smooth
   sauce)

Try with cold fish; e.g., salmon.
Also good with green and mixed
vegetable salads.

Coleslaw Cream Dressing

1 cup Whipping Cream
1 Egg
1 Tbsp. grated fresh Horseradish
1 tsp. Sea Salt
1/2 tsp. Honey
1/4 tsp. Paprika
2 Tbsps. Lemon Juice
1 tsp. Dry Mustard
   (optional)

Blend until thick and smooth.
 (H) speed

Fruit Dressing

3 Tbsps. Lemon Juice
3 Tbsps. Orange Juice
4 Tbsps. cold-pressed Oil
1 Tbsp. Honey
Liquefy until well blended.
           (H) speed

Sophisticated Dressing

1/2 tsp. Dry Mustard
1/2 tsp. Vegetable Seasoning
1/4 cup Cider Vinegar
1 Egg
2 Green Onions, with tops, all
   cut in pieces
Thin sliver Garlic
2 Hard-cooked Egg Yolks
1/2 bunch Watercress
(H) speed
Blend about 30 seconds, then
   add gradually:

1-1/2 cups Safflower, corn, or
   Soy Oil.

Blend till smooth and thick.
 (H) speed

Banana Dressing

1/2 cup Pineapple Juice, unsweetened
1/2 cup Oil, unheated
1 tsp. Sea Salt
1 Tbsp. Lemon Juice
1 medium-sized ripe Banana

Place all ingredients in the
   container in order indicated.
   Blend till smooth. (H)

Cottage Cheese Dressing

1/2 cup Cottage Cheese
1/2 cup Buttermilk
1/4 cup Lemon Juice
1 tsp. Vegetable Seasoning
1/2 tsp. Paprika
3 Hard-cooked Egg Yolks
Sliver Garlic
1/2 Green Pepper, cut in pieces
4 Radishes

Blend till Green Pepper and radishes are finely chopped but not till
   minced too fine to show in the
   dressing. Use on green salads.
(L)

156

Honey-of-a-Celery Seed Dressing

3/4 cup good Salad Oil
3/4 cup Honey
½ cup Lemon Juice
1 tsp. Lemon Rind, grated
1 tsp. Paprika
1 tsp. Celery Seed
½ tsp. Sea Salt
½ thin slic Onion
Put above ingredients in blender
and mix at (L) speed for 15-20
seconds, or until well mixed.
This makes a delicious dressing
for your vegetable salads.

Buttermilk Dressing

½ cup Buttermilk (if none avail-
    able, add little lemon juice
    to milk)
½ cup Cottage Cheese
½ tsp. Sea Salt
½ tsp. Paprika
½ Green Pepper cut up (remove
    seeds)
Dash Cayenne Pepper may be added
With exception of green pepper, put
ingredients in blender at speed (H)
until smooth. Then turn to (L)
speed, add green pepper and run
blender until chopped as desired.
Serve on vegetable salads.

Celery Sour Cream Dressing

1 cup Sour Cream
2 tbsps. Lemon Juice
1 tbsp. Honey
½ tsp. Sea Salt
1 tsp Celery Seeds

Put all ingredients in blender.
Turn to (H) speed until smooth.
Delicious served with vegetable
salads.

Sour Cream Dressing with Herb Touch

1 cup Sour Cream (if not on
    hand, add little extra
    lemon juice)
2 tbsps. Lemon Juice
1 tsp. Honey
Pinch Sea Salt if desired
3/4 tsp. Celery Seeds
¼ tsp Thyme
Blend all together on (L)
speed. Chill and serve with
vegetable salads.

Tomato Avocado Dressing

1 large ripe Avocado
1 med. size tomato, cut in
    pieces
1 small piece Onion
3 tbsps. Lemon Juice
1 tbs. Olive Oil
½ tsp. Vegetable Seasoning
1 tbs. Lecithin Granules
Shake Cayenne Pepper
    Blend all together until
    smooth. Lemon protects the
    color of the avocado.

Tomato Avocado Dressing

1 large ripe Avocado
1 med. size Tomato cut in piece
1 small piece Onion
3 tbsps. Lemon Juice
1 tbsp. Olive Oil
½ tsp. Vegetable Seasoning
1 tbsp. Lecithin Granules
Shake Cayenne Pepper
Blend all together until smooth
Lemon protects the color of
Avocado.

Tuti Fruiti Cream Dressing

3/4 cup Pineapple or orange juice
2 Eggs
2 tbsps. Honey
2 tbsps. Soy Flour
$\frac{1}{4}$ tsp. Sea Salt
$\frac{1}{4}$" slice unpeeled Orange,
    quartered
$\frac{1}{4}$" slice unpeeled Lemon,
    quartered
1 cup Whipped Cream
Put all ingredients, except
whipped cream, into blender,
and mix on (M) speed until well
blended. Pour into heavy saucepan. Cook over low heat, stirring constantly until thickened.
Remove. When thoroughly cool
fold in whipped cream. (See
recipe on page   for whipping
cream.)

Yogurt or Sour Cream Dressing

1 cup Yogurt or Sour Cream
2 tbsps. Lemon Juice
1 thin slice Onion
$\frac{1}{2}$ tbsp. Sea Salt
2 tbsps. Honey
$\frac{1}{4}$ tsp. Paprika or Pimento
Blend all together on (M) speed
until finely blended. (A tangy
dressing for any vegetable salad.)

Avocado Salad Dressing

1 large ripe Avocado, peeled
   and pitted
1/4 small Onion
1 medium sized Tomato,
   quartered
3 Tbsps. Lemon Juice
1 Tbsp. Olive Oil
1 tsp. Vegetable Seasoning
Dash Soy Sauce, Paprika
 (H) speed
Blend until smooth. Lemon
   protects the color of Avocado.
   Nice on tart salads and greens.

Sour Cream and Pineapple

Juice of 1/2 Lemon)
2 Tbsps. Raw Sugar) Blend
1 cup Sour Cream   )   to
1/2 cup Pineapple) mix
                    (L)

Peanut Butter Dressing

2 Tbsps. blender-made Peanut Butter
1 Tbsp. Olive Oil
1-1/2 Tbsp. Lemon Juice
 (L)
Blend to combine, then gradually add 1 cup Health
   Mayonnaise.

- - - - - - - - - - -

DIPS

Avocado-Cheese Dip

6 ounces Health Cream Cheese*
1 fully ripe Avocado, cut in
   pieces
1 Tbsp. Lemon Juice
Thin slice of Onion
1/2 tsp. Vegetable Seasoning
3 Tbsps. Cream
Liquid Chlorophyl--a few drops

Blend ingredients to make
   smooth, using rubber spatula
   to push down top of mixture
   if necessary. The Chlorophyl
   will give a pretty pale green
   color to the dip, helping
   to accentuate the avocado color.
   (M)

Cottage Cheese Dip

1 cup Cottage Cheese
1/4 lb. Blue Cheese, crumbled
1 thin slice Onion
Good dash of Soy Sauce
Tiny sliver of Garlic   (Cont'd.)

Cottage Cheese Dip   (Cont'd.)

2 Tbsps. Sour Cream

Beat until very smooth. Makes
   a delicious dressing too. (H)

Herb Dip

Into container put:

2 Tbsps. Water
1 Tbsp. Lemon Juice
1/3 cup Sour Cream
1-1/2 cup Cottage Cheese

Blend on high speed for 1/2
   minute. Add:

1/2 tsp. Dry Basil
1/2 tsp. Dry Tarragon
1/2 tsp. Dry Parsley
1 tsp. Vegetable Seasoning
1/2 tsp. Dill Weed
1 clove Garlic
Blend a few seconds on high speed

* See recipe page 51

Horseradish Dip with Cheese

Scant 3/4 lb. Cottage Cheese
1 Tbsp. fresh Horseradish, grated
1/2 tsp. Paprika
1/2 tsp. Dry Mustard
5 or 6 sprigs Parsley
1/2 tsp. Poultry Herbs
1/2 tsp. Vegetable Seasoning
(H) speed
Blend thoroughly. The flavor is unusual and delicious

Avocado Dip

1 soft ripe Avocado, peeled and cut in pieces
Slice of Onion
Juice of 1/2 Lemon
3/4 tsps. Vegetable Seasoning
Very few drops Soy Sauce
3 Tbsps. Mayonnaise, health variety

When blended smooth, leave in refrigerator for an hour for flavors to blend. This also makes an excellent dressing.
(H)

Green Dip

1/2 lb. Cottage Cheese (or Tofu--may need a little cream)
1 slice small Onion
Sliver Garlic
1 Tbsp. Horseradish, freshly grated

1 bunch Watercress, washed and dried
3 Tbsps. Lemon Juice
2 tsps. Vegetable Seasoning; dash Cayenne
(H) speed

Blend until smooth, using spatula now and then when getting started. For a salad dressing (lovely with fish or slaw) thin with sour cream or mayonnaise. — — — — — — —

SPREADS

These delicious tasting spreads can, with a little imagination, be used as a spread on anything from a circle of carrot to a slice of green pepper, to say nothing of cucumber or zucchini circles, large mushrooms, celery, dates, figs, prunes, apple slices, bananas (after removing seeds), Romaine lettuce or cabbage leaves. Try some of your own ideas as a change from bread and crackers, especially for the cheese and nut spreads.

Carrot Spread

Chop at low speed
2 large Carrots, cut in pieces
Turn out and then chop
1/2 cup Raw Peanuts
Mix Carrots and Nuts with
1/4 cup Mayonnaise (Cont'd.)

(Cont'd.)

1/2 tsp. Vegetable Seasoning

Coarse-cut cabbage and some diced celery can be added with a little more dressing to make a crunchy variation.

160

Avocado Spread

1 ripe Avocado, coarsely
    diced
2 tsps. Soy Sauce
Vegetable Seasoning
Garlic and Onion Seasoning

Put in liquefier and blend
    smooth. Use rubber scraper
    to help. (H)

Watercress Butter Spread

1/2 bunch Watercress, washed
    and dried
1/2 cup soft Butter
1 Tbsp. Lemon Juice
1/2 clove Garlic (optional)
Vegetable Seasoning

Blend until cress is very fine.
    Beautiful on fresh whole
    wheat bread or spread over
    cooked Brussels Sprouts,
    Cauliflower, etc.

Mushroom Butter Spread

1/2 lb. steamed or canned Mush-
    rooms
1/2 cup Butter
1 Tbsp. Apple Cider Vinegar
2 Tbsps. Grape Juice
1/2 tsp. Vegetable Seasoning
1/4 tsp. Paprika

Blend till smooth. (H)

Nut-Olive Spread

1/2 cup Olives--blend only to
    chop fine
1/2 cup Nut Butter--blender made

Mix the two gently together with
Vegetable Seasoning for flavoring

Garlic Butter Spread

1 cup Heavy Cream
Blend on low speed until
    whipped. Add:

1/2 cup Ice Water
1 clove Garlic

Blend till butter forms. Fresh
    cream may take some time,
    of course, but if you can re-
    member to put it in the refri-
    gerator for a day or two, it
    is faster. Drain butter,
    and save "buttermilk".

Almond Nut Spread

To 1/2 cup ground Almonds, or
    Almond Butter, add 1 ripe
    Banana and blend to spread-
    ing consistency. (L)

Fruit Nut Spread

1 Apple, cut in pieces
1 cup soaked Raisins
1 cup Walnuts, soaked
1/2 cup Orange Juice
Dash Vegetable Seasoning

Blend until mixture is spread-
    able. Try on toasted rye.
    (M)

Apricot and Nut Spread

1 cup well-drained revived
    Dried Apricots
1/4 cup Walnuts, soaked
1/4 cup Mayonnaise
(L) speed
When blending, do not allow nuts
    to become minced; stop when
    they are just chopped.

Very nice on Whole Wheat Bread.

Date-Nut Spread

Into container put:

1/4 cup unsweetened Pineapple Juice
Pulp from 1/2 Orange

Cover and blend on high speed for
5 seconds. Add:

1/3 cup Nuts, soaked
3/4 cup pitted Dates (softened in
Pineapple Juice

Blend on high speed for 20
seconds. Chill.

Peanut-Jelly Spread

Into container put:

1/2 cup Peanuts, raw,
unsalted
1 Tbsp. Vegetable Oil

Cover and blend on high speed
until peanuts are pureed.
Add 1/4 cup tart Jam or
Jelly, health varieties.

Blend until mixed, stopping to
stir down if necessary.

BASIC CHEESE SPREAD AND VARIATIONS

Basic Cheese Spread

3 oz. Cottage Cheese
2 Tbsps. Sour Cream
1-1/2 tsps. Vegetable Seasoning
1 slice Onion

Blend onion in sour cream to
make fine. Add seasoning
and then cottage cheese a
little at a time, scraping
down sides of blender frequently. Blend until a
smooth spread is obtained.
(M) speed

Cheese Variations with Above

Blender-grate your favorite
cheeses--Jack, Swiss, Roquefort, Edam, etc. Gradually
add basic spread, continually
blending until desired consistency is reached .

Fancy Variations on Basic

To basic spread, add:
1/4 cup crumbled Blue Cheese
1/2 tsp. Soy Sauce
Add 1/4 cup blender-chopped Nuts

Other Variations

When blending the Sour Cream,
make one of the following
additions for variety:

Parsley
Chives
Radish
Garlic
Herbs
Celery
Cucumber
Watercress
Mushrooms

Sweet-Sour Spread

Basic spread
2 Tbsps. Soft Butter
2 Tbsps. Raw Sugar
2 Tbsps. blender-chopped Almonds
2 Tbsps. blender-chopped Orange
and Lemon Peel
2 Tbsps. Chopped Raisins

Blend on   low speed, scraping
down sides of container often.
Stop when ingredients are
mixed. Chill.

Sweet Spread

Make Basic Spread but omit
Onion. Blend in Fruit Juice
Concentrates, such as Apple,
Grape, and Cherry Concen-
trate. Sliced fresh fruits,
such as Peaches, Apple, or
Berries in small quantities are
worth trying. A little Honey
or Vanilla may be added.

Party Specials

Make Basic Spread, omitting
   Onion

2 Tbsps. Butter
1 Tbsp. Date Sugar
1/2 tsp. Cinnamon
1/4 tsp. Pure Vanilla
   (M)
Blend briefly to mix. Spread
on rye or soy toast and heat
in moderate oven.

Canape Spread

1 cup Blue Cheese--crumbled
   in blender
1/4 cup Buttermilk
Slice Onion
3/4 tsp. grated Horseradish

Add and blend fine: (H)

2 Tbsps. Sour Cream
1/3 cup Cottage Cheese (L)

Blend above in briefly.

Fresh "Garden" Spread

1/4 cup Health French Dressing
1/4 lb. Sharp Cheese, cubed
1/2 Cucumber, cut up
Vegetable Seasoning, to taste
1 Carrot, cut up
   (H)
Blend until Carrots are fine.
For a change, add a few crisp
pieces of Cabbage or Cauliflower florets.

- - - - - - - - - -

Egg Spread au Grautin

4 hard-cooked eggs, cut in pieces
¼ lb. Cheddar Cheese
½ cup Mayonnaise (health recipe, see page (154)
1 slice Green Pepper
¼ tsp. Sea Salt
1 dash Cayenne Pepper
1 thin slice Onion

Blend all together at (H) speed, but watch so that Green Pepper is still recognizable.

Autumn Glory

12 oz. Cottage Cheese
2-3 sprigs Parsley, with heavy stems removed
1 thin strip Green Pepper
8 small stuffed Olives
3 one inch pieces Cheddar Cheese
3 tbsp. soft Butter or Margarine
1 shake Cayenne Pepper, if desired
½ tsp. Paprika
1 Pimiento
1 very thin slice of Onion

Put Cottage Cheese and Cheddar Cheese in blender and blend on (H) speed until smooth. Add remaining ingredients. Add while motor is running by using opening on top to add ingredients, or move lid to one side. Use (H) speed, but turn motor on and off once or twice, as the food is only to be in chopped state when finished. Use as spread for your favorite Rye or other health breads or crackers. Best used on Melba toast or other toasted crackers. Use as a garnish for salads.

Honey Spread

½ cup Liquid Honey
½ cup Margarine or Butter, softened
1 dash of Cinnamon, if desired

Blend on (M) speed until well blended. Use spatula if necessary to push mixture into blades. Store in small jar until ready to use. Delicious as a spread on Melba toast, Rye-Krisp or any other small wafers.

ENTREES

It is not the province of the Blender to tenderize or improve the flavor of roast beef or sirloin steaks, foods which in the health food realm we do not stress anyway. But when it comes to meat substitutes, accompanying sauces and toppings, it excels. Such nut preparations as Nuttose and Protose can be used for vegetable roasts. These vegetarian loaves may be made very tempting and delicious. Vary the moisture by adding tomato juice or other vegetable juices to soften them, or dried whole wheat bread crumbs to make them more solid. Shredded wheat, rice, or lentils may be used instead of crumbs. Eggs will also hold the loaf together. Your loaf will resemble a meat loaf and will be more delicious when the nuts that are used are ground fine.

Vegetables or any pureed left-over vegetables can help make delicious entree dishes and casseroles. Remember, when the loaf predominates in vegetables, if the pan is left uncovered during cooking valuable nutrients are lost.

NUT DISHES

Baked Nut Loaf

1 cup Whole Wheat Crumbs
  --make in blender
1/2 cup Walnuts or Raw Peanuts
  --grind in blender
1 Tbsp. Tomato Juice
1 Egg
2 Tbsps. Melted Butter
1 Onion, roughly sliced
(L)
Blend till onion is chopped. Add nuts and crumbs and turn motor on just to mix. Pack into greased pan and bake 1/2 hour in moderate oven. Turn out onto platter and serve with home-made tomato sauce.

Nutburgers

Crumb in blender and turn into bowl

3 slices Whole Wheat Bread, torn apart (L) (Cont'd.)

Nutburgers (Cont'd.)

Place in blender container

1 cup Milk
1 Egg
1 slice Onion
1/4 cup packed Parsley
1-1/2 tsps. Vegetable Seasoning
2 cups Pecans or Walnuts
(M)
Blend until nuts are chopped fairly fine. Add to crumbs and shape into 8 to 12 patties. Dip into additional buttered crumbs and brown in oven. Serve with mushroom sauce.

Walnut-Vegetable Roast

1 cup Walnuts - blender chopped
   Set aside. (L)

Blend to chop: (L)

1 small Onion
1 stick Celery
Sage
Vegetable Seasoning to season
1 cup Milk or Water

Gradually add:

2 cups Soybeans, cooked,
   and reduce to juice. Pour
   into bowl. Add:

3 cups Mashed Potatoes with
   peelings. Add Nuts, as above.

Use enough toasted bread crumbs
(blender made) to make thick
enough to roll. Bake 1 hour
in loaf pan. Serve on platter
with sliced tomatoes and parsley.

Nut Apple-Celery Roast

1 cup Whole Wheat Bread
   Crumbs
1/2 cup Almonds--blend to
   chop. Add to crumbs.
   (L)

1 cup Milk
1 Egg
1 tsp. Vegetable Seasoning
1 cup Celery Tops
1 cup cut Celery
1 cup cut Apples

Blend to chop vegetables (M)
   finely. Add crumbs and
   nuts. Bake in oiled
   casserole in moderate
   oven for 1 hour.

VEGETABLE LOAVES, CASSEROLES, ETC.

"Nuttose" Mushroom Loaf

2 cups Tomatoes, slice in blender
2 Eggs - add

1 cup Green Pepper)
1-1/2 cups Celery   )
1/2 cup Parsley   )
1 large Onion   )

Shred above coarsely. Add to
   blender and blend to chop
   fine. (M)
1-1/4 lbs. Nuttose
1 lb. Mushrooms, sliced
Mix all together, place in baking
dish and bake 35 minutes. Slow oven.

Baby Lima Bean Loaf

2-1/2 cups whole grain bread
   crumbs. Blender made. Add:
2-1/2 Tbsps. Melted Butter;
Whizz to Butter Crumbs.
3 Eggs   )
1 clove Garlic   )
1-1/2 Tbsps. Vegetable   )
   Seasoning   )
Pinch Sage; 1 Tbsp. Parsley)
Blend above ingredients. (L) Add:

3 cups cooked Baby Limas (not
   mushy), drain. Mix into liquids,
   fold in Buttered Crumbs. Bake
   brown in buttered loaf pan.

Raw Vegetable Loaf

2 cups Raw Peanuts - grind
  in blender (H)
2 cups Carrots, sliced. Put
  in blender and cover with
  water. Blend a few seconds
  then strain off water. Keep
  aside. Put Carrots in bowl.

2 cups Celery pieces. Blend,
  using water off carrots. Put
  in bowl after straining.

1 cup Cabbage. Shred as Celery.
  (Save water for soup.)

1/2 cup Almonds--blend to Almond
  Butter (L) increase to (H)

1/2 Onion   ) Add and blend
1 clove Garlic) till minced (L)

Mix all ingredients in bowl.
Press into loaf form, turn out
on platter when ready to serve.
Sprinkle Parsley along middle.

Vegetarian Roast

1/2 cup Whole Wheat Bread
  Crumbs--blender made. (L)
  Set aside.

1 cup Milk
1 Egg
1 small Onion, sliced
1 cup cut Carrots
1/2 cup String Beans
1/2 cup cut Celery
1 tsp. Vegetable Seasoning

Blend till vegetables are finely
  chopped. (H)

3 Tbsps. Pecan Butter--blender
  made. Blend in. Add crumbs.
  Bake in buttered casserole
  1 hour in moderate oven.

Eggplant Casserole

1 large Eggplant, cubed
1 Onion, chopped
1/2 Green Pepper, chopped
2 Tomatoes, diced
1 cup graham bread or crackers
  --blender crumbled
1/2 cup Cheese--blender
  grated (L)
2 tsps. Vegetable Seasoning
1 tsp. Dulse Powder

Mix all together and place in a
  greased casserole dish.

Mix and sprinkle on top:

  1/4 cup extra cracker
    crumbs
  1/4 cup blender grated
    Cheese

Bake in a slow oven, and when
  nearly done, increase heat
  or pop under broiler to
  brown topping.

Carrot Loaf

2 cups cooked Brown Rice
3 Eggs
1 cup thick Soy Milk
2 cups diced Raw Carrots
1 small Onion
1/2 tightly packed cup Celery
  Leaves
2 tsps. Vegetable Seasoning

Put rice into separate mixing
  bowl. Place other ingredients
  in container in order indicated.
  Blend thoroughly 3 minutes. (H)
  Fold mixture into rice. Place
  in greased loaf pan or ring
  mold. Bake in moderate
  oven at 350° F. for 1 hour,
  15 minutes. Serve with
  Cheese or Tomato Sauce.

Asparagus Cheese Loaf

1-1/2 cups Cheese--blender
   grated . Put aside. (L)

1/4 cup Cream   )
2 Eggs   )
1 Tbsp. Melted Butter)
1 small Onion, sliced)
1 Green Pepper, sliced)

Blend to chop Vegetables. (L)

Add and blend very briefly: (L)

1-1/2 cups cooked Asparagus
1/2 tsp. Vegetable Seasoning
1 Tbsp. Soy Flour

Add Cheese. Bake in loaf
   pan or casserole about
   45 minutes.

Broccoli Loaf

Chop in blender enough cooked
   Broccoli to make 2 cups
   chopped Broccoli. Turn
   into pan.

Into blender place:

2 Eggs
1 cup sliced Tomatoes
1 slice medium-sized Onion
1 cup diced Celery
3 Tbsps. Butter
1/2 tsp. Vegetable Seasoning
1/4 tsp. Paprika
(L) speed
Blend to chop vegetables. Add
   to Broccoli with:

1 cup Graham Crackers. Bake
   in greased loaf pan in 350°
   oven about 40 minutes. Serve
   with Cheese Sauce.

Soy Noodles and Cheese Mousse

Cook about 12 minutes in boiling
   salted water and drain:

8 ounces Soy Noodles or Macaroni

Crumb in blender and set aside:

2 slices Whole Wheat bread, torn
   apart. (L)

Place in blender container:

3 Eggs
1-1/2 cups Milk
1 tsp. Vegetable Seasoning
1/3 cup Butter
1/4 packed cup Parsley
1 small Onion, quartered
2 Pimentos
1/2 lb. American Cheese, diced

Blend about 30 seconds and mix
   with Soy Noodles. Add crumbs.
   Place in greased shallow baking dish and set in a pan of
   hot water. Bake in moderate
   oven, 350° F., for an hour
   or until the custard sets.
   Serve plain or with Tomato
   Sauce.

Mock Scalloped Oysters

Blend the following ingredients
   until pureed. Then pour into
   baking dish and bake in moderate oven about 45 minutes:
     (M)
3 cups cooked Salsify
3 Eggs
1/2 cup Raw Cream
1/4 cup Olive Oil
1 Tbsp. Vegetable Seasoning.

RICE DISHES

Mock Veal Chop Suey

Chop up in blender:
 1 cup Celery
 2 large Onions
 Water to cover   (L)

Add and blend briefly: (L)
 1/2 cup Walnuts or
 Water Chestnuts
 2 cups Bean Sprouts
 1 tsp. Vegetable Seasoning

Chop up a little   (L)
 1/2 lb. "Protose" or
 "Nuttose"
 1 cup Dried Mushrooms
 --soaked 3 - 4 hours

Put all together in saucepan
 and simmer gently. Do
 not overcook. It is better
 if it is "chewy". Serve
 with Soy Sauce.

Wild Rice Souffle

 cup Wild Rice   )
 -1/2 cups Water)
 Steam till tender or
 cook overnight in thermos.
 Drain.

 cup Milk
 Tbsps. Soft Butter
 Egg Yolks
 /2 tsp. Sea Salt
 Tbsp. Arrowroot
 /4 tsp. chopped fresh
 Basil (or dried)
 Green Onion, rough-chopped
 stalk Celery
 (H)
Blend until the vegetable is
 finely chopped. Pour into
 a double boiler and cook,
 stirring, until thickened.
 Cool slightly and fold
     (Cont'd.)

Wild Rice Souffle

 in cooked rice and

4 stiffly beaten Egg Whites

Turn into ungreased casserole,
 stand in a pan of hot water,
 and bake in a slow oven,
 300° F, for 1 hour or until
 set. Serve immediately.

Baked Rice

1/2 cup Rice. Brown dry in
 skillet or in a moderate
 oven, stirring occasionally.

Blend fine the following:

2 cups Boiling Water
1/2 stalk Celery, chopped
1/2 small Onion, chopped
1/2 small Carrot, chopped
2 - 3 sprigs Parsley
2 tsps. Vegetable Seasoning
1 tsp. Dulse Powder (H)

Put Rice in a deep casserole
 dish. Pour hot broth over
 and place on tight fitting
 lid. Bake 30 to 40 minutes
 (until Rice is tender) in a
 moderate oven. Stir in
 when cooked:

2 Tbsps. Butter.

Can be used with a sauce,
 vegetable, vegetable casserole, or curry.

Spanish Stuffed Peppers

4 Green Peppers, with a slice
   removed to extract seeds and
   pulp. Parboil and drain.

1 slice Whole Wheat Bread,
   torn apart.
2 fresh Tomatoes, sliced
1 medium sized Onion
1 tsp. Paprika
1 tsp. Chili Powder
1 tsp. Vegetable Seasoning
1 small clove Garlic
1 slice Green Pepper
 (M)
Blend for short period. Pour
   over:

2 cups cooked Unpolished Rice

Mix and stuff Peppers, dot with
   Butter and bake, covered, at
   350° for 40 minutes.

Apple-Raisin Bake

Crumb in blender, 2 slices at
   a time: (L)
8 slices Whole Wheat Bread
   Empty crumbs into mixing
   bowl.

Fill container to top with:

2 large Apples, sliced (uncored)
   Add water to cover. Blend
   on high speed until apple
   slices are pulled through
   blades. Drain apples and
   add to crumbs. Add:

1 cup Seedless Raisins
Vegetable Salt
1/2 tsp. Dry Marjoram
1/2 tsp. Thyme
1/2 cup Melted Butter

Mix lightly. Bake in greased
   casserole.

SOY BEAN AND LENTIL LOAVES, ETC.

Quick Method for preparation of Soy Beans and Lentils: in the
following recipes, soak the legumes, blend using the soaking
water, and cook in the Thermos for 2 hours.

Soy Bean Loaf - No. 1

2 Eggs
1/4 cup Soy Sauce
3 Tomatoes, sliced
2 Tbsps. Butter
2 Tbsps. Parsley
2 stalks Celery, sliced
1 Onion, sliced
 (M) speed
Blend above to fine-chop
   vegetables

4 tsps. Vegetable Seasoning
1 tsp. Dulse Powder
A little Garlic Powder
A little Basil
   (Cont'd.)

(Cont'd.)
2 cups cooked Soy Beans with
   some of the liquor. Gradually
   add, continuing to blend.
   Scrape down sides of blender
   container frequently.

(Consistency of loaf can be
   varied by amount of bean
   liquor incorporated.)

Bake in well-greased casserole
   in a moderate oven for about
   30 minutes.

170

Soy Bean Loaf - No. 2

2 cups Soy Beans - soak overnight

Blend, using the soaking water
and more, if necessary.
Cook in a double boiler or
bring to boil and thermos
cook 2 hours. (H) speed

1 cup Breadcrumbs, blender-made
1/4 cup Whole Wheat Cereal (L)
--blender ground. Set aside.

1 cup Vegetable Broth or Herb
Tea
2 Carrots, chopped (other vegetables may be used)
(H) speed
Blend to reduce Carrots to a
pulp. Add:

2 Tbsps. Vegetable Oil
4 Green Onions, sliced
Small bunch Spinach
A little Thyme
4 tsps. Vegetable Seasoning
1 tsp. Dulse Powder
Garlic Powder

Blend to chop vegetables. (L)

Mix all ingredients throughly,
bake in an oiled loaf or ring
pan 30 to 40 minutes, moderate
oven.

Soy Bean Patties

1 Onion, sliced
1 Egg
4 tsps. Vegetable Seasoning
1 tsp. Dulse Powder
Fresh Bay Leaves, Thyme
and Dill Herb.

Blend finely.
(Cont'd.)

Soy Bean Patties (Cont'd.)

1-1/2 cups cooked Soybeans
(M)
Add gradually, continuing to
blend. (A little of the Bean
Liquor may be necessary.
Stop frequently to scrape
down sides of container.)

1/2 cup Nuts--blender ground
1/2 cup Soy Bread Crumbs--
blender made.

Shape into patties and dip in
Sesame Seeds or extra
Breadcrumbs. Bake on an
oiled baking sheet for 25
to 35 minutes in a moderate
oven.

Lentil Loaf DeLuxe

1/2 cup Milk
1 clove Garlic
1 Onion, sliced
Fresh Thyme, Mint and Parsley

Blend to chop Onion (L)

2 cups cooked Lentils
1 Egg
4 tsps. Vegetable Seasoning
1 tsp. Dulse Powder
1 Tomato, sliced

Add and blend smooth, scraping down sides frequently (H)

Put in a buttered baking dish
and bake in a moderate
oven 3/4 of a hour to 1
hour. Serve with Tomato
Sauce.

Lentil Patties

1 Onion, sliced
1 Egg
3 tsps. Vegetable Seasoning

1 tsp. Dulse Powder
Fresh Thyme, Mint and
  Parsley

Blend fine. (H)

1-1/2 cups cooked Lentils,
  drained

1 Tbsp. Butter

Add and blend, scraping down sides frequently. (L)

3/4 cup Whole Wheat Breadcrumbs, dry (blender made)

Stir in. This is a very soft mixture, but it can be rolled in more breadcrumbs; carefully shape into patties and bake on an oiled oven sheet in a moderate oven until firm and browned.

Variation:

Replace some of breadcrumbs with blender-ground nuts. A little firm nut butter (blender-made) changes the flavor.

Egg/Cheese Dishes

CHEESE DISHES

Twice a week, use cheese for your main protein: either cottage cheese or an unprocessed hard cheese which breaks. Cheese lends zest and variety to any healthful dinner.

Any cheese can be grated in your Blender. Place in a tightly covered glass jar and store in the refrigerator for handiness in future meals.

To grate:

Dry Cheese: Grate only 1 cup at a time. Put 1/2 cup diced cheese in dry container, cover, blend on high speed 6 seconds.

Soft Cheese: Grate 1/2 cup at a time. First, put into blender 3 or 4 small chunks of soft bread to absorb the oil from the cheese. Then the cheese grates evenly and does not pack together. Blend on high for 6 seconds.

Cottage Cheese Bake

3/4 cup Cottage Cheese
1 oz. Jack Cheese--blender grated
2 Tbsps. Whole Wheat or Rye
   Cracker crumbs, blender made
2 tsps. Vegetable Seasoning
 (L)
Stir together to mix. Place in a
greased overware dish and bake
in a moderate oven for 20
minutes. (1 serving.)

Cheese and Nut Loaf

1 cup Whole Wheat Breadcrumbs
  --blender made. Set aside.
 (L)
Place in container:

2/3 cup Hot Water
2 Tbsps. Lemon Juice
2 Eggs
Vegetable Seasoning to taste
1/2 Onion, sliced
1 cup Walnuts
1/4 lb. Cheese

Blend till cheese is grated
   and walnuts are chopped.
 (L) speed
Add crumbs which were set
   aside. Put in oiled baking
   dish and bake 30 minutes.
   Serve with Health Tomato
   Sauce.   3-4 servings

Cottage Cheese Patties

1 cup Whole Wheat or Rye Bread-
   crumbs--blender made (L)

Blend to chop fine (L)

1 small Onion.   Add:

1 lb. Cottage Cheese

Combine ingredients. Form into
   small cakes and bake on greased
   baking sheet in moderate oven for
   20 minutes.

Cheese Rarebit

Into container put:
  1/3 cup Hot Milk
  1 cup diced Cheddar Cheese
  1 Tbsp. Arrowroot
  1/2 tsp. Dry Mustard
  1/4 tsp. Vegetable Seasoning
  Dash Capsicum Pepper
  1 Tbsp. Soft Butter

Blend on high speed for 10
   seconds. Heat over
   simmering water and serve
   on cooked spinach, or use as
   a sauce with vegetarian
   loaves. Nice on thin slices
   of baked Protose or Soybean
   Loaf. Garnish with Parsley.
   Serves 2.

Cheese Souffle

1 cup Milk   ) Heat in a
3 Tbsps. Butter) saucepan

1 thin slice Whole-grain Bread
1/2 tsp. Dry Mustard
1/2 tsp. Vegetable Seasoning
Pinch Nutmeg

 (M)
Blend, then with motor still
   running, add hot milk mixture and

1 cup diced Cheddar Cheese

Continue blending. Add:

4 Egg Yolks
Blend a further 12 seconds. In
   a souffle dish beat till stiff:

4 Egg Whites

Gradually pour cheese mixture
   over whites, folding cheese into
   them with a rubber spatula until
   lightly blended. Bake at 375°
   F. for 35 minutes. 4-5 servings

Once a week have an egg dish. Blender-beaten eggs develop a
new crepe-like texture. Additions of cooked and raw vegetables
as you blend, give different flavors to the usual omelets or
scrambled egg dishes. When making a souffle, place it in a pan
containing water, as it requires gentle cooking. Eggs also require
gentle cooking for easy digestion.

Plain Omelet

2 Eggs   ) Blend on high
1 Tbsp. Water) for 3 seconds
Seasoning   )

In a small frying pan, heat 1
  Tbsp. Butter. When hot,
  pour in egg mixture and stir
  rapidly with a fork until mixture begins to set. To set the
  top, put under grill a few
  moments. Roll up or fold
  over and serve.

(2 tsps. Skim Milk Powder adds
  extra value to omelets.)

Cheese Omelet:

  2 Tbsps. Sour Cream
  2 Tbsps. diced Cheese
  2 Eggs; Seasoning

Puffy Omelet with Cheese

1/3 cup Milk or Water
1 cup diced Cheddar or Swiss
  Cheese
1 tsp. Vegetable Seasoning
1/4 tsp. Paprika
6 Egg Yolks
Sprig of Parsley
(M) speed
Blend for 3 seconds. Fold in:

6 stiffly beaten Egg Whites

Cook very gently in a   (Cont'd.)

Puffy Omelet with Cheese (Cont'd.)

  well-buttered skillet
  until puffed and delicately
  browned underneath. Trans-
  fer to oven, 375°, to brown
  top. Place on a warm serving dish and accompany with
  creamed vegetables.
             5-6 servings

Bean Sprout Omelet

3 Eggs
1/2 cup raw Sweet Cream
1 pinch Vegetable Seasoning
1 cup cooked Bean Sprouts
Cook as for omelets. Or like
  scrambled eggs in a double
  boiler. Garnish with crisp
  red Radishes.

Filled Omelet

Make a plain omelet, allowing
  it to barely set, then spread with
  a filling of creamed vegetables,
  grated cheese, etc. Roll up
  and turn out on hot serving dish.
  Choose a suitable savory sauce
  to go with it.

Herb Omelet: 2 Tbsps. Milk
             2 Tbsps. Parsley
             1 Green Onion
             1/2 tsp. Dry
               Tarragon
             2 Eggs; seasoning

Cook as plain omelet.

Cottage Cheese Omelet

2 Tbsps. Sour Cream
2 Tbsps. diced Cheddar
  Cheese
2 Eggs
Seasoning

Place in liquefier and run to
  blend. Cook as usual
(M)   2-3 servings

Firm Banana Omelet

1 large ripe Banana
6 Eggs
2 Tbsps. Cream
2 tsps. Raw Sugar or Molasses
1/2 tsp. Sea Salt
 (M)
Blend 3 seconds and cook as
  usual.   5-6 servings

Half-Baked Omelet

3/4 cup Hot Milk
3 Tbsps. Skim Milk Powder
(M) speed
Blend. Pour over:

3/4 cup soft Whole Wheat
  Breadcrumbs, blender
  made   (L)
1/4 cup Wheatgerm

Stand till cool.

6 Eggs
3/4 tsp. Sea Salt

Blend all ingredients well.
  Cook in heavy oiled skillet
  until bottom is light brown.
  Remove to 300° oven and
  bake until top is dry.

Orange Omelet

4 Eggs
1/4 cup Milk
1/2 tsp. Vegetable Salt
1/4 cup Orange Juice
Small piece of outer peel of
    Orange, grated
  (H)
Blend for 3 seconds. Cook
  as for omelets. 3-4 servings.

Spinach Souffle

3/4 cup Milk
1/4 cup Soft Butter
4 Egg Yolks
1/2 cup Cooked Potato
1 slice Onion
1 tsp. Sea Salt
Dash Cayenne
1/2 cup diced Hard Cheese
2 cups packed, washed raw
  Spinach, or
  1-1/2 cups diced raw Carrot
 (H)
Blend until vegetables are
  finely chopped. Fold in:

4 stiffly beaten Egg Whites
              5-6 servings
Gently pour into greased
casserole, sprinkle with
    Paprika and bake at 325° F.
    about 50 minutes to 1 hour.
    Serve immediately.

Green Bean Souffle

2/3 cup sweet Raw Cream
2 Egg Yolks
Pinch Sea Salt
3 cups cooked Green Beans. Add
    gradually to above ingredients
    in blender and blend.(H). Fold in:
2 Egg Whites stiffly beaten

Bake in moderate oven for
    25 minutes. 3-4 servings

Scrambled Eggs a la Jensen

3 Eggs   1/2 tsp. Vegetable Seasoning
1/2 cup Raw Sweet Cream   (Tomato Rings to garnish)

Blend on high speed for 3 seconds. Cook in a little butter in a
double boiler, stirring occasionally until eggs are thick and
creamy. Garnish with tomato rings.

Variations can easily be made by additions of green peppers, onion,
cooked mushrooms, cheese, etc.

VEGETABLES

Vegetables

Even in the field of vegetable preparation, the Blender can be
very useful. It can chop or grate raw vegetables, reduce them to
the fine state required for souffles and vegetable rings, and also
puree the cooked vegetables. Casserole dishes with the aid of the
Blender can be new flavor sensations for the family.

For their valuable minerals, vitamins, and roughage, let us increase the number of vegetables in our diet. Remember the golden
rule: four to six vegetables every day, and at least two of these
green.

However, vegetables should be eaten raw as often as possible. Shred carrots, zucchini, beets, cabbage, turnips, radishes; slice cucumbers or Jerusalem artichokes, or just wash raw celery, asparagus, okra, Chinese peas, young broccoli, young string beans, fresh young corn, cauliflower, spinach, all green leaf lettuce, onions, scallions, and anything else you can think of.

And, try them with some of our tasty blended Health Dressings (see Dressings Section).

You may steam your vegetables, just to tenderize, and add a simple health sauce, such as the Blended White Sauce, Cheese Sauce, or Nut Sauce. Try any of the other tempting sauces in the Savory Sauce Section which may appeal to you.

Basic Recipe for Blending Vegetables

Blended Asparagus - or other vegetables:

1 cup sliced Asparagus)   Steam briefly until just tender.
1/3 cup Water   )

1/2 tsp. Vegetable Seasoning
2 tsps. Butter

Put all in blender and run until completely blended. (H) Serve immediately.

Mixed Vegetables, Vegetarian

1/3 cup sliced Beets
1/3 cup sliced Carrots
2 leaves Escarole
1/3 cup sliced Sweet Potato
2 Tbsps. sliced Leek
1/4 cup Vegetable Water

Blend until completely blended,(H) then cook in covered saucepan over low heat for 5 minutes. Serve with knob of butter.   3 servings

Carrot Ring

1 slice Whole Wheat Bread

Prepare crumbs and set aside. Place in container: (Cont'd.)

Carrot Ring   (Cont'd.)

3 Eggs
1 slice Onion
4 sprigs Parsley
1 Tbsp. Melted Butter
1 tsp. Vegetable Seasoning
Dash Capsicum Pepper
2-1/2 cups Raw Carrot
1 Tbsp. Maple Syrup or Raw Sugar

Blend until carrots are fine.(H) Fold in breadcrumbs and turn into an oiled ring mold. Set in a shallow pan of water and bake in moderate oven, 375° F. for 30 minutes or until firm. Unmold on serving plate and fill with creamed peas.
4-5 servings

178

Vegetable Casserole

1 package frozen Vegetable
   (Limas, Asparagus, etc.)

Lay in oiled shallow casserole.

1/4 cup Peanuts or Cashews.
   Blend 6 seconds.(M)

Make a Mushroom Sauce (see
   Sauce Section), and pour over
   vegetables. Bake at 350° for
   30 minutes. Sprinkle with
   chopped nuts. 3-4 servings

Cauliflower and Nuts

Cook only until tender, whole or
   broken apart:

1 medium sized head Cauliflower

Break into blender and cut into
   fine crumbs:

1 slice Whole Wheat Bread
(L)
Empty crumbs into saucepan
   with

1/4 cup melted Butter. Add:

1/4 cup Nuts, ground fine (H)
   in blender (Pecans preferably)

Sprinkle crumb-nut mixture over
   cauliflower and brown slightly
   in oven if desired.

Piquant or Orange-Beets

cups scrubbed, sliced Raw
   Beets
1/4 cup Water
Pulp of two Oranges
2 Tbsps. Butter
1 tsp. Vegetable Seasoning (Cont'd.)

Piquant or Orange-Beets (Cont'd.)

1/8 tsp. Capsicum or Cayenne
1/2 cup Raw Sugar
2 Tbsps. Arrowroot
   (L)
Blend until beets are chopped
   coarsely. Turn into saucepan and cook, stirring over
   gentle heat until thickened.
                4-5 servings

Baked Eggplant

1 Eggplant. Steam tender.
   Drain.
1 slice Whole-grain Bread,
   crumbed (Save).
1/4 cup Cream
2 Tbsps. Soft Butter
1/2 small Onion
1 small clove Garlic
2 Eggs
1/2 tsp. Vegetable Seasoning
Dash Paprika
1 tsp. Lemon Juice
Prepared Eggplant
1 slice Whole-grain Bread

Blend rapidly for 20 seconds.(H)
   Pour into greased casserole
   and top with other breadcrumbs.
   Bake at 325° in oven for about
   30 minutes.   4-5 servings

String Beans with Cheese

Place 2 cups cooked String
   Beans in a buttered casserole
   dish.

1/4 cup Milk
1/4 cup Cream
1/2 tsp. Vegetable Seasoning
1 cup cubes of Cheddar Cheese
(L) speed
Blend to grate cheese; pour over
   beans, dot with butter, and
   bake in a moderate oven for
   15 minutes.   3-4 servings

Zucchini with Cheese

1 cup Cheddar Cheese, blender grate and set aside (L)

Blend to puree the following: (M)
2 cups Vegetable Water
2 tsps. Vegetable Seasoning
1 tsp. Soy Sauce
1 lb. Ripe Tomatoes, sliced

Add and blend till chopped: (L)

1 Onion, sliced
1 Green Pepper, sliced

1 lb. Zucchini, sliced. Place in pan. Add sauce and simmer, covered, for 15 minutes. Remove from heat. Stir in cheese and a little butter if desired. Serve plain or over cooked soy noodles for a main dish.
3-4 servings

Stuffed Rice Peppers

Dry Whole Wheat Bread--blended to crumble. Set aside. (L)

1 Egg
1/2 Onion, sliced
1 tsp Vegetable Seasoning
(M)
Blend and pour over:

1 cup cooked Brown Rice

Mix, adding enough crumbs to make firm.

Peppers: remove stem and fibers. Stuff with rice mixture. Bake in moderate oven till tender. (Peppers may be parboiled a few minutes to lessen baking time.)

Potato Pancakes

Place 3 Eggs in blender. Start blender and slice in:

6 Potatoes, unpeeled
3 slices Onion
2 large sprigs Parsley
(H) speed
Blend until vegetables are minced fine. Add:

1/3 cup sifted Whole Wheat Flour
1/4 tsp. Baking Powder
1-1/2 tsps Vegetable Seasoning

Blend just enough to mix. Cook on an oiled skillet.

Baked Potato Continental

Bake your potatoes in the usual way, but instead of serving them with butter, prepare accompaniment as follows:

1/2 cup Yogurt
1/4 cup Garden Cress
1/2 small Onion, sliced
1/2 small stalk Celery
1 tsp. Vegetable Seasoning

Blend to chop vegetables, (L) scraping down blender frequently. Stir into

1 cup Sour Cream.

A dash of Lemon Juice makes a tasty variation. Or try herbs for a change.

Spicy Sweet Potatoes

1 cup diced Sweet Potatoes, raw
1/2 cup Cream or Milk
2 Eggs
1/4 cup melted Butter
1/2 cup Raw Sugar
1/2 tsp. Ginger
1/2 tsp. Cinnamon
1/2 tsp. Vegetable Seasoning
 (M)
Blend these, and with blender
  running, add:

2 cups diced Sweet Potatoes, raw

Bake in oiled casserole at 325°
  for 45 minutes.   3-4 servings

Apple and Sweet Potato Scallop

3 cups sliced, cooked Sweet
  Potato. Place in oiled
  casserole.
  (H)
Thoroughly blend, about 1
  minute, the following:

1/4 cup cold-pressed Oil
1/2 cup Maple Syrup
Peel of 1/2 Orange
1-1/2 cups Apples, diced
1/2 tsp. Vegetable Seasoning

Pour over sweet potatoes, bake
  in moderate oven about 1
  hour.   3-4 servings

Sweet Potato Tropical

1/3 cup Almonds) Blender
1/3 cup Walnuts) chopped (L)
2 cups Sweet Potatoes,
  blender mashed (L)
1 Tbsp. Raw Sugar
Pinch Vegetable Seasoning
1 Tbsp. Butter
1/2 tsp. Pure Vanilla

Mix all these ingredients in a
  bowl.

1 slice Whole Wheat Bread.
  Crumb.

2 Bananas, mash in blender
  (L)
Add to other mixture, shape
  into small mounds in
  well-oiled pan. Bake
  in moderate oven, 350° F.,
  for 15 minutes. Top with
  walnut halves. 3-4 servings

For Vegetables, Vegetarian or Nut Loaves, Casseroles, Etc.

Avoid all artificial seasonings, flavorings, and stimulants, such as table salt, black and white pepper, vinegar, alcoholic flavorings, artificial extracts, ketchup, mayonnaise, and hot sauces. Use sea salt, if you need salt.

Green peppers, red peppers, onions, garlic, celery salt, vegetable seasoning, horseradish, tomatoes, nuts, mushrooms, lemon and lemon peel, and all herbs are delightful and healthful flavorings for sauces.

No more lumpy sauces with the blender at your side. Extra flavor from natural ingredients, minimum-cooked--in fact, many uncooked sauces--are possible. Most of these sauce recipes need just be heated over water before serving, if desired. Blend first, and then cook is the rule to apply usually, and never overheat.

Don't use the common white sauce made from white flour, but try our tasty Health "White" Sauce. The following recipes should give you plenty of other tasty, nutritious sauces to choose from.

Basic "White" Sauce

3 Tbsps. Rice Polishings
1 cup Milk
3/4 tsp. Vegetable Seasoning
Dash Dulse Powder
1 small slice Onion
Small sprig Thyme

Blend smooth in liquefier. (H)

Bring to a boil, stirring.

1 Tbsp. Sweet Butter--stir in.

Variations on Above

(a) Parsley Sauce: Add:

1/2 cup Parsley Sprigs, place with
sauce in heated blender container and re-blend to chop
Parsley without cooking.

(b) Cheese Sauce: Add:

1-1/2 oz. Cubed Cheese and a
pinch Capsicum Pepper with
first group of ingredients.

(c) Mushroom Sauce: Add:

4 to 6 fresh Mushrooms, sliced.
Heat blender container, put
in sauce and mushrooms and
re-blend 2 to 3 minutes to
allow mushrooms to soften
and disperse. Extra Vege-
table Seasoning.

(d) Cream Sauce: Re-blend,
adding:

3 Tbsps. Sweet Raw Cream
Omit butter.

Nut Sauce

1/2 cup Almonds
1 tsp. Vegetable Seasoning
1 cup Vegetable Broth, boiling

Blend very smooth (H)

1 Tbsp. Butter or Oil, add
and blend in.

1 - 2 tsps. Soy Sauce--optional

If preferred, use other varieties
of nuts.

Nut Butter Sauce

1/4 cup raw Nut Butter, made
in blender. (L) to start
then on (H)
Gradually, with blender running,
(L)add hot herb tea or water until sauce consistency is
reached.

Nut Gravy

3 Tbsps. Pecan, Almond, or
Cashew Butter, in liquefier
1 cup hot Vegetable Broth (see
--add and blend well. (H) 141)

Cook gently in double boiler,
stirring until thick. Serve
over cooked vegetables,
nut and vegetarian loaves.

Simple Cheese Sauce

1 cup Vegetable Broth--bring
to boil. (see recipe page 141)

2 cups cubed Cheese

Whirr in the blender until a
smooth creamy sauce is
obtained. A little Vegetable
Seasoning and Herbs may be
added if desired. (M)

Basic Cheese Sauce

A very simple and most healthful cheese sauce is made by
blender-grating your choice
of cheese, and melting it in
a double boiler over hot
--not boiling--water. Keep
the heat low and continue
to stir until the cheese has
melted to a smooth sauce
consistency. Use over
lightly cooked vegetables,
etc.

Tangy Cheese Sauce

2 cups Sour Cream
2 Tbsps. Lemon Juice
2 cups cubed Sharp Cheddar
(M)
Blend in liquefier, scraping
down sides frequently to ob-
tain a smooth creamy sauce.
Gentle heat in a double boiler
may be used for a hot sauce.

Delicious over vegetables or
vegetable loaves, with a
dash of Paprika for garnish.

Butter Sauce

1/2 cup Butter
1 Tbsp. Lemon Juice
1-1/2 tsp. Grated Rind
(M) speed
Blend above ingredients well.

Heat over boiling water till butter
is melted.

Variations: Add one or more
of the following:
2 tsps. Chopped Chives or Dill
1 tsp. Paprika
1 Tbsp. Parsley
1/2 cup sharp Cheese,
blender grated (Cont'd.)

Butter Sauce (Cont'd.)

Serve over Asparagus,
Broccoli, French Arti-
chokes, or anywhere a
plain sauce is necessary

Vegetable Sauces

Any cooked vegetable may be
blended with vegetable
liquid, milk or nut milks,
adding a slice of onion,
vegetable seasoning, and
herbs for seasoning. When
heated enough to serve as
a sauce, dress with a tablespoon of raw cream, sweet
butter, or nut butter. No
thickening necessary. (M)

Parsley Sauce

2 cups cooked Tomato)
1 very small Onion   ) Blend
1/2 cup Parsley   ) to puree
(M) speed
Heat over hot water. Add:

1 Tbsp. Sweet Butter. Serve

Cucumber with Lemon

2 medium Cucumbers, cut up
Juice of 1 Lemon
1 tsp. Vegetable Seasoning
1/4 tsp. Paprika

Blend to finely shred cucumber. (H)

Add a little Mayonnaise or
Sour Cream if desired.

Herb Sauce

1 large bunch Parsley
1/2 as much Chives as
  Parsley
Juice of 4 Lemons
  (L)
Blend till "minced". Then
  allow to infuse for 1 hour.

1/4 tsp. dried Thyme or Basil
4 Tbsps. Sweet Butter
1 tsp. Vegetable Seasoning
1-1/2 cups boiling water

Add and blend shortly.
  Simmer over low heat for 5
  minutes. Serve immediately.

Hollandaise Sauce

The blender excels in the quick
  preparation a Hollandaise
  Sauce that does not curdle;
  nothing simpler, nothing
  tastier, almost uncooked.

3 Egg Yolks or 2 Whole Eggs
2 Tbsps. Lemon Juice
1/4 tsp. Sea Salt
Pinch Cayenne
1/4 cup Parsley
1/2 cup Butter
  (M)
Heat butter really hot in saucepan while blending other
  ingredients except Parsley. With blender running,
  pour hot butter on Eggs,
  etc. Add parsley for a
  moment's blending. Turn
  off motor. Done!

Hollandaise Variation

3/4 cup Hollandaise Sauce, made
  in blender
1 Tbsp. Orange Juice
  (Cont'd.)

Hollandaise Variation (Cont'd.)

1 to 2 tsps. grated Orange Rind

Stir in.

Good on cooked vegetables,
  especially carrots and beets.

Tomato Sauce I

2 cups Tomato Juice
2 tsps. Soy Bean Flour
1 tsp. Vegetable Seasoning
1 Onion, small--roughly
  chopped
1 Green Pepper--roughly
  chopped
1 small clove Garlic, chopped
2 tsps. Sweet Butter
  (H)
Blend tomato juice and soy
  flour. Bring to boil in
  saucepan, stirring till the
  mixture thickens. Pour
  into blender with all other
  ingredients and run till
  finely chopped--or smooth,
  if you prefer. Cook a few
  more minutes, or just heat
  for serving over hot water.

'Fresh Tomato Cream Soup'
  (from Soup Section) makes a
  very nice tomato sauce also.

Tomato Sauce II

1 cup cooked Tomatoes
1 clove Garlic
1/2 cup Parsley
1 Onion
1/2 cup Green Peppers
Vegetable Seasoning to taste

Chop coarsely on (L) speed
then turn to (H) to make finer
mixture. Cook very slowly for
15 minutes. Or just heat for
serving.

Spanish Sauce

1 clove Garlic
1/2 cup Ripe Peppers, sliced
1 large Onion, sliced
1/2 cup Celery, chopped
1/2 cup Tomato Juice
  (L)
Blend till vegetables are chopped.
Add and blend very briefly:

1-1/2 cups Tomatoes
1 tsp. Vegetable Seasoning

Cook over very low heat for a
  few minutes. Add 2 Tbsps.
  Sweet Butter. Good for
  vegetables and vegetarian
  loaves.

Pesto Italian Sauce

1/2 cup Olive Oil
1/4 tsp. Basil
1/4 cup Parsley clusters
2 cloves Garlic
Sprinkle Oregano
1/2 tsp. Vegetable Seasoning
1/2 cup Walnuts
1 Tbsp. Hard Cheese,
  grated in blender

Blend till smooth. (H)

Speedy Mushroom Sauce

3/4 cups Cooked Mushrooms
1/2 cups Vegetable Broth*(page 141)
1/2 cup Sour Cream
2 Tbsps. Soft Butter
1/2 cup cooked Potato, or
  Potato Powder

Blend above, then heat over
  hot water to serving point,
  stirring occasionally.(M)

Cream of Horseradish

1/2 cup Heavy Cream--partly
  whip in blender.
1/4 tsp. Vegetable Seasoning
2 Tbsps. Horseradish

Add and flick the motor on and
  off so as just to blend without
  turning cream to butter. (L)

Tartar Sauce

1 cup Mayonnaise) Blend
1 small clove Garlic) to
1 small Cucumber) grind (L)

2 stalks Watercress
5 ripe Black Olives

Add just to chop and mix in
  sauce.

Barbecue Sauce I

1/4 cup Lemon Juice
1/4 cup cold-pressed Oil
1/2 tsp. Vegetable Seasoning
1/4 tsp. Ginger
3/4 cups drained revived Dried
  Apricots (see page 22)
  (L)
Blend for half a minute. Heat
  till really hot. Nice for chops,
  duckling, spareribs, and nut
  roasts.

Barbecue Sauce II

Juice of 1 Lemon
1/4 cup Oil
1 tsp. Vegetable Seasoning
1 tsp. Dry Mustard
3 Dashes Soy Sauce
2 Tbsps. Raw Sugar
1 Tbsp. Molasses
1 cup Tomato Juice
1 tsp. Chili Powder
1 tsp. Horseradish, grated
    fresh
1 tsp. Tarragon
1 tsp. Oregano
1 clove Garlic
1 Onion, chopped
 (L)
Blend to sauce consistency.
    Baste on chops and roasts
    and vegetarian roasts
    before cooking.

Curry Sauce

1-1/2 cups Milk
2 Egg Yolks
1 Tbsp. Arrowroot
2 Tbsps. Butter
1 tsp. Vegetable Seasoning
1 tsp. real Indian Curry Powder
(L) speed
Blend until smooth. Pour into
    double boiler and heat, stir-
    ring until thickened.

Mock Cranberry Sauce

Juice of 1 Lemon
2 cups Raspberries or Olallie
    Berries
6 Apples, chopped

Liquefy, adding apples gradually.
    Run for three minutes. (H)

When we change our body chemistry through natural living, we will soon lose the need for the stimulation of highly seasoned pickles and sauces. The commercially "embalmed" foods, sparking the appetite with their harsh spices, peppers, table salt, vinegars, and heated oils, are usually harmful to the body.

For a change, though, we can sometimes use a healthful preserve, incorporating natural ingredients for zip, to cheer up an otherwise bland meal.

The blender is reliable for mashing, chopping or pureeing fruits and vegetables for preserves. Homemade, they can be healthful, more flavorful, much cheaper, and quick and easy.

Never use preserves or relishes to camoflage the dullness of poorly cooked food or salads no longer fresh. Our aim should always be to develop in ourselves an appreciation of the genuine goodness of flavor of well-prepared, natural food.

Health Catchup

1 Red Pepper with a few
    seeds
1/2 large Sweet Green Pepper
1 large Onion
2 cloves Garlic
3/4 cup Apple Cider
    Vinegar
1/2 bunch Parsley

Put in blender and finely
    chop. (M)

8 Tomatoes--add and blend
    fine. (H)

1 Tbsp. Vegetable Seasoning
3/4 tsps. Dry Mustard
Pinch Cayenne
3/4 cup Raw Sugar

Add and blend 2 to 3 seconds.
    Put together in baking dish
    and hang, having placed in
    muslin bag, inside the dish
    the following:

1/2 tsp. Allspice, whole
1/2 tsp. Cloves
1/2 tsp. broken Cinnamon Sticks

Have a very slow oven, and
    cook sauce with lid partly
    off pan to allow catchup to
    reduce to half volume.
    (May be strained to give
    smooth texture). Pour into
    hot sterilized jars. Seal

Beet Relish

Sliced Raw Beets--fill lique-
    fier almost to the top.

1 cup Water
1 tsp. Vegetable Seasoning
1/4 cup Apple Cider Vinegar
            (Cont'd.)

Beet Relish (Cont'd.)

2 Tbsps. Arrowroot
1 Tbsp. Raw Sugar
2 Tbsps. Soft Butter
    (H)
Add to beets, and blend until
    all beets are blended. Then
    cook gently for 15 minutes.
    Stir occasionally. When beets
    are tender and sauce thick,
    chill.

Hot-Pepper Chutney

1 stalk Celery
2 sweet Red Peppers, seeded
2 Green Peppers, seeded
1/2 large Onion
3/4 tsp. Vegetable Seasoning
1/4 cup Raw Sugar
1/4 cup Apple Cider Vinegar
1/2 tsp. Red Pepper
1/8 tsp. Nutmeg
1/8 tsp. Cinnamon
    (L)
Blend briefly to chop up. Boil
    gently for 20 minutes. Cool
    and serve, or pack hot into
    hot jars and seal.

Marmalade

If you are not too insistent on
    meticulously sliced oranges
    and lemons for your marma-
    lades, the blender can take
    much of the slavery out of
    this task by chopping the fruit.

Raw Apple Chutney

2 Apples, cut up
1 medium Green Pepper, cut
1 clove Garlic
 (L)
Barely cover with water and
 blend 2 to 3 seconds just to
 chop. Drain and empty
 vegetables into bowl.

1/2 cup Raisins
3/4 tsp. Paprika
Shake Cayenne
1/4 tsp. Ginger
1/2 tsp. Vegetable Seasoning
1 Tbsp. Lemon Juice
1 Tbsp. Apple Cider Vinegar
(M) speed
Blend and add to chopped
 vegetables & apple. Chill.

Spicy Apple Preserve

2 lbs. Cooking Apples, roughly
 sliced
1/2 cup Oatstraw Tea or Apple
 Juice   (See page 20)
1/2-inch slice Lemon
1/4 tsp. Cloves, ground
1/2 tsp. Nutmeg
1/4 tsp. Allspice
1/2 tsp. Vegetable Seasoning
1 cup Raw Sugar
1 tsp. Cinnamon

Blend till mushy. Then put in
 saucepan and cook over very
 low heat about 30 minutes,
 stirring occasionally. Have
 sterilized jars ready, and
 pour into these. Seal.

Variations: Quince, Winter
 Pears or Plums will also make
 nice preserves.

Apricot Jam

1/2 lbs. Dried Apricots, revived.
 (H)
Liquefy, using the juice and
 more water if necessary.
 There should be about 5
 cups of puree. Put in large
 saucepan with:

1/4 cup Lemon Juice
7 cups Raw Sugar

Bring to a full rolling boil.
 Boil hard 1 minute, stirring
 constantly. Turn off heat.
 Pour in:

1 bottle Fruit Pectin

Cool slightly, removing froth,
 then ladle into hot, sterilized
 jam jars. Cover.

Apricot-Date-Ginger

1/2 cup revived Dried Prunes,
 pitted, drained
1/2 cup revived dried Apricots,
 drained
1/2 cup revived Raisins, drained
1/2 cup Crushed Pineapple with
 juice
2 thin strips peel of Orange
2 slices Preserved Ginger
 (L)
Blend, using rubber spatula to
 help get all fruit to blend.
 Add and blend just enough to
 crush:

1/4 cup Walnuts

Serve as preserve with roast
 turkey, mock meat roasts,
 etc.

If you can grind the whole grains in your own kitchen at the time you are ready to use them, you will derive greater nutritional value. Sift the flour to the desired fineness, keeping the remaining "bran" for your cereal preparations. As you eat more of the whole grain in simple cereal form, you will gradually lose the desire for baked goods, which contain less food value. Flour-containing products should be served only with those foods which are compatible with a carbohydrate meal.

See the following pages for recipes of variety, flavor and the maximum food values. These will become basic in your kitchen.

BREADS

Bread

1 package Dry Yeast	) Let stand 5 minutes
1 cup Lukewarm Water or Herb Tea	) in blender

Blend at high speed for 20 seconds.

1/4 cup Soy Oil	1 Tbsp. Raw Sugar
1 Egg	1 tsp. Sea Salt

Add and blend to mix well.

3 cups fresh-ground Whole Wheat Flour·have warm in warm bowl.

Pour in yeast batter, stir thoroughly until elastic. Knead a little; shape into loaf, place in loaf pan, let rise until double in bulk.

Bake at 375° to 400° for 30 to 40 minutes or until done. On removing from pans, brush over with melted butter.

Variations of Above:

Onion Bread: At second blending add:

> 1 small Onion, sliced
> 1/4 tsp. Sage
> 1/2 tsp. Celery Salt

Raisin Bread: Stir in 1 cup raisins with the flour and increase the sugar to 1/2 cup.

Nut Bread: Stir in 3/4 cup blender-chopped nuts with the flour. Increase sugar to suit taste.

Soy Bread: Replace part of the flour with soy flour.

Barley Bread: Replace part of the flour with barley flour.

Herb Bread: Fresh or dried herbs will give great variety of flavor.

See suggestions on the following page.

Herb Breads (Cont'd.)

Add with flour:

(a) 1/2 tsp. Nutmeg
    1/2 tsp. Sage
    2 tsps. Caraway Seed

(b) 1/2 tsp. Oregano
    1/2 tsp. Thyme

(c) 3/4 tsp. Summer Savory
    (or Rosemary, Thyme,
    or Marjoram)

(d) Sprinkle Poppy Seed
    lightly over bread before
    baking.

Corn Bread

1 cup Milk
2 Eggs
1/4 cup Olive Oil
2 Tbsps. Raw Sugar
2 tsps. Vegetable seasoning

Blend above well.

1 cup Yellow Corn Meal
  --add and blend to mix

Allow to stand 1/2 hour

3/4 cup Whole Wheat Flour
3 tsps. Baking Powder
    Sift together

Combine ingredients, stirring just enough to mix.
  Pour into shallow, greased
  baking pan and bake 20 to
  30 minutes at 400° F.

Cheese Bread a la Casserole

1 cup lukewarm Water
2 packages Yeast   (Cont'd.)

Cheese Bread a la Casserole

Let yeast and water stand in
  blender 5 minutes. Blend
  at high speed for 20 seconds.

1 Cup Milk - scald
3 Tbsps. Raw Sugar)
2 tsps. Sea Salt   )
1 Tbsp. Oil   )

Stir above ingredients into
  milk, cool to lukewarm and
  add to yeast mixture.

4 ounces Cheddar Cheese,
  cubed. Add to above

Blend to mix and grate cheese

4-1/2 cups sifted Whole Wheat
  Flour--warm in a large bowl.

Stir in yeast mixture very well,
  blending with a spoon for about
  2 minutes. Cover. Let rise
  in a warm place until more
  than double in bulk.

Stir batter down. Beat vigorously
  for about 1/2 minute. Turn
  into oiled 1-1/2 quart casserole
  and bake uncovered at 375°
  for about 1 hour.

Vegetable Bread

1 package Yeast)	Stand in blender for 5 minutes,
1/3 cup Lukewarm Water)	then blend briefly. (M) speed
1 tsp. Raw Sugar)	

Set aside in warm place to "work".

3/4 cup Hot Water)	Blend very fine. (H) speed
1/2 cup sliced Carrots)	

2 cups sliced Celery, Carrots,)	Add and blend to chop
Green Peppers, and Parsley)	vegetables. (M) speed
1/3 cup Vegetable Oil)	

4 cups Whole Wheat Flour)	Sift and warm.
1 Tbsp. Vegetable Seasoning)	
1 tsp. Sea Salt)	

Pour liquids into flour, mix, knead till smooth. (Add more flour if needed). Place bowl in a warm place and allow to rise until double in bulk. (About 1 hour).

Knock down, knead again. Shape into loaf and place in a greased pan. Again let rise until double in bulk, then bake at 350° to 375° F. for about 1 hour.

Note: A very good bread results with only one rising period; i.e., after the first kneading, shape into loaf, allow to rise till double, then bake.

Vegetable Rolls

Use above recipe, but instead of making into a loaf, shape into about 15 rolls. Place in an oiled and lightly floured pan 1 inch apart (or use muffin pans).

Allow to rise until double in bulk. Then bake at 400° F. for 5 minutes. Lower temperature to 350° and bake 35 minutes longer, or until done and crusty brown.

ROLLS

Make delicious, nutritious homemade rolls easily now with the help of your blender. Just learn the technique of the blender-made yeast batter from the following recipe. Then go ahead converting any of your own favorite breads or rolls.

Basic Rolls

Place in blender container and let stand for 5 minutes:

> 1 package Dry Yeast
> 1 cup Lukewarm Water

Blend at high speed for 20 seconds. Add to mixture:

> 1/4 cup Soy Oil
> 1 Egg
> 1 tsp. Vegetable Seasoning

Blend at high speed for a few seconds. Pour into bowl over cups whole wheat flour. Stir until thoroughly mixed. Cover and let rise for 1-1/2 hours, or until double in bulk. Stir down. Fill greased muffin tins half full of dough and let rise another 5 minutes, or until double in bulk. Brush with beaten egg yolk and bake at 375° for 25 minutes. If desired, top the rolls with poppy or sesame seeds, or a mixture of nuts, raw sugar, and butter. Makes about 2 dozen rolls

Variations on Above

After the dough has risen once, you may add any one of the following simply by mixing into the dough in a bowl. Then fill the greased muffin tins half full and proceed just as directed above.

1. 1 cup drained, Crushed Pineapple, unsweetened.
2. 1 cup Raisins, blended for a few seconds.
3. 1 cup Walnuts, chopped in blender with
     1 Tbsp. Cinnamon
     2 Tbsps. Raw Sugar
4. 1 cup grated Cheddar Cheese
5. Variations as for bread (See variations following
     basic bread recipe, page 164)

Millet Muffins

1 cup Millet Flour)
1 cup Whole Wheat Flour)
4 tsps. Baking Powder)
1 tsp. Vegetable Seasoning)

Sift above together and add:

2 Tbsps. Raw Sugar

1-1/4 cups Milk)
1 Egg, well beaten)
2 Tbsps. Butter)
1/2 cup   Pitted Dates)
(L)
Blend above to chop dates and
stir into flour mixture.

Beat thoroughly. Spoon into
oiled muffin pans. Bake at
425° F. for 20 minutes.
6-8 muffins

Ginger Muffins

Sift together in bowl:

1-1/2 cups Whole Wheat Flour
1 tsp. Soda

Place in blender:
(L) speed
1/4 cup soft Butter
1 Egg
1/2 cup Strong Dandelion
 Coffee (see page 93)
1/2 cup Molasses
1/2 cup Raw Sugar
1/4 tsp. each :
    Vegetable Seasoning
    Nutmeg
    Ginger
    Cinnamon

Blend until smooth. Pour in-
to dry ingredients and stir (Cont'd.)

Ginger Muffins (Cont'd.)

lightly together. Fill greased
muffin pans two-thirds full and
bake at 375° about 20 minutes.
12muffins
*See recipe in "Drinks Section",
page

Date-Walnut Muffins

Sift together into a bowl

2 cups Whole Wheat Flour
4 tsps. Baking Powder
1/2 tsp. Vegetable Seasoning

Place in blender

1-1/2 cup pitted Dates, soaked
1 cup Soy or Sesame Milk (L)

Blend then add:

1/4 cup soft Butter
1 Egg
1/4 cup Raw Sugar

Blend a minute and add:
(L) speed
1/4 cup Walnuts , to chop only.

Pour into dry ingredients and
stir until dry ingredients are
dampened. Spoon into greased
muffin pans, filling two-thirds
full. Bake in 400° oven 20
to 25 minutes. 1½ dozen

Cereal Muffins

1 cup cooked Corn Meal Mush)
1 Egg   )
1/2 cup Milk   )   Blend (M) speed
1 Tbsp. Butter   )
2 Tbsps. Raw Sugar   )

3/4 tsps. Baking Powder   )
1 tsp. Vegetable Seasoning)   Sift Together
1/2 cup Soy Bean Flour   )

1 cup rolled Oats
1/2 cup Bran
1/2 cup Sunflower Seed Meal
2 Tbsps. Raisins

Mix all dry ingredients well. Pour in liquids. Stir lightly but
do not over-mix. Turn into greased muffin pans. Bake about
30 minutes at 375° F.

GRAINS AND CEREALS

Whole grains, as nature gave them to us, grind dry in the liquefier beautifully; so do flaxseeds, sunflower seeds, apricot kernels,
dry melon seeds, etc. These deteriorate rapidly once powdered
or made into meals, so keep your liquefier handy, and grind them
as needed.

The grains, thus ground, are delicious served as they are, with
a drizzle of honey over them. In this form they invite good masti-
cation so necessary for starch digestion.

Grain Drink:

To make a drink, put 1 Tbsp. of Flaxseed Meal with each serving
of whole-grain. Use a Herb Tea for the base (huckleberry aids
digestion of starches), sufficient for smooth blending of thick
consistency. Season with vegetable seasoning, or a sweet cereal
may be made with Carob Powder for flavoring. Soy Milk is a
good base for cereals, except wheat, with which it is not compatible.
Soaked, sprouted or cooked grains may be similarly liquefied.

Soaked dried fruits, such as Prunes, Apricots, Raisins, Dates or
Figs may be liquefied with Carob Powder or Fresh Coconut ground
in the liquefier and served with any liquefied cereal for breakfast.

For other carbohydrate meals, serve liquefied grain with vegetables, including leafy greens, of which you should have at least twice as much as of the concentrated carbohydrate.

— — — — —

Muesli

This is the delicious " raw breakfast" formulated by the late Dr. Bircher-Benner of the famed sanatorium in Switzerland.

The basis is oats:

(a) Whole Oats soaked overnight then blended in your liquefier
        to a smooth consistency. (H)

(b) Rolled Oats soaked overnight.

(c) Liquefier-ground Whole or Rolled Oats soaked overnight.

In the morning blend: (M)

> 1 Tbsp. Top Milk or Cream
> Juice of 1/2 Lemon
> Honey to taste

Add and blend fairly small: (L)

> 1 large Apple, cut up

Pour this blended mixture over the oats in a bowl. Mix. Set out in serving dishes. Sprinkle the tops with

> 1 Tbsp. Almonds or other Nuts, liquefier-ground. Start on
> (L) speed then turn to (H) for finer mixture

Variation: Soaked Raisins may be added to Muesli.

Muesli with Fruits

2 Apples, cut in quarters	1 cup Milk
1/2 Orange, peeled	2 Tbsps. Honey
1/2 Lemon, peeled	1 cup Oat Flakes

Place apples, orange and lemon in the blender with the milk. Switch on for 20 seconds. (M)

Put Oat Flakes in a plate or bowl, pour ingredients from blender, mix well. Serve with cream. (M)   2 servings

Muesli with Berries

3 Tbsps. Hazel Nuts
1 cup Yogurt
1 cup Cottage Cheese
4 Tbsps. Raw Sugar
(L)

2 cups Berries; e.g.,
   Strawberries, Raspberries etc.
2 cups Oat Flakes

Rough-chop hazelnuts first. Add yogurt and berries; blend briefly.
Add sugar and cottage cheese. Turn blender on and off and carefully push ingredients down with rubber scraper. When blended
pour over oats in bowl. Stand a while for flavors to mingle.

2-3 servings

THERMOS COOKING OF GRAINS

To cook grains, either, whole, cracked or milled, try using a
   Thermos.

Use 1/2 cup to 1-1/2 cups boiling water. This is a good proportion
for a ONE-PINT THERMOS.

(1) WHOLE: Try this simple procedure.

    (a) To wash: Measure your cereal into the
                    Thermos. Add water and wash.
                    Drain off water. If necessary,
                    use a small strainer.

    (b) To scald: Pour in boiling water and leave
                    a few moments to heat both
                    grain and Thermos. Drain
                    again.

    (c) To cook: Immediately fill to the top with
                    boiling water, close tightly and
                    leave 12 hours for most varieties.
                    (Rice and buckwheat will cook in
                    2 to 3 hours).

(2) GRITS: For greatest value, fresh-grind your own grain.
             Preheat your Thermos. Put in 1/2 cup grits and
             fill with boiling water. Then give it a quick,
             gentle stir so that no uncooked layer remains on
             the bottom. Close and leave 2 to 3 hours, depend-
             ing on the fineness of the grind, or overnight.

(3) MEALS: Again, grind meals yourself just before using.

             Take 1/2 to 3/4 cup of meal, mix it to a cream
                                  (Cont'd.)

3) MEALS: in a warm bowl using hot water, then pour into
(Cont'd.) a pre-heated pint Thermos.

Top with boiling water, then close and leave
1-1/2 to 2 hours, or overnight. Vegetable Seasoning may be added prior to cooking, but we prefer
that any butter, honey, or other seasoning be
added to taste on serving.

Cereal for Breakfast

3 cups Water
1 cup Redwheat Kernels
5 Tbsps. Skimmed Dried Milk (Optional)
1-1/2 cups Milk
4 to 6 Tbsps. Wheat Germ
(H)
Blend the water, kernels, and skim milk powder for 3 minutes.
Cook in double boiler for 2 to 3 minutes, stirring constantly
till thickened.

Add gradually the liquid milk and the wheat germ. Serve with
honey or raw sugar. For variety, dates or raisins or 1-1/2
Tbsps. Molasses may be added.   5-6 servings

Blended Cooked Cereal

Run any cooked cereal through the liquefier to make smooth and
creamy. Serve with a little butter and honey. (M) speed

Cereal Cream

Liquefy any cooked cereal, using milk or nut-milk for the liquid.

Heat to serving temperature, but do not boil.

Whole Wheat Yeast Pancakes

Dissolve and let stand for 10
  minutes

1-1/2 Tbsps. Dry Yeast
2 Tbsps. Honey
1/2 cup Lukewarm Water

Blend together. (M)

3 cups Water
1 Tbsp. Honey
3 Tbsps. Molasses
1/3 cup Soy Milk Powder
2 Tbsps. Soy Oil

Sift together

3 cups Whole Wheat Flour
  (or part Buckwheat)
3/4 tsp. Vegetable Seasoning

Combine liquid ingredients.
  Add sifted dry ingredients.
  Bake well on oiled griddle.
         8-10 servings

Orange Pancakes

1 cup Orange Juice
1/4 cup Milk
3 Tbsps. Soft Butter
1 Egg
3 Tbsps. Raw Sugar
1 tsp. Vegetable Seasoning)
1 cup Whole Wheat Flour)
2-1/2 tsps. Baking Powder)
1 Tbsp. Rice Polishings)
1 Tbsp. Sunflower Seed)
  Meal)

Sift together above dry ingredients in brackets, then
  place all ingredients in
  blender and blend smooth, (H)
  stopping to scrape down (Cont'd.)

Orange Pancakes (Cont'd.)

sides often. Pour from blender
on to hot, lightly greased
griddle and cook. makes 3-4

Serve with Orange Sauce.

Orange Sauce

3/4 cup Orange Juice)
1/8 slice Orange) Blend
1 Tbsp. Arrowroot) Orange
1/4 tsp. Sea Salt) fine.
              (H)

Cook in a double boiler, stirring until thick. Stir in:

1/3 cup Honey

Carrot Waffles

1-1/4 cups Buttermilk) Blend
1 cup chopped Carrots)   fine (H)

3 Egg Yolks
1/4 cup Salad Oil
2 tsps. Raw Sugar
1 tsp. Vegetable Seasoning

Add above and blend smooth. (H)
  Sift together:

2 cups Whole Wheat Flour
3 Tsps. Baking Powder

Stir liquids into flour. Mix
  lightly.

3 Egg Whites, stiffly beaten
  --fold in.

Bake in a hot waffle iron.
       10-12 medium size

Cornmeal Waffles

Sift together in a bowl:

1 cup Whole Wheat Flour
1 cup Corn Meal
3 tsps. Baking Powder

Place in container and blend:
 (M)
3 Egg Yolks
1-¼ cups Milk
¼ cup Soy Oil
2 tsps. Raw Sugar
½ tsp. Vegetable Seasoning

If desired, add to this mixture:

1 cup diced Cheese

Pour over dry ingredients,
mixing gently. Fold in
stiffly beaten Egg Whites.
Bake in waffle iron.
 5-6 servings

Protein Hot Cakes

2 large Eggs - -blend to beat
1 cup Cottage Cheese
1 heaped tbsp. Soy Flour

Add Cottage Cheese to well
mixed Eggs and blend on very
low speed so as just to mix.
Stir in Soy Flour. Cook on
lightly greased griddle.
        2 servings

Corn Hot Cakes

1 cup Buttermilk
¼ tsp. Soda

Let stand 10 minutes

3 Eggs
1 dash Sea Salt
2 tbsp. Oil

Blend together and add:
        (M)
½ cup Corn Flour or Corn Meal
¼ cup Wheat Flour or use half
    and half Buckwheat flour
3/4 tsp. Baking Powder

If too thin add just a little
flour, if too thich add more
milk.
Bake on hot griddle with plenty
of T.L.C. (Tender Loving Care)

  2 -3 servings

The blender has revolutionized the health-dessert field. Recipes which were once difficult to make are now quick and easy. Although I do not generally approve of desserts, there are times when they are permissable and some of the following recipes are so nutritious and satisfying they can become complete meals on a hot summer's day. Other ideas suggest welcome changes for simple breakfast fruit dishes.

With Starch Meal - Desserts made from dried fruits, starchy fruits, coconut or whipped cream are best eaten with starch and vegetable meal.

Health Desserts

With Protein Meal - Desserts made with fresh fruits, baked, stewed, steamed, and frozen fruits should be eaten at a protein meal. Custards and puddings in which eggs predominate, and whipped cream, also come under this classification.

When whipping cream to top desserts, add a dash of cinnamon and maple syrup.

White Velvet Cream

1/2 cup Warm Water
3 Tbsps. Soy Milk Powder
(M) speed
Blend above. Add gradually:

1/3 cup Safflower Oil, continuing to blend.

Sweet White Velvet Cream

1/2 cup Warm Water
3 Tbsps. Soy Milk Powder
Blend above, add gradually continuing to blend: (L)
1/3 cup Safflower Oil
Few drops Pure Vanilla
Honey to sweeten .Run just to blend in.

Cherry Velvet Cream

1/2 cup warm Water
4 Tbsps. Soy Milk Powder
1 tsp. Cherry Concentrate
Honey to sweeten

Blend above ingredients. (M)
Add gradually, continuing to blend (L)

1/2 cup Safflower Oil.

Green Velvet Cream

1/2 cup warm Water
4 Tbsps. Soy Milk Powder
1/2 tsp. Chlorophyl (more, if desired)
Few drops Pure Vanilla
Honey to sweeten (Cont'd.)

Green Velvet Cream (Cont'd.)

Blend above ingredients. Add gradually, continuing to blend: (L)
1/2 cup Safflower Oil.

White Velvet Whipped Cream

1/2 cup warm Water   ) Blend
4 Tbsps. Soy Milk Powder) (M)

1/2 cup Safflower Oil--add gradually, continuing to blend. (L)

Few drops Pure Vanilla
Honey to sweeten

Blend until smooth whipped "cream" is obtained.

Mock Whipped Cream

1 chopped tart Apple
Juice of one Lemon
1 cup Raw Sugar
1 Egg White
     (M)
Blend until beautiful whipped "cream" is arrived at. Chill.

Nut Toppings

Thin any nut butter with water to consistence of a thick sauce. (Easily done in the blender). Delicious served over baked apples or stewed fruit.

"Mock-Choc" Sauce

4 squares Carob-Chocolate cut in pieces
1/2 cup Raw Sugar
2/3 cup warm Milk & Cream
1 tsp. Pure Vanilla
Dash Vegetable Seasoning
Blend until smooth. (H)

Mocha Sauce

2 Tbsps. Whey Powder
1 Tbsp. Carob
1 Tbsp. Rice Polishings
1 Tbsp. Sunflower Seed
  Meal
2 Tbsp. Honey
2 Tbsps. very strong
  Dandelion Root Coffee
1 Tbsp. Butter
Dash of Sea Salt
1/2 tsp. Pure Vanilla

Blend on (L) to a smooth
sauce. Delicious over Health
Ice Cream or Milk shakes

Lemon Sauce

1/2 cup Raw Sugar
1 cup Warm Water
1 Tbsp. Arrowroot
Dash of Vegetable Seasoning
Dash of Nutmeg
Outer skin of 1/2 Lemon
Peeled 1/2 Lemon, cut up
  (M)
Blend until Lemon Peel is
  finely grated; pour into
  saucepan and cook, stirring
  constantly until thickened
  and clear. Add:

1 Tbsp. Butter

Serve warm on steamed
  puddings.

Custard Sauce

1/2 cup Milk
1/2 cup Blanched Almonds
1/4 cup Raw Sugar
Dash of Vegetable Seasoning
(M) speed
Blend until almonds are chopped.
Add and blend just a second or
  two:

2 Eggs
1-1/2 cups additional Milk

Pour into double boiler, cook
  and stir over hot water until
  mixture will just coat a spoon.
  Add:

1/4 tsp. Pure Almond Extract

Chill immediately. Serve over
  baked or steamed puddings.
  Nice with Date Pudding.

Banana Cream Sauce

1 ripe Banana, cut up
2 Tbsps. Raw Sugar
1 cup Sour Cream

Blend on high speed until
  smooth. Good on hot spice
  cake or gingerbread or
  carob chocolate ice cream.

Banana-Fruit Sauce

Blend until smooth: (M)

1 cup Pineapple Juice, unsweetened.
3/4 cup single or mixed revived
  dried fruits. Add:

Part of a Banana (as much as
  desired)

Continue to blend until thick.
  (M)

Pear Sauce

1/2 cup Water
1/8 cup Crystallized Ginger
1 Tbsp. Lemon Juice
1 strip Lemon Rind
1 Pear--whole, washed, and
   quartered
(L)
Blend a few seconds, then
   gradually add:

3 medium Pears--whole,
  washed and quartered

Blend until mixture is smooth.
Stir in 1/4 cup Honey.

Raw Applesauce

3 red Apples--thinly sliced
1 Tbsp. Lemon Juice
1/4 cup Honey
1/4 tsp. Spice
(M) speed
Place in blender (add apple
  gradually). Blend till
  smooth. Chill.

Orange-Honey Butter

1/4 cup Honey
3 Tbsps. Orange Juice Concentrate, unsweetened
1/4 pound Butter, soft
(M) speed
Blend until smooth and creamy.
Good on waffles, pancakes and
  gingerbread.

Cream Fruit Sauce

1 cup Milk
1 Egg Yolk
Sliced Peaches or Pears

Continue adding the fruit with
  blender running until a thick
  puree is obtained. (M)

    * See recipe Page 20

Strawberry Sauce

1 pint Fresh Strawberries
  or Frozen Strawberries
Honey to sweeten

Blend till smooth. (M)

Prune Coconut Sauce

Liquefy pitted prunes and
  fresh coconut in a little
  pineapple juice to sauce
  consistency. (M)

Apple Concentrate Sauce

Place in container and blend

  1 cup Oatstraw Tea*
  Peel of 1 Lemon
  1 Tbsp. Lemon Juice
  (H)
Add and partially blend:
  (M)
1/4 cup Raw Sugar
1/2 cup Raisins
2 Tbsps. Arrowroot

Pour into saucepan and cook,
  stirring constantly until
  sauce thickens. Stir in
2 Tbsps. Apple Concentrate

Sweet Sauce for Fruits, Puddings

1 cup Milk
2 Tbsps. Rice Polishings
1 Tbsp. Whey Powder
1 Tbsp. Soy Milk Powder
1/2 tsp. Vegetable Seasoning
Dash of Pure Vanilla
(H) speed
Blend smooth, heat over boiling water, stirring till
  thick.
Add Honey to taste
1 Tbsp. Cream or Butter
  --stir in.

Honey-Maple Butter

½ cup Honey
⅓ cup Maple Syrup
½ cup Butter or Margarine

Blend on (M) speed until smooth. Can be used as a spread or sauce.
If nut flavor butter is desired, simply add ½ to 3/4 cup Pecans.

Blueberry Syrup

2 cups fresh Blueberries, or frozen berries, thawed
2 tbsp. Honey
½ cup Water
1 dash Sea Salt, or 1 tbsp. Lemon Juice

Put all in blender and blend on (H) speed until smooth. Pour into
saucepan and heat, just to boiling point, stirring constantly.
Boil and stir constantly for 5 minutes. Serve warm or cold over
any desired dessert or waffles.

Cake Topping a la Whip Cream

½ tsp. unflavored Gelatin
2 tbsp. cold Water
1 cup icy cold Whipping Cream
2 tbsp. Honey
1 tsp. Lemon Juice
1 tsp. gratted Lemon Rind

Stir Gelatin into cold Water, add 2 tbsp. Cream and mix well.
Place over boiling water until Gelatin dissolved thoroughly.
Pour this Gelatin mixture into blender container and add Honey,
Lemon Juice, and Lemon Rind. Blend on (H) speed until well
blended. Put in bowl and let set until mixture looks like egg
whites. Now, whip remainder of Cream in blender on (L) speed.
Fold whipped cream into Gelatin mixture. Serve as topping for
cakes or serve with gelatin salads or desserts.

Blender Whipped Cream

Put 1 cup chilled whip cream into blender container. Run on (L).
Be careful not to overwhip which could result in butter. Add liquid
Honey and a little Vanilla. Do not make more than 2 cups at a time.
  Flavor may be varied by adding Mint flavoring, a few drops of
chlorophyl coloring. Or for Lemon flavor, add: 1 tbsp. Lemon
with a little rind,1 tbsp. Honey and run at (L) speed.

PUDDINGS

Many of these rich starch puddings can sometimes take the place of a main starch at mealtime.

Steamed Date Pudding

(L)
Tear whole-grain bread into coarse pieces and blend a slice at a time (empty each time) to get 2 cups crumbs --not too fine.   Add:

1-1/2 tsp. Baking Powder
1/3 cup blender-chopped Nuts

1/4 cup Milk   )
2 Eggs   )
1/2 tsp. Vegetable Seasoning)
1/3 cup Raw Sugar   )
2 Tbsps. Soft Butter   )
1 tsp. Pure Vanilla   )
3/4 cup Dates, softened in   )
   juice or Honey Water   )
   (M)
Blend until smooth and add to crumbs and nuts.   Turn into well greased pan or pudding mold, cover tightly and steam 2-1/2 hours.   Let stand in mold several minutes and turn out.   Slice and serve with a lemon sauce. 4-6 servings

Fig Pudding

Blend and bake in a pudding pan in a moderate oven

1 cup Whole Wheat Bread Crumbs
   --blender made (⌐) speed
1 cup Milk
1 cup softened Figs, roughly chopped
1 Egg

To serve with pudding, whip on low speed:
3/4 cup Cream with 1/4 cup Honey
   5-6 servings

Sweet Potato Dessert

1 cup diced raw Sweet Potatoes
1/3 cup Milk
1/2 cup Melted Butter
3 Eggs
3/4 cup Molasses
1/2 tsp. Vegetable Seasoning
1/2 tsp. Nutmeg

Blend high for a few seconds, then gradually add, with liquefier running

2-1/2 cups diced raw Sweet Potatoes

If necessary, very carefully stir mixture while it is blending with a rubber spatula.   Stir in

1/2 cup Walnut pieces
1/2 cup soaked Raisins

Pour into a buttered baking dish.   Bake at 325° for 1-1/2 hours.   Serve hot with whipped cream.
   5-6 servings

Rice and Date Pudding

Blend until dates are just broken: (L)

3 cups warm Milk
3 Eggs
3 Tbsps. Honey
1/2 cup pitted Dates

Add and blend for 1 or 2 seconds (M)

1 cup cooked Brown Rice

Pour into custard cups and bake in pan of hot water gently till set.   Use Raisins instead of dates if desired.   5-6 servings

Apple Pudding

Sift together:

2 cups Whole Wheat Flour
1 tsp. Baking Powder
1/2 tsp. Soda
1/2 tsp. Vegetable Seasoning

Add:

1/4 cup unsalted Pecans

Blend (M)

4 Tbsps. Sour Milk
2 Eggs
1/2 cup Vegetable Oil
1 tsp. Pure Vanilla
1 cup Raw Sugar
1 cup diced, whole Apples

Add to first mixture. Bake
30 minutes at 375º in 2
8" layer pans. Serve with
pudding sauce or whipped
cream.
6-8 **serv**ings

Hawaiian Pudding

Grate fresh Coconut in blender
to make 6 cups grated Coconut.
Add:

3 cups Hot Milk and Coconut
Water

Place in cheesecloth and squeeze
all the liquid out. Keep liquid,
discard coconut (for use elsewhere).

Blend till smooth: (M)

1 cup Coconut Liquid
6 Tbsps. Arrowroot
6 Tbsps. Raw Sugar

Pour into saucepan, add rest
of coconut liquid, and cook
until thick. Pour into 8"
square pan and chill till firm.
Cut into squares and serve.

Pure Vanilla, Cherry or Grape
Concentrate may be used for
flavoring. Pureed fruit can
be added before setting.

A creamy pudding can be made
by using only 3 Tbsps. Arrowroot. 5-6 servings

PROTEIN PUDDING DESSERTS

Nut Honey Dessert

Chop finely in blender 1 cup
Nuts. Mix together thoroughly with 1 Tbsp. Honey. (L)

Cover with whipped cream and
garnish with half a nut meat.
(Protein dessert or breakfast
dish.)

Fruit Cottage Cheese Mix

1 cup Wheat Germ
4 Tbsps. Raw Sugar
1/2 cup Cottage Cheese
3/4 cup Favorite Fruit
1 Tbsp. Lemon Juice

Put all ingredients into blender,
emulsify and serve cold. Very
good for breakfast. (M)

3-4 servings

Orange-Nut Cup

cups Yogurt
Egg Yolks
/2 cup finely grated Carrot
Honey to taste
(M) speed
Blend creamy. Chill, serve
in dainty sundae dishes.

Orange sections, Nuts,
--blender grated

prinkle generously with
nuts and garnish with orange
sections.   4-5 servings

Avocado Boats

2 Avocados, halved
1 cup Cottage Cheese
1/3 cup Yogurt
Cherry Concentrate to tint
(M) speed
Blend smooth. Chill.
Fill avocado halves with
cheese-yogurt mixture. Garnish with blender-grated
coconut.   4-5 servings

WHIPS

Coffee Taste Whip

-1/2 cups Milk
/2 cup very strong Dandelion
Root Coffee   (see page 93)
Eggs
Tbsps. Rice Polishings
Tbsps. Soy Milk Powder
Tbsp. Arrowroot
Tbsps. Whey Powder
tsp. Vegetable Seasoning
(H) speed
Blend very thoroughly in
liquefier. Pour into
double boiler and cook over
gentle heat until thick,
stirring. Add:

Tbsps. Butter
Tbsps. Honey
-1/2 tsps. Pure Vanilla
     4-5 servings
Chill.

Mocha Pudding Whip

1-1/2 cups Milk
1/2 cup very strong Dandelion
  Root Coffee *
2 Eggs
2 Tbsps. Rice Polishings
2 Tbsps. Soy Milk Powder
2 Tbsps. Carob Powder
2 Tbsps. Whey Powder
1 tsp. Vegetable Seasoning
(H) speed
Blend very thoroughly in liquefier. Pour into double boiler
  and cook over gentle heat until
  thick, stirring. Add:

2 Tbsps. Butter
3 Tbsps. Honey
1-1/2 tsps. Vanilla

Chill.   4-5 servings

"Mock-Choc" Whip

2 cups Milk
2 Eggs
2 Tbsps. Rice Polishings
2 Tbsps. Soy Milk Powder
3 Tbsps. Carob Powder
2 Tbsps. Whey Powder
1 tsp. Vegetable Seasoning
(H)

Blend very thoroughly in
liquefier. Pour into double
boiler and cook over gentle
heat until thick, stirring.
Add:

2 Tbsps. Butter
3 Tbsps. Honey
1-1/2 tsps. Pure Vanilla

Chill. 4-5 servings

Raspberry Cream Whip

2 cups Raspberries
1/2 cup Honey

Liquefy just to combine (H)

1 cup Cream--blender whipped
(L)
Fold in and freeze in refrigerator tray. Stir occasionally.
The same method can be used
for plums, pineapple, peaches,
etc. 3-4 servings

Make a date cream using 3/4
cup pitted dates and 3/4 cup
Applesauce as foundation.
Dates with freshly grated
coconut is also nice.

Persimmon Whip

Liquefy whole, washed persimmons
in a little goat or soy milk to desired consistency. No sweetening
needed. Sour or whipped cream may
be folded in if so desired. Delicious.

Almond Cream Apple Whip

4 Apples, roughly chopped
Honey to sweeten
1/2 cup Milk
1 tsp. Almond Butter
(M)
Blend until smooth above ingredients. Fold in

1 cup Cream--blender whipped (L)
Chill. 4-5 servings

Fresh Fig Whip

2 cups sliced fresh Figs

Blend smooth, adding Honey,
if desired. (M)

1 cup blender-whipped Cream

Fold in. Serve in dainty sundae
dishes, topped with blender-
chopped nuts. 4-5 servings

Raisin Whip

2 cups soaked Raisins, with
juice
Dash of Nutmeg or Cinnamon

Blend smooth. (M)

1 cup blender-whipped Cream

Fold in. Serve in attractive
dishes, garnishing with
grated coconut. 5-6 servings

Papaya Whip

Choose very ripe Papaya. Blend
thoroughly to liquefy. Blend in
equal quantity of Sour Cream. (L)
Top with Strawberry.

Golden Sunset Apricot Dessert

2 cups revived Apricots (see page 22)
1-¼ cups Milk
2 tbsp. Lemon Juice
2 tbsp. Honey
2 Egg Whites
6 Apricot Halves, for garnishing

Put revived Apricots into blender. Add Milk, Lemon and Honey.
Blend on (H) until smooth. Beat Eggs in separate large bowl.
A little Honey can be added to Egg Whites if desired. When
Egg Whites are beaten sufficiently, peaks form, gradually add
the mixture from blender. Chill and serve with Apricot Halves,
if desired. 5-6 servings

Lime Avocado Fluff

½ cup Lime concentrate (thawed)
2 Tbsp. boiling water
1 tbsp. Unflavored Gelatin
2 tbsps. Honey
1 tbsp. Lecithin Liquid or Granules.
2 Avocados, ripe, peeled and cut in pieces
   about 1" size,
1 cup Whipping Cream
Heat Limeade almost to boiling point. Put in blender with
gelatin. Blend at (L) speed until gelatin is well dissolved.
Add honey and avocados. Blend on (H) speed until very smooth.
Cool. Fold whipped cream into this mixture. (Make whipped
cream in blender, using (L) speed and being careful not to
whip too long or mixture might turn into butter. Spoon into
serving dishes and top with date if desired.(4-5 servings)

Apricot Whip

2 cups fresh mashed or
  revived Dried Apricots *
A little Honey
A little Almond Extract

Blend until smooth. (H)

2 cups Heavy Cream, whipped

Fold in. Spoon into glasses
  and top with a red grape or
  cherry. Use the same method
  with prunes, peaches, nectarines, dates, bananas, etc.

Nuts may be added for last 10
  seconds of blending, so they
  are chopped only, not ground.
  For an apple whip, use raw
  applesauce. Decorate with
  nuts. 6-8 servings

Banana Whip

1 cup Pineapple Juice
1 Tbsp. Cashews
1 Tbsp. Raisins
1/2 Apple, diced
  (H)
Blend in liquefier until fine.
  With motor running, remove
  lid and add:

2 ripe Bananas, sliced

When whipped sufficiently,
  pour into dainty sundae dishes,
  top with whipped cream and
  serve immediately.
        5-6 servings

CUSTARDS, SOUFFLES, ETC.

Plain Custard

1 cup Milk
2 Tbsps. Honey
1 tsp. Pure Vanilla
1 Egg
1/2 tsp. Cinnamon or
  1/2 tsp. Nutmeg

Two Egg Yolks may be substituted
  for 1 Egg for a smoother, finer
  grained custard, which is better
  for you.
  (M) speed
Place first 4 ingredients in liquefier and blend 3 seconds. Pour
  into greased dish, sprinkle spice
  on, and set in a pan of hot water
  to bake--300° F for 25 minutes
  to 30 minutes, or until set.
        3-4 servings

Apple Custard

3/4 cup Hot Milk
1 Egg
1 Tbsp. Honey
1/3 cup raw diced unpeeled
  Apples
(M)
Place all ingredients, except
  the egg in the container. Blend
  about 1 minute. Add egg and
  blend a few seconds. Pour into
  3 greased custard cups. Put in
  a pan of hot water. Bake in a
  moderate oven, 325° F. for
  about 20 minutes.

For variation, try the same
  recipe with peaches, cherries,
  strawberries, revived dried
  fruits, cottage cheese, or
  pumpkin (cooked or finely grated
  raw) in place of apples.

* See recipe Page 51

Apricot Blancmange

1-1/2 cups Milk or Soy Milk
2 tsps. Raw Sugar
Thin slice Orange rind
Pinch Vegetable Seasoning
3 Tbsps. Arrowroot
1-1/2 cups Apricots, dried,
  revived   (see page 22)

Put 1 cup milk on to heat; remaining 1/2 cup in liquefier
with sugar, vegetable seasoning,
rind and arrowroot. Blend to
shred rind. Pour hot milk in
and blend. Return to saucepan
and heat, stirring until thick.
Puree apricots, add arrowroot
mixture, and whip together.
Pour into a dish and put in
cool place to set. Serve garnished with chopped nuts, a
sprinkle of spice, or a dab
of yogurt. (If more sweetening is desired, add honey.)
                    4-5 servings
Variations: Replace apricots
and orange rind with raw apple
liquefied with a little cinnamon;
bananas and nutmeg; pureed
prune; try apple concentrate
or cherry concentrate for
flavoring in a plain arrowroot
blancmange.

Tangy Dessert

1/3 cup Lemon Juice
2 Tbsps. Honey
2 medium sized Beets, diced
1 small Apple, diced
1-1/2 tsps. Vegetable Seasoning
3/4 tsp. Dulse Powder
  (L) speed
Blend till very smooth, often
stopping to scrape down sides.

3/4 cup Yogurt--stir in. Chill.
Serve in dainty sundae dishes, garnishing with rosettes of cream.
                    4-5 servings

"Mock-Choc" Souffle

Prepare in blender and set aside

1/2 cup fine Whole Wheat Bread
  Crumbs   (L)
  (Use toasted bread.)

Place in container:

3/4 cup Milk
2 Tbsps. Arrowroot
2 Tbsps. Soft Butter
5 Egg Yolks
2 squares Carob Chocolate,
  cut in pieces.
1/2 cup Raw Sugar
  (M)
Blend until smooth and pour
  into saucepan. Cook and
  stir until thickened and
  smooth, over moderate
  heat or in top of double
  boiler.

Cool and add:

Reserved crumbs
1 tsp. Pure Vanilla

Fold above mixture into:

5 Egg Whites beaten stiff with

1/4 tsp. Vegetable Seasoning
1/2 tsp. Cream of Tartar

Bake in greased casserole which
  has been set in pan of hot
  water for 1-1/4 to 1-1/2
  hours at 300° F. Serve hot
  with plain or whipped cream
  or custard sauce. 6-8 servings

Apricot Bavarian Cream

1 cup Apricots or revived dried
   Apricots (see page 22)
2 cups Apricot or other juice
  (M)

1 tsp. Lemon Juice
2 Egg Yolks
1/2 cup Raw Sugar

Blend till apricots are completely broken up. Bring mixture up
to boil. Meanwhile soak:

1-1/2 Tbsp. Plain Gelatin in
1/2 cup Cold Water

Add to hot apricots and stir in well. Chill until mixture begins to
thicken, fold in:

2 Egg Whites, stiffly beaten
1-1/2 cups blender-whipped cream

Pour into mold and chill till firm. 4-5 servings

MOLDED DESSERTS

Agar Agar

Blend (L) speed
2 Tbsps. Agar Agar
1/4 cup Cold Water
Add
1/2 cup Boiling Water

Bring to boil, stirring for 1
  minute to dissolve agar. Add

2 cups pure fruit juice
Honey, if desired

Sets very quickly without
  refrigeration. 4-5 servings

Juices may be: orangĕ or
  grapefruit, lemon, blackberry, canned pineapple; or
  try apple, cherry or grape
concentrates diluted.

Apricot Gelatin

Use basic Agar recipe, but use
  1 cup fruit juice with 1-1/2
  cups apricot pulp from fresh
  apricots or revived dried
  apricots. Set.

Apricot Gelatin Fluff

When above jelly has begun to
  set, fold in a stiffly beaten
  egg white.

Pineapple Gelatin

(Using basic Agar Recipe above)

When pineapple gelatin has set
  return to liquefier and whip;
  reset.

216

Pineapple Gelatin Fluff

To plain pineapple after
   beginning to set, fold in stiffly
   beaten egg whites.

Lime Foam

1 package lime flavored health
   gelatin
1/2 cup hot canned Pineapple
   Juice, unsweetened

Blend on high speed for 20
   seconds. Add:

2 cups crushed ice. Blend for
   30 seconds. Pour into mold
   and chill till firm.
            3-4 servings

Nut Gelatin Ring

2 tsps. plain Gelatin dissolved
   in 1 Tbsp. cold water

Melt over boiling water.

1 cup Pineapple with juice,
   canned, unsweetened
1 cup Nuts
1 Tbsp. Maple Syrup

Place all ingredients in blender
   and run until nuts are chopped.
   (M) speed
1 cup Cream, blender-whipped,
   fold in. (L)

Pour into wet ring mold. Chill.
   Unmold and fill center with
   fresh berries.   6-8 servings

Quick Health Gelatin

1 package flavored Health
   Gelatin
1/2 cup Boiling Water

Blend on high speed for 6
   seconds. Add:

1-1/2 cups crushed ice. Blend
   for 30 seconds. Pour into
   a ring mold and chill for 5
   minutes.   3-4 servings

"Mock-Choc " Gelatin

1 Tbsp. Carob Powder
1 Tbsp. Rice Polishings
2 Tbsps. Whey Powder
2 Tbsps. Honey
1/2 tsp. Pure Vanilla

Soften in 1 Tbsp. Cold Water
2 tsps. Gelatin

1 cup boiling Mint Tea--add to
   Gelatin and dissolve.
   (H) speed
Gradually add to other ingredients
   and blend thoroughly till light
   and smooth. Set in refrigerator.
   When serving, garnish with
   grated nuts (prepared in liquefier) and blender-whipped
   cream.   3-4 servings

"Tri" Fruit Gelatin

1-½ tbsp. Clear Gelatin
½ cup hot Water

Blend until Gelatin is well dissolved, using (L) speed.
Then add the following:

2 tbsp. Honey
1 cup fresh Peaches, or frozen Peaches, thawed
1 cup Pears
1 cup chilled Pineapple Juice

Blend all together until smooth, using (H) speed. Put in mold
to "set". Serve topped with a little Whipped Cream and a Date.

4-5 servings

HEALTH PIES

For some pie fillings, crumb crusts are perfect. Graham crackers are probably the most popular. Try a nut crust, but be sure to use a filling that has a firm texture and holds its shape.

For Cracker Crumbs: While blender is running, remove cap and gradually add 8 graham crackers at a time. You may need to flick motor on and off quickly a few times. Repeat for larger quantities.

Quick Pie Crusts

Graham Cracker Crust

16 to 18 Graham Crackers, blender-crushed
1/2 cup Melted Butter
3 Tbsps. Raw Sugar
1/2 tsp. Cinnamon (optional)

Combine ingredients and pack firmly over bottom and sides of 9-inch pie pan.

Nut Crust   (Do not Bake)

1 cup blender-ground Pecans, Walnuts, Black Walnuts or Brazil Nuts
3 Tbsps. Raw Sugar

Combine and press over bottom and sides of pie plate. This crust clings to the filling but doesn't hold its own shape very well. Best with cream fillings.

Cooky Crumb Crust

1-1/4 cups blender-crushed cookies (whole grain health cookies) (L) speed
1/3 cup Melted Butter

Combine crumbs and butter, and pack firmly over bottom and sides of 9-inch pie pan. Keep out a few crumbs to sprinkle over the top of the
(Cont'd.)

Cooky Crumb Crust (Cont'd.)

pie if you like. Chill crust. Don't bake it. If desired, use crumbs only for the bottom of the pie and stand whole cookies up around the rim.

Quick Lemon Pie or Lemon Dessert

1/3 cup Cold Water
1 Tbsp. Plain Gelatin

Soften the gelatin in the water, then dissolve over hot water. Place in blender with:

1/2 large Peeled Lemon, cut in pieces
All outer peel without bitter white part
4 Egg Yolks
1/2 cup Honey or Raw Sugar
(H) speed
Blend smooth. Chill until thick, not stiff.

4 Egg Whites, beaten stiff
1/2 cup Raw Sugar

Fold together, then fold into thickened lemon custard. Turn into crumb crust and freeze until firm.

For a change, serve as a dessert without crust--no need to freeze.

Quick Cheese Pie

Graham Cracker Crust:
  Crumble Graham Crackers
in the blender, five at a time.
Use a total of 16. Empty into bowl and stir in

1/2 cup Raw Sugar
1/2 tsp. Cinnamon
1/4 cup Melted Butter

Press into 8-inch pie plate.

Filling:

Place in the blender

2 envelopes Plain Gelatin
A few thin strips Lemon Peel
Juice of 1/2 Lemon
1/2 cup Hot Milk
  (M) speed
Blend for 40 seconds. Turn off
  motor and add:

1/4 cup Raw Sugar
2 Eggs
8 oz. Cream Cheese
  (L) speed
Blend for 10 seconds and without stopping motor add

1 cup cracked ice
1 cup Raw Cream

Pour immediately into Graham
  Cracker crust. Let set for
  5 minutes before serving.
  May be garnished nicely
  with fruit.

Whipped Prune Pie

Place in the blender:

1/4 cup Orange Juice
1 tsp. Lemon Juice
Small piece Lemon Rind (Cont'd.)

* See recipe Page 42.

Whipped Prune Pie (Cont'd.)

Begin blending and add gradually

1 lb. pitted, Revived Prunes (see
(M)   page 22)
When blended smooth, add:

1 cup Walnuts or Pecans. Blend
  just a few seconds to chop. Pour
  in mixing bowl and stir in

1/2 cup Raw Sugar
1/2 tsp. Vegetable Seasoning

Fold in stiffly beaten whites of
  2 Eggs. Pour into baked
  9-inch pie shell and bake at
  325° F. for 30 minutes. When
  cool you may top with whipped
cream flavored with Pure Almond
Extract.

Pumpkin or Squash Pie

Piece of Outer Orange Peel
1/2 cup Milk
(M) speed
Blend fine. Add

3/4 cup Raw Sugar
1 tsp. Cinnamon
1 tsp. Nutmeg
1/2 tsp. Vegetable Seasoning
1/2 tsp. Ginger
3 Eggs
1 cup Milk, or milk and cream,
  or Sesame Milk

Add gradually with blender running 1-1/2 cups cooked pumpkin
  or squash. Blend till smooth. (M)
  Pour into whole wheat pastry
  pie shell. Bake at 450° F. for
  10 minutes, then reduce heat
  to 350° F. and bake for 30
  minutes more, or until firm.

Cherry Taste Cheese Pie

Put in blender container and liquefy

2 Eggs
1 tsp. Lemon Juice
1 tsp. grated Lemon Rind
3/4 cup Raw Sugar
4 Tbsps. Cherry Concentrate
(M)

Add and blend until velvety smooth

8 oz. Health Cream Cheese

Pour into Graham Cracker Crust

Crust:

12 to 14 crackers finely crumbled
   in liquefier. (L)

Combine with 1/4 cup Melted
   Butter. Bake in 9-inch pie
   pan in moderate oven, 350°,
   25 to 30 minutes. Remove
   from oven and cool for 5
   minutes.

Topping:

Blend 2 cups Sour Cream
3-1/2 Tbsps. Raw Sugar
2 tsps. Pure Vanilla (L)

Pour over pie. Refrigerate
   for 5 hours. Serves 10 to
   12.

Orange Coconut Pie

1 Tbsp. Plain Gelatin
1/4 cup Milk

Soften the gelatin in the milk,
   then dissolve over hot water.
   Put in blender. Add:
   (M)
2 Egg Yolks
1/2 cup Orange Juice
   (Cont'd.)

Orange Coconut Pie
(Cont'd.)

1/3 cup Raw Sugar or Honey
1 cup more Milk
2 Tbsps. Lemon Juice
1 small strip Lemon Rind
Outer rind from 1/2 Orange
1/4 tsp. Sea Salt
(M)

Blend until rinds are cut fine.
   Pour into saucepan and cook
   on low heat or over hot water,
   stirring constantly until thick.
   Cool, then chill until slightly
   thickened. Make meringue of

2 Egg Whites
1/4 cup Raw Sugar

Fold in. Pour into baked whole
   wheat pie shell or graham
   cracker crust. Sprinkle with

1/3 cup Shredded Coconut

Chill until firm.

Date Custard Pie

1 cup Hot Milk
1 cup Pitted Dates (soaked)
   (M)
Blend smooth. Add:

1-1/4 cups more Milk
1/8 tsp. Nutmeg
Dash of Sea Salt
2 Eggs

Blend briefly and pour into whole
   wheat pastry-lined pie pan.
   Bake in hot oven, 450° F., for
   10 minutes, then at 350° F for
   25 minutes longer

Cream of Coconut Pie

4 Eggs	7 Tbsps. Arrowroot
1/2 cup Raw Sugar	1 cup Coconut--blender shredded
1 cup Milk	1/4 tsp. Sea Salt
(M)	

Blend a good quarter of a minute, then pour into saucepan with

1 cup additional Milk. Cook, stirring constantly, over gentle heat until thickened and quite stiff. Remove from heat and add

1 Tbsp. Honey
1 tsp. Pure Vanilla
2 Tbsps. Butter

Cool and spread in baked whole-grain pastry-lined pan. Chill and top with 1 cup heavy cream, blender whipped.

CAKES AND COOKIES

If on occasion you feel you must indulge in cakes or cookies, choose the most natural ingredients and the most natural way of preparing them. (See instructions in section on Bread). Do not have them with acid fruits or proteins, but eat them with foods compatible with carbohydrates.

You can save considerable time in preparation by blending the liquids, fats, eggs and sugar and stirring them into the dry ingredients. Keep a rubber spatula handy for scraping the sides when necessary. Have ingredients at room temperature and the butter soft.

Fats and oils should be used sparingly. It is important that they be the cold-pressed oils, highest in unsaturated fatty acids, safflower being the highest in linoleic acid content. It is best to avoid the heated fats.

Flavorings should be natural. Use vanilla that is alcohol-free; nut flavorings, such as almond or black walnut. Carob powder is versatile and should be used instead of cocoa, and carob chocolate can be used instead of ordinary chocolate, which harms the body. Buy fresh coconut, but store it in the refrigerator and use quickly, as it is very perishable. Use fruit juice concentrates, such as apple, cherry or grape (available in Hidden Valley Brand Products).

For sweetening, use dates, date sugar, pure maple syrup, unsulphured molasses, raw sugar or honey. (Note: it is better to use raw sugar in cooking as honey is altered by the heat processes.)

CAKES

Date Torte

Place in blender container
(Ⓜ)
1 cup Warm Water
1 Tbsp. Butter
2 Eggs
1 cup Raw Sugar
1 cup Dates

Blend until smooth and add:

1 cup Nuts

Blend just a second or two to
chop nuts. Sift into bowl:

1 tsp. Soda
1 cup sifted Whole Wheat Flour

Fold in blended mixture. Turn
into wax-paper-lined, greased
pan. Bake in slow oven, 300°
F., for 45 to 55 minutes. Cut
into squares when cool and
serve with whipped cream or
whipped soy cream.
6-8 servings

Carrot Torte a la Hidden Valley

Beat until very thick and light:

6 Egg Yolks
1 cup Raw Sugar

1 cup very finely ground Raw
Carrot
1 cup finely ground Walnuts
(blender-prepared)
1/4 cup dry Whole Wheat Bread
Crumbs, blender-ground
1 tsp. Cinnamon
1 tsp. Lemon Rind

Add above ingredients to eggs
and sugar and beat till well
blended.   (Cont'd.)

Carrot Torte a la Hidden Valley
(Cont'd.)
3/4 cup Sultanas--stir in
6 Egg Whites, beaten stiff but
not dry--fold in.

Pour batter into 9" tube pan
prepared by greasing and
shaking with breadcrumbs.

Bake at 325° F for about 50
minutes or until just baked.
Invert pan until cake is cool,
then remove. 10-12 servings

Mock-Choc Cake

1 cup Milk
1-1/2 cups old-fashioned Brown
Sugar
3 Eggs
1 tsp. Vegetable Seasoning
1 tsp. Pure Vanilla
(Ⓜ) speed
Begin blending, and with motor
running, add:

3/4 cup Soft Butter--blend smooth

2-1/2 cups sifted Whole Wheat
Flour
3 Tbsps. Carob Powder
2-1/2 tsps. Baking Powder
1/2 tsp. Baking Soda

Sift together. Add liquid ingredients and beat a little to mix
well.

Divide evenly into 2 greased 9"
cake pans. Put in a 350° F.
oven and bake for 30 minutes.

Devonshire Cheesecake

5 double Graham Crackers
--blender crumble with:
1 Tbsp. Raw Sugar
2 Tbsps. Butter, melted. Stir
  into crumbs.

Press firmly against the bottom
  of a 1-1/2 qt. oblong casserole
  and bake in a 300° F. oven for
  8 to 10 minutes, or until
  lightly toasted. Cool thoroughly.

Blend until very smooth: (M)

4 Eggs
1/4 cup Yogurt
10 oz. Cottage Cheese
4 oz. Sour Cream
1-1/2 Tbsps. Lemon Juice
1 tsp. Pure Vanilla

1/2 cup Raw Sugar--add and
  blend to mix.

Pour into prepared crust and
  bake the cake in a moderate
  oven, 350° F., for about 40
  minutes to set filling. Cool
  thoroughly before chilling
  overnight.

Just prior to serving, spread with

1 cup heavy Sour Cream)
1 Tbsp. Honey   ) Mixed

Sweet strawberries or orange
sections in orange juice should
accompany cheesecake.

Orange-Date Loaf

Sift together in a bowl

2 cups Whole Wheat Flour
1-1/2 tsps. Baking Powder
            (Cont'd.)

Orange-Date Loaf (Cont'd.)

1/2 tsp. Baking Soda

Place in blender container

1/2 cup Strawberry Tea
2/3 cup Dates

With blender at high speed, drop
  in, a piece at a time:

1 Orange, seeded

Then add and continue to blend:

1 Egg
2 Tbsps. Soy Oil
1/2 tsp. Vegetable Seasoning
3/4 cup Raw Sugar

Add and blend briefly: (L)

1/2 cup Nut Meats

Turn off the motor as soon as
  the nuts are drawn into the
  blades. Pour this mixture
  over dry ingredients and mix
  together gently. Turn into an
  oiled pan, 9-1/2" x 5-1/2",
  and bake in 350° oven for one
  hour.

Apricot-Date Filling for Cakes or Pies

1/2 cup Dried Prunes, pitted,
  (revived)
1/2 cup Dried Apricots, (revived)
1/2 cup Raisins
1/2 cup Crushed Unsweetened
  Pineapple with Juice
2 thin strips Orange Peel
  (M)

Blend to grate the peel. At last
minute add:

1/4 cup Walnuts--blend just to
chop.

Natural Fruit Cake

3/4 cup Nuts--rough grind in
    blender   (L) speed
25 Graham Cracker Crumbs
    --make in blender. Place
    together in bowl.

Blend briefly and add to in-
    gredients in bowl:
    (M)
6 Graham Crackers
1/2 cup soft Pitted Dates
1/2 cup Dried Apricots (re-
    vived)

Blend following briefly and add
    to other ingredients in bowl:
    (M)
1/4 cup soft Butter
1/4 cup Raw Sugar
2 Tbsps. Honey
1/2 cup Health Marmalade
1/2 tsp. Cinnamon
1/2 tsp. Vegetable Seasoning
1/8 tsp. Ground Cloves

Stir in following and mix
    thoroughly:

1/2 cup Raisins
1/4 cup Diced Citron
1/4 cup Candied Cherries
1 tsp. Pure Vanilla

Pack into mold and refriger-
    ate a day or two before cut-
    ting for service.

Applesauce Cake

Sift into mixing bowl:

2 cups sifted Whole Wheat Flour
1 tsp. Cinnamon
1/2 tsp. Cloves
2 tsps. Baking Powder
1/4 tsp. Vegetable Seasoning
        (Cont'd.)

Applesauce Cake (Cont'd.)

Into blender container put:

1/2 cup Shortening
1 cup Old fashioned Brown Sugar
1 Egg
1 tsp. Pure Vanilla
1-1/2 cups Applesauce

Cover and blend on high speed,
    Add: 1 cup Raisins
Blend for 15 seconds. Combine
    with dry ingredients. Turn into
    greased 8-inch square pan and
    bake in a preheated 350° oven for
    40 minutes.

Pecan Topping

1 cup Pecans
1/2 cup Brown Sugar
4 Tbsps. Melted Butter
2 Tbsps.   Milk

(M) speed
Blend a few seconds. Spread
on top of cake and place under
broiler heat for 3 to 4 minutes
until brown.

Spice-Nut Cake

1/2 cup Soft Shortening   )
1 cup Clabber Milk or Buttermilk   )   Blend Smooth.
2 Eggs   )
1-1/4 cups Old-Fashioned Brown Sugar)   (M)

2 cups sifted Whole Wheat Flour)
1 tsp. Baking Soda   )
1/2 tsp. Vegetable Seasoning   )
1 tsp. Cloves   )   Sift into a bowl.
1 tsp. Cinnamon   )
1 tsp Nutmeg   )
1 tsp. Allspice   )

Add: 3/4 cup blender-chopped Nuts.(L) speed

Pour blended liquid over dry ingredients and mix thoroughly. Spread
in 2 greased floured layer pans and place in an oven heated to 350°
F. for 25 to 30 minutes.

Pan may be wax paper lined if you feel the cake may stick.

COOKIES

Banana Cookies

Into blender container put:

3/4 cup Soft Butter
1 cup Raw Sugar
1 Egg
 (M)
Blend until fluffy. Add:

2 large Bananas--blend until
 bananas are whipped then
 add:

1/2 cup Pecans or Walnuts

Blend until nuts are chopped.
 (M)
Sift together in a mixing bowl:

1-1/4 cups Whole Wheat Flour

(Cont'd.)

(Cont'd.)

1 tsp. Vegetable Seasoning
1/2 tsp. Soda
1/4 tsp. Nutmeg
3/4 tsp. Cinnamon

Add:

1-3/4 cups Rolled Oats

Pour liquids into dry ingredients
 and stir until smooth. Drop
 by teaspoonsful, about 1-1/2
 inches apart, on to ungreased
 cooky sheet. Bake at 400° F.
 for 15 minutes or until done.
       3-4 dozen

olden Carrot Cookies

/2 cup Sour Milk
Eggs
/3 cup Soft Butter
cup Raw Sugar
tsp. Pure Vanilla
M)
lend until mixed. Sift into
mixing bowl the following:

-3/4 cups Whole Wheat Flour
tsp. Baking Powder
/2 tsp. Soda
/2 tsp. Vegetable Seasoning
tsp. Cinnamon
/4 tsp. Nutmeg
/4 tsp. Cloves

dd:

cups Rolled Oats
cup Raw Carrots--blender-
grated
/2 cup blender-chopped Nuts

:ir liquids into dry ingredients,
mixing carefully. Drop in
small balls from the tip of
a spoon on to greased cooky
sheet. Bake at 400° F. for 12
to 15 minutes. Makes about 5 dozen

innamon Cookies

Eggs
/3 cup Sour Cream
/2 cup Soft Butter
-1/2 cups Raw Sugar
M)
lend above until thoroughly
mixed. Sift and add:

cups sifted Whole Wheat Flour
tsp. Baking Soda
tsps. Cinnamon

cup Nuts--coarsely blender-
chopped   (Cont'd.)

Cinnamon Cookies (Cont'd.)

1 cup Raisins

Add blended mixture and mix
   well. Drop in teaspoonsful
   on an ungreased baking sheet.
   Bake 18-20 minutes in a 350°
   F. oven. Makes about 5 dozen

Old-Fashioned Nut Cookies

3 cups Filberts-grind in blender
   and set aside.   (M)

2 Eggs
1 cup Raw Sugar
1 tsp. Vegetable Seasoning
1/2 tsp. Pure Vanilla
   (M)
Blend until thick and lemon
   colored. Add to nuts. Mix
   well. Chill thoroughly. Roll
   into small balls and place on
   a greased tray. Bake at
   325° F. for 15 minutes or
   until done. makes about 1½ dozen

HEALTH ICE CREAM AND SHERBETS

I believe that the commercial ice cream today is doing more harm
in this country than anything else, because of the unnatural ingredients from which it is made. Nearly all modern ice cream
has synthetic sweeteners, artificial flavorings and coloring, with
stabilizers added to prevent it from melting. As these ingredients
are not bio-chemical, they are harmful. There is no reason why
ice cream cannot be wholesome, if good materials are used. And
with the blender, you can make delicious healthful ice cream for
less than the cost of the commercial commodity. Your homemade
ice cream can also be made quickly and easily: a wonderful dessert
for company.

The secret of success is to use yogurt or cottage cheese, or both,
as a base; in fact, any kind of cheese. Try using a Jack cheese and
see how all of the cheesy taste is eliminated. However, the dry
or Farmer's Type cottage cheese is best.

For sweeteners use only the natural sugars, such as date powder,
grape sugar, molasses, maple sugar, honey or raw sugar. Sweet
syrups, such as apple, cherry, or grape concentrates are also
good--or try a fig concentrate for a change. And for flavoring, use
natural fruits, which make the ideal flavoring agents.

Health ingredients, such as rice polishing, rice bran syrup, sunflower
seed meal, or wheat germ can be added without detection in the
finished dish. This is very good, especially for children.

Simple Ice Cream

1/2 cup Cottage Cheese
1/2 cup Cream
1/2 cup Yogurt
1 Tbsp. Grape Concentrate
Honey to sweeten
Chopped Nuts
 (M)
Blend. Freeze to "mush"
 stage; re-blend and freeze
 completely. 5-6 servings

Banana Ice Cream

1/2 cup Grape Juice
1/2 cup Cream
1/4 cup Soy Milk
2 Bananas, sliced
(M)
Begin blending, then add:

1/2 cup Cottage Cheese
1/4 cup Yogurt

Blend smooth. Freeze to
"mush" state, then re-blend
and freeze completely.
           5-6 servings

Vanilla-Fruit Ice Cream

1/2 cup Milk
1/2 cup Cream
1/2 cup Apples, sliced
6 Dates, cup up
1 Tbsp. Honey
1 tsp. Pure Vanilla
  (M)
Blend to pulverize apple and
  dates.   Add and blend:

1/2 cup Cottage Cheese

Freeze to "mush" stage. Re-
blend and freeze completely.
          4-5 servings

Apple Grape Ice Cream

1/2 cup thick Soy Milk
1/2 cup Cream
2 Tbsps. Apple Concentrate
1 dozen Grapes
2 oz. Jack Cheese, cubed

Blend to reduce grapes and
  cheese.   Add and blend
  smooth: (M)

1/2 cup Yogurt

Freeze to "mush" stage. Re-
blend and freeze completely.
            5-6 servings

Grape or Black Cherry Ice Cream

4 Tbsps. Nuts or Coconut, blender-
  grated. Set aside.

1 tsp. Gelatin) Dissolve.
1 Tbsp. Milk   )

Melt over boiling water.

1/2 cup Cottage Cheese
1/2 cup Sour Cream
1/2 cup Yogurt
 1 Tbsp. Grape or Black
 Cherry Concentrate (Cont 'd.)

Grape or Black Cherry Ice Cream
                              (Cont'd.)

Honey to sweeten
  (M)
Blend to smooth creaminess, then
  with blender still running add
  gelatin. Stir in nuts or coconut,
  pour into freezing tray.   When
  partially frozen, re-blend and
  freeze again. In fact, if this
  is repeated once or twice, a
  better texture is obtained.
            6-8 servings
Other suggested flavors:

Carrot Juice and Coconut
Carob or Soy Chocolate
Pineapple

Pumpkin Ice Cream

1/2 cup thick Sesame Milk
1 cup cooked Pumpkin
4 Tbsps. Honey
1/4 tsp. Cinnamon
1/4 tsp. Ginger
1/8 tsp. Sea Salt
1/2 cup Whipping Cream, stiffly
  beaten
  (H)
Place all ingredients except cream
  in blender. Blend thoroughly.
  Freeze until beginning to stiffen,
  then fold in cream. Freeze
  again, stirring once more if a
  smoother product is desired.
            5-6 servings
Date Ice Cream

1-1/2 cups Top Milk
15 - 20 Pitted Dates
  (H)
Blend until completely liquefied.
  Pour into freezer tray and half
  freeze. Beat again and re-freeze
  two or three times to insure
  smooth texture.   4-5 servings

Banana-Pineapple Ice Cream

1-1/2 cups Thin Cream
4-1/2 cups Yogurt
1 cup Crushed Fresh Pineapple
4 Bananas
1/2 cup Honey
1 cup Raw Sugar or Maple
  Syrup
1-1/2 tsp. Pure Vanilla
A little Lemon Juice
  (M)
Put all ingredients in blender
and run till smooth. Freeze.
                    10-12 servings

Pineapple Yogurt Ice Cream

1 cup unsweetened Pineapple
1 cup Yogurt
1 cup Thick Cream
  (M) speed
Beat smooth and creamy in
blender. Partially freeze.
Reblend. Repeat two or
three times before finally
freezing solid, as this gives
superior texture.

Variations: Replace pineapple
with your favorite fruit or
berry.

Mock-Choc" Ice Cream

1/2 cup Cream
2 tsp. Honey
1/4 cup Cottage Cheese
1/4 cup Yogurt
1 Banana
1/4 cup Carob Sauce
1/4 cup Soy Milk
1 tsp. Plain Gelatin
  (M)
Blend thoroughly, scraping
down sides of container
frequently. Pour into
freezer tray and freeze
to "mush" stage. Re-
blend and freeze completely.
                 6-8 servings

Quick Carob Sauce:

1 Tbsp. Carob Flour
1 Tbsp. Arrowroot
1 Tbsp. Raw Sugar
3 Tbsps. Water

Blend well.   (H)

Vanilla Ice Cream

1/3 cup Raw Sugar) Boil for
3 Tbsps. Water   ) 3 minutes.

4 Egg Yolks   ) Blend
1/4 tsp. Sea Salt   ) briefly
2 tsps. Pure Vanilla) (M)

With motor still running, gradually pour in hot syrup in a
steady stream.

Fold mixture into:

1-1/2 cup Heavy Cream, whipped

Freeze in refrigerator tray,
covered with waxed paper.
               5-6 servings

Variation: "Mock-Choc"

Replace vanilla with 1/2 cup
carob sauce.

Ice Cream Blancmange

1 cup Cream
1 cup Yogurt
2 Tbsps. Honey
1-1/2 tsps. Pure Vanilla
1 cup Cottage Cheese

2 tsps. Gelatin   ) Soften
1/4 cup Raw Milk)
  (M)
Blend well. Do not freeze--put
in refrigerator to set.
                8-10 servings

Regular Ice Cream I

1-3/4 cup Milk
2 Tbsps. Milk Powder or
   Soy Milk Powder
4 Egg Yolks
1/2 cup Raw Sugar
1/8 tsp. Sea Salt
   (M)
Blend to mix thoroughly.
   Cook over hot (not boiling water, stirring constantly, until the mixture
   coats the spoon. Strain
   through cheesecloth and
   cool. Add:

1 cup Heavy Cream)
1 tsp. Pure Vanilla)

Pour into freezing trays.
   For good texture it is
   necessary to re-blend
   the partially frozen ice
   cream at least twice before completing the process. 5-6 servings

Variations:

Instead of vanilla, use different fruit juice concentrates,
   such as grape, cherry and
   apple.

Any number of different fruits,
   blender-pulped, and nuts
   blender-chopped can be
   added.

Regular Ice Cream II

1-3/4 cups Milk
2 Tbsps. Milk Powder or
   Soy Milk Powder
3 tsps. Arrowroot
3/4 cup Raw Sugar
1/4 tsp. Sea Salt
2 Egg Yolks   (Cont'd.)
(M) speed

Regular Ice Cream II (Cont'd.)

Blend to mix ingredients. Cook
   over hot (not boiling) water,
   stirring constantly, until the
   mixture coats the spoon.
   Strain through cheesecloth and
   cool. Add:

4 cups Thin Cream
1-1/2 tsps. Vanilla

Pour into freezing trays and
   freeze, but for good texture
   it is necessary to re-blend
   the ice cream at least twice
   before it is completely frozen.
         12-14 servings

Banana Freeze

3 cups Water or favorite Herb
   Tea
6 rounded Tbsps. Whey Powder
3 tsps. Brewer's Yeast
1 tsp. Vegetable Seasoning
1/2 tsp. Dulse Powder
1/4 cup Honey--or to taste
3 ripe Bananas
1 Tbsp. Rice Polishings
(H) speed
Blend in liquefier until very
   smooth and creamy. Pour
   into freezing tray and freeze
   solid.   6-8 servings

Variations:

Chopped nuts may be added.
   "Revived" Dried Fruits may
   replace banana.
   Try other fresh fruits.
      * * * * * * * * * * * *
To freeze fruit, separate the very
ripe part and liquefy. Added liquid may not be necessary. Then
slice remainder of fruit and freeze
in this base. This gives extra
value and flavor. Can be used as a
breakfast fruit, in drinks, sauces
or salads.

Avocado Sherbet

3 strips Orange Rind
1/3 cup Lemon Juice
(M)
Blend to grate rind.

1-1/2 Avocados
1 cup Milk
Dash of Vegetable Seasoning
2/3 cup Honey or Raw Sugar
(M) speed
Add to orange and lemon and
blend until smooth. Pour
into refrigerator tray and
freeze, stirring once or
twice during freezing. This
is nice to serve on a fruit
plate, also for dessert.
5-6 servings

Apricot Sherbet

1/2 Tbsp. Gelatin }
4 Tbsps. Cold Water } Dissolve

When dissolved melt over
boiling water.

1 cup Milk or Light Cream
1/2 cup "Revived" Dried
Apricots   (see page 22)
1/3 cup Honey
(M) speed
Place in blender container,
add gelatin and blend about
1 minute. Pour into freezer
tray and freeze, stirring
occasionally. 5-6 servings

Orange Cream Sherbet

3 cups Orange Juice)
3 Tbsps. Lemon Juice)
1/2 cup Honey)   ) Blend
1/2 cup Water)
2 strips Orange Rind)
(Cont'd.))

Orange Cream Sherbet   (Cont'd.)

Freeze to "mush" stage. Return
to blender and add:

1 cup Light Cream

Beat into fruit mixture on low
speed. Return to freezer
tray. Finish freezing.
8-10 servings

Tangy Green Sherbet

1/4 cup Honey
1-1/2 cups Pineapple Juice,
unsweetened
1/2 package Lime Flavored
Health Gelatin
1 tsp. Lemon Juice
1 bunch Watercress (leaves only)

Dissolve gelatin in 1/2 cup of
pineapple juice which has been
heated. Cool. Place all ingredients in container and
blend thoroughly. Freeze in
refrigerator tray until mixture begins to stiffen.

1/2 cup Whipping Cream, whipped

Add to frozen mixture, stirring
slightly and freeze, stirring
once more, until stiff.
5-6 servings

Pineapple Yogurt Sherbet

1 cup Crushed, unsweetened, Pineapple with 1 cup Yogurt. Blend
to mix thoroughly. Pour into
freezing tray and partially freeze.
Re-blend. Freeze Solid.
5-6 servings
Variations: Replace pineapple with
different berries, fresh peaches,
etc., sliced; fruit juices or concentrates.

Supplement Candy

Blend to grind seeds: (H)

1/2 cup Honey
1/4 cup Sunflower Seeds
1 tsp. Vegetable Seasoning
1 tsp. Powdered Dulse

1/4 cup Wheat Germ
1/4 cup Flaxseed Meal

Combine ingredients in a bowl and mix in sufficient rice polishings to make a stiff paste. Chill. Shape into balls and roll in whey powder. Eat several a day to supplement nutrition.

"Mock-Choc" Nut Candy

1/2 cup Nuts--chop in blender. Set aside.
1/4 cup Sunflower Seeds--grind in blender (H)
1 tsp. Vegetable Seasoning
1 tsp. Dulse Powder   (Cont'd.)

1/2 tsp. Pure Vanilla
1/3 cup Honey
  (M)
Add to sunflower seeds and blend smooth. Pour into:

1/4 cup Carob Powder
1/4 cup or more Whey Powder

Mix to a stiff consistency. Cream well. Chill. Roll thickly in chopped nuts.

Fig Candy

1/2 cup Fresh Coconut, blender-grated
1/2 cup Sunflower Seeds, blender-ground

Mix to a paste with a little honey, 10 or 12 "Revived" White Figs --cut off about 3/4 of stem end and open fig.

Stuff with mixture and garnish with walnut halves.

Fruit Candy

1/4 cup Orange Juice
1 Egg White

Blend frothy (H) speed

1/2 cup Seedless Raisins
1/2 cup Pitted Dates, chopped

Add gradually, continuing to
blend, and scraping down sides
frequently.

1 cup Nuts, blender-ground
1/2 cup Sunflower Seeds,
blender-ground

Mix all ingredients well in a
bowl, adding a little Wheat
Germ if not firm enough.
Chill. Roll into balls in
Coconut or Sesame Seeds.

Grape Candy

2 Tbsps. Grape Concentrate
1 Tbsp. Honey
1/2 tsp. Lemon Juice
2 Tbsps. Soft Butter
1 tsp. Vegetable Seasoning

Blend Smooth   (M)

4 Tbsps. Rice Polishings
4 Tbsps. Whey Powder

Pour in blended ingredients
and mix to a stiff paste.
Roll into balls in coconut.

Date Porcupines

Soften dates overnight in orange
juice. Blender-chop pea-
nuts and roll dates firmly
in these so as to coat well.

Sesame Candy

2 Tbsps. Nuts--blender chop
and set aside.
2 tsps. Gelatin)
2 tsps. Water)   Dissolve

Melt gelatin, when softened,
over boiling water.

4 Tbsps. Honey
2 tsps. Molasses
2 tsps. Butter
1 Egg White
1/2 tsp. Pure Vanilla
1/8 section of Orange
1/4 tsp. Vegetable Seasoning

Blend above to pulp orange.(M)

Add gelatin and blend in. Then
blend in the following:

2 Tbsps. Flaxseeds
2 Tbsps. Sunflower Seeds (H)

2 Tbsps. Rice Polishings) In
2 Tbsps. Carob Powder) bowl
4 Tbsps. Whey Powder   )

Combine all ingredients and mix
to a stiff paste. Sprinkle
waxed paper with sesame seeds,
toasted or plain, and shape mixture into candy bars. Wrap in
waxed paper and chill.

Laxative Candy

2 "Revived" Figs, chopped)
2 tsps. Fig Juice)
1 Tbsp. Honey)   Blend (M)
2 tsps. Molasses)
1/2 tsp. Pure Vanilla)

2-1/2 Tbsps. Flaxseed Meal
1 Tbsp. Rice Polishings
1 Tbsp. Whey Powder
1 Tbsp. Sunflower Seed Meal

Mix all ingredients thoroughly. Chill. Roll in balls in any of the following:

Sesame Seeds, Whey Powder, Date Sugar, or Coconut.

LECTURE REPRINTS

1. **HOW TO ENJOY BETTER HEALTH FROM NATURAL REMEDIES**
   Tonics that can be used for different conditions in the body. A discussion of foods precedes it.

2. **HOW TO RELAX AND RELIEVE TENSION**
   How to relieve tensions of the day. Learn to live without tranquilizing drugs as nature intended you to.

3. **HOW TO REVITALIZE YOUR GLANDS**
   How the glands control the rest of the body, giving foods, exercises and a new concept of living.

4. **A NEW SLANT ON HEALTH AND BEAUTY - SLANT BOARD**
   To overcome fatigue, prolapsus, pressure symptoms in the lower abdominal organs by using the slant board.

5. **A HEALTH PATTERN TO LIVE BY**
   A new concept of living; of physical, mental and spiritual relationship to keep us in good health.

6. **HOW TO BUILD A BETTER BODY FROM YOUR KITCHEN**
   Prepare good health for your children in school lunches. Keep your husband well and on the job. The whole family is considered in beginning good health.

7. **HOW THE BREATH OF LIFE SUSTAINS YOU & IMPROVING THE EYES** - Learn to breathe correctly. Learn the value of your lung structure. Improve your eyes. Exercises for improving the eyes.

8. **PHYSICAL, MENTAL AND SPIRITUAL BALANCE**
   No life is complete without considering the three-fold balance.

9. **DEVELOPING INWARD CALM**
   To keep the body motor running smoothly is to know how to be calm under all circumstances.

10. **THE NEED FOR A NEW ATTITUDE**
    Your attitude is your altitude. Learn the many different levels of consciousness you can live on.

11. **THE HEART AND CIRCULATORY SYSTEM**
    A plan to help heart conditions, to help dissolve cholesterol, complete dietetic advice and how to live to regain a healthy heart.

12. **THREE STEPS TO HIGHER LIFE (PART I, II, III)**
13. These are spiritual lessons helping you to find
14. the higher values in life. Learn what the staff of life is, what to lean on in times of trouble and problems.

15. **HEALTH FOR OUR CHILDREN**
    Don't raise your child to be a doctor bill. Start him out right. Mental and physical health ideas for your child. How to wean the baby.

16. **SPECIAL FOODS FOR SPECIAL NEEDS & BLOOD, THE ESSENCE OF LIFE** (Two popular lectures) The fundamentals in getting well. Changing the blood stream to build toxic-free tissue.

17. **LET'S BEGIN AT THE BEGINNING**
    MAN NEEDS GOOD EARTH   (Three lectures given
    GRAINS FOR THE BODY   at the Health Center)

18. **YOUR LOVE LIFE**
    What attracts us to another person? Fundamental causes of divorce. For all ages, before and after marriage.

19. **INTESTINAL DISORDERS & FASTING AND ELIMINATIVE DIETS** - A wealth of information on two vital subjects.

    VOLUME I - SECRETS I CAN SHARE WITH YOU

    VOLUME II - MORE SECRETS I CAN SHARE WITH YOU

YOU CAN FEEL WONDERFUL, ENJOY IT NOW! $3.95
An all around book for the whole family and one that will make a wonderful gift.

JOY OF LIVING AND HOW TO ATTAIN IT 4.75
This will get you started on the Royal Road to Health.

VITAL FOODS FOR TOTAL HEALTH 4.50
Know the foods you can get well with by using the Science of Nutrition. Know your "ONIONS", know the berries, know how to make sandwiches, salads, soups and broths. A book dedicated to changing your kitchen to a health kitchen where the whole family can start the healthy body everybody wants.

YOU CAN MASTER DISEASE 4.75
This gives all the work used at the Health Ranch. Illustrates and gives the treatments and the philosophy used.

BEAUTY & CHARM AT A GLANCE 2.00
This book helps you to do many things for yourself to raise your health level. Reducing diets — a complete plan for Health and Beauty.

OVERCOMING ARTHRITIS OR RHEUMATISM 3.00
Water treatments, fasting, elimination, diets, sunbathing and the natural phases of the Nature Healing Arts discussed.

Buy them at your health food store, or if not available, order direct from:

BERNARD JENSEN PRODUCTS
PUBLISHING DIVISION
P.O. Box 8, Solana Beach, California 92075

ORDER FORM

Please Ship My Order To: Name _____

Street _____

City _____ State _____ Zip ____

	Quantity	Amount

BLENDING MAGIC **3.95**
Blend your way to health and happiness. 650 prize winning recipes. A must for those interested in preparing meals, drinks and special food combinations by way of blending.

CREATING A MAGIC HEALTH KITCHEN **1.95**
A doctor's manual for his patient. Clear directions and lists for the best proteins, starches, vegetables, etc. Start your life and health the right way in a revised kitchen prepared by a nutritionist.

HEALTH MAGIC THROUGH CHLOROPHYLL **3.95**
Gives the true value of greens and how to use. Many case histories and remedies are presented. The most definitive text on greens, grasses and sprouts. First in the series of Survival Books. Following this will be BERRIES AND YOUTH FOODS and SEEDS AND SPROUTS (enlarged edition).

HEALTH TIP BOOKS
All include recipes along with practical advice:
1. HONEY—The natural sweet. Ancient and modern usage. Types of honey for beauty and health. 1.00
2. SEEDS AND SPROUTS FOR LIFE— How to grow and use these vital foods. Recent discoveries, descriptions. 1.50
3. YOUR LIFE IN YOGURT — Special benefit to the intestinal tract. Used by oldest men in the world. How to make yogurt at home. 1.00

4. CHEESE IT! — How to make, buy, prepare, serve. Advantage of raw milk cheese. 1.50

5. SOUP'S ON! — Special ingredients. Thermos soups. Blended soups. 1.00

6. CANDY FOR YOUR SWEET TOOTH — Natural candy making for all ages. . . 1.00

7. PROTEIN — What is the best? How much protein do you really need? 1.00

8. DRIED FRUIT—A natural way of preservation. Sun drying, storing, reviving. . 1.00
9. SALADS AROUND THE WORLD — Gathered from Dr. Jensen's travels. New twists for serving. How to select around the seasons. 1.50
10. NUTS FOR YOU — Nuts in their natural state. Nut Milk Drinks. Growing, planting, Descriptions. 1.50

11. HEALTH DESSERTS — Tasty and nourishing for your family. 1.00
12. HOME FREEZING — Another natural method of preservation. Learn how to retain vitamins and minerals with proper freezing. 1.50

DR. JENSEN'S HOME STUDY COURSE
Health encyclopedia in 56 lessons. This complete course in healthy living covers the physical, mental and spiritual aspects of life.
Individual Lessons 1.50
Complete Encyclopedia 75.00

Volume I	Lessons 1 – 10	14.00
Volume II	Lessons 11 – 20	14.00
Volume III	Lessons 21 – 30	14.00
Volume IV	Lessons 31 – 40	14.00
Volume V	Lessons 41 – 50	14.00
Volume VI	Lessons 51 – 56	8.50

SEND FOR FREE OUTLINE AND INDEX

DR. JENSEN'S LECTURES on CASSETTE TAPES
1. Chemical Story 6. Seeds
2. Building a Way to Eat 7. Natural Healing
3. Replacement Therapy 8. Key to Inner Calm
4. Regularity Management 9. Breathing Exercises
5. Divine Order *$6.95 EACH!*

IRIDOLOGY, The Science and Practice of
Full-color Photographs, $18.50
Wall Chart, 27"x22", 2 color photos *$7.50*
Plastic Desk Chart, 4"x8" plastic cover *$3.50*

Ask For FREE Folder ☐

Subtotal _____
6% CA Sales Tax _____
TOTAL _____

DR. JENSEN'S LECTURES ON CASSETTE TAPES

60 to 90 Minutes

Inspirational! ★ Informative!

9 of Dr. Jensen's Many Lectures are now available at

$6⁹⁵ Per Tape

MORE LECTURE TAPES AVAILABLE SOON

1. Chemical Story
2. Building a Way to Eat
3. Replacement Therapy
4. Regularity Management
5. Divine Order

6. Seeds
7. Natural Healing
8. Key to Inner Calm
9. Breathing Exercises

If you need a Cassette Player order ours at cost! We will be happy to pass along to you, at our cost, a high quality cassette tape player. We make this offer possible because we feel that to deny anyone the opportunity to listen to Dr. Jensen's valuable lectures for lack of a recorder would be unjust. Indicate if you would like us to send additional information on the cassette player.

The words and wisdom of one of the nation's leading nutritionists can now be yours to enjoy at your leisure. Eight inspirational and informative lectures that can change your life to a more productive and enjoyable way of living. Order one or all of the above lectures today and take your first step on the wonderful road to health.

Notes